CRITICAL INSIGHTS

Langston Hughes

CRITICAL INSIGHTS

Langston Hughes

Editor
R. Baxter Miller
University of Georgia

SALEM PRESS
A Division of EBSCO Publishing
Ipswich, Massachusetts

Cover Photo: © CORBIS

Editor's text © 2013 by R. Baxter Miller

Copyright © 2013, by Salem Press, A Division of EBSCO Publishing, Inc. All rights reserved. No part of this work may be used or reproduced in any manner whatsoever or transmitted in any form or by any means, electronic or mechanical, including photocopy, recording, or any information storage and retrieval system, without written permission from the copyright owner. For permissions requests, contact proprietarypublishing@ebscohost.com.

∞ The paper used in these volumes conforms to the American National Standard for Permanence of Paper for Printed Library Materials, Z39.48-1992 (R1997).

Library of Congress Cataloging-in-Publication Data
Langston Hughes / editor, R. Baxter Miller.
    p. cm. -- (Critical insights)
  Includes bibliographical references and index.
  ISBN 978-1-4298-3724-8 (hardcover) -- ISBN 978-1-4298-3772-9 (ebook) 1. Hughes, Langston, 1902-1967--Criticism and interpretation. I. Miller, R. Baxter.
  PS3515.U274Z6687 2012
  818'.5209--dc23
                            2012019660

PRINTED IN THE UNITED STATES OF AMERICA

Contents

About This Volume, R. Baxter Miller   vii

Career, Life, and Influence

On Langston Hughes, R. Baxter Miller   3
Biography of Langston Hughes, Donna Akiba Sullivan Harper   20

Critical Contexts

The Critical Reception of Langston Hughes, 1924–2012,
    R. Baxter Miller and Dolan Hubbard   31
The "Diamond Stair" Within: Black Female Inspiration
    in Hughes's Poetry, R. Baxter Miller   55
History and Historicity in the Work of Langston Hughes, Hans Ostrom   69
In the Shadow of the Blues: Aesthetic Discoveries by Ma Rainey,
    Langston Hughes, and Sterling A. Brown, John Edgar Tidwell   87

Critical Readings

Reassessing Langston Hughes and the Harlem Renaissance: Toward
    an African American Aesthetic, Christopher C. De Santis   105
The Creative Voice in the Autobiographies of Langston Hughes,
    Joseph McLaren   121
I'm Lonely: I'll Build Me a Family: Functional Family Relationships
    in the Life and Art of Langston Hughes, Carmaletta M. Williams   138
Hughes and Lynching, W. Jason Miller   158
The Blues I'm Not Playing?: Langston Hughes in the 1930s,
    David Roessel   176
Hughes's Stories and the Test of Faith, Sharon L. Jones   194
Madam Alberta K. Johnson and the Women of the "Simple" Tales,
    Donna Akiba Sullivan Harper   207
Without Respect for Gender: Damnable Inference in
    "Blessed Assurance," Steven C. Tracy   223
Inspired by Hughes: Hughes's Dramatic Legacy in the
    Twenty-First Century, Leslie Sanders   238

"Yo también soy América": Latin American Receptions of Langston
    Hughes's American Dream, Laurence E. Prescott   255
Langston Hughes, Modernism, and Modernity, John Lowney   275

Resources

Chronology of Langston Hughes's Life   297
Works by Langston Hughes   301
Bibliography   304

About the Editor   309
Contributors   311
Index   317

About This Volume

R. Baxter Miller

The seventeen essays in this volume explore, in great detail and fluency, both the extrinsic and intrinsic implications of Hughes's work: the informative history of his artistry in general and of genre, of the literary kind, and of engaging intellect; the comparative and even international biography and autobiography across the Americas, Europe, and Africa; the family and, indeed, the psychology of Hughes's personal motivation; the cultural impact of music, identity, and the Christian church on his literary form; the imaginative conversion of African American *modernity*, the forces engendering his temper and his times, into the literary artistry of African American *modernism*, the works themselves, without cheapening the times or the texts; and, finally, the appreciation of Hughes's literary form as well as his literary per*form*ance of literary insight in both the imaginary world of theater and the real life of world politics.

In many ways the current volume follows several of the exemplary editions on Langston Hughes published during the last twenty-five years, particularly those edited by Edward Mullen in 1986, Steven C. Tracy in 2004, and John Edgar Tidwell and Cheryl R. Ragar in 2007. Rather than taking up the varied and timely concerns of the important volumes, the current edition proposes new (and a few old) angles of inquiry for a new generation of readers. Initially Hughes recognized his agency, his own force, in American history and eventually his role as a subject within it. Over time he became an inspiration in racial affirmation on a global scale. On the personal front, he hid the troubled path of a family life that led him ironically to reach for a power of writing. Often he used fictive, dramatic, or poetic situations to test gendered norms, revealing more enlightened ways of living. And more than is often recognized, he converted a sense of history into aesthetic form, the beautiful. Therefore, he became quite talented in transforming historical sources into his own lyric power. In many ways, then, he represented black women through his varied forms. He was a master of Socratic and African American irony, of a sophisticated literary structure in which a story or poem says one thing, but its teller suggests a contradictory subtext quite well. Hughes created an imaginary landscape out of many international journeys. Ultimately, he achieved a reinscription in which African Americans—and perhaps most people of color—were not hapless victims to *modernity*, the economic causes of the times. Rather, he recognized intuitively that it was indeed modernity, the force of historical change over time, that produced the fragmentations of his age, the dislocations in geography and history. Through these essays as a whole, Langston Hughes rearticulates his democratic and aesthetic perceptions of African American modernism.

In the first essay, R. Baxter Miller considers African American modernism as a measure of Hughes's growth over forty years. Building on the early renditions in musical forms of *The Weary Blues* (1926), Hughes reached a lyrical pinnacle in *Fields of Wonder* (1947) and a modernist highpoint in *Ask Your Mama* (1961). Even as an early romanticist during the 1920s, he was already on a four-decade path toward modernity. Yet, in pursuing a modernist path marked by the displacement of linear time, the profound sense of aging, and the democratic paradox, he almost never lost the great reflections that distinguished the personal epiphanies of world history. Despite his increasing playfulness with modernist forms, he recognized the political reality in culture and therefore the artist's moral responsibility to history. He showed that the dramatic monologue, an experimental poetics adopted by the likes of Alfred Tennyson, Robert Browning, and T. S. Eliot in which an intimate speaks to an undramatized listener, had become much more than an Anglo-American terrain. Langston Hughes helped establish a black modernism that transformed American democracy.

Hans Ostrom observes Hughes's concern for social change. In representing the radical roots of the 1930s, Hughes set the stage for an appreciation of political concerns during the civil rights movement of the late 1950s and the 1960s. On the cultural front, he was crucial in the establishment of the Harlem Renaissance or New Negro movement of the 1920s, which featured such writers as Countee Cullen, Claude McKay, Georgia Douglas Johnson, Wallace Thurman, and Zora Neale Hurston. In *The Weary Blues*, he depicts the Great Migration of blacks from the South to the North. By the tumultuous decades of the 1930s and 1940s, he observed the effects of the Bolshevik Revolution that transformed Russia from a feudal state into a communist regime. In the concurrent rise of fascism that helped provoke World War II, he expressed a radicalism somewhat tempered by the atrocities of his time. Intrigued by the revolutionary possibilities of Marxism as a theory, he covered the Spanish Civil War for the *Afro-American*, a black newspaper. The travel that energized him in Western or Eastern nations, in the Caribbean and West Africa, made history appear to him so clearly. Sensitive to the plight of the oppressed, he rebelled against the New Critical dictum that arbitrarily divided politics from literature. Instead of retreating from history, he actually encapsulated it in his literary art.

Donna Akiba Sullivan Harper narrates the development of the person within history. While Hughes achieved fame during the Harlem Renaissance, his lasting impact on African American cultural tradition supersedes a particular time and place. Though his accomplishments as an essayist, novelist, playwright, and poet were certainly centered in Harlem, his world travels, as Ostrom concurs, informed his life and work. Hughes, who had dropped out of Columbia University in 1922 to explore Africa and Europe, returned to Lincoln University, the nation's first African American college, in 1926, the same year that brought the publication of *The Weary Blues*, his first volume of poetry. Despite Hughes's well-deserved acclaim in verse, the middle-class black intelligentsia was not particularly pleased with *Fine Clothes to the Jew* (1927), which presented sensual portraits that were not particularly uplifting for the race. Motivated by the advice of the legendary educator Mary McLeod Bethune, he received a grant to read his poetry on a Southern tour. While in Alabama he visited the nine Scottsboro boys accused falsely of raping two white women on a train. In 1932 he visited Russia with a contingent of African Americans to produce an ill-fated film about race in the United States. Later he wrote many poems and columns that captured the adventures of those years in the *Chicago Defender*, a black newspaper, and in *I Wonder as I Wander* (1956), his second autobiography. In 1936 he was awarded a Guggenheim fellowship to work on several plays with Karamu House in Cleveland. His interest in drama persisted in the founding of the Harlem Suitcase Theater in 1938. While he continued to have poetry published widely in volumes such as *Shakespeare in Harlem* (1942), *Fields of Wonder* (1947), and *One-Way Ticket* (1949), he was busy doing various translation projects in French and Spanish. In 1953, during the Cold War between the United States and the Soviet Union, he was subpoenaed to testify before Wisconsin senator Joseph McCarthy's Permanent Subcommittee on Investigations. Inducted into the National Institute of Arts and Letters in 1961, the same year in which his experimental volume *Ask Your Mama* was published, Hughes died on May 22, 1967, due to infection following prostate surgery.

Rather than recount the same events in Hughes's life, Joseph McLaren seeks to rediscover the literary voice that articulates the historical occasions in the autobiographies. He proposes that *The Big Sea* (1940) and *I Wonder as I Wander* (1956) become imaginary moments that transcend historical details. What distinguishes Hughes's voice is that it encapsulates an era through the complementary perspectives of race, gender, and culture. Hughes journeyed to Africa in 1922 and then witnessed the jazz greats in Paris. In addition to visiting the Soviet Union in 1932, Hughes ventured to Cuba and Haiti as well as the Far East. With an eventual return to Paris in 1937, he retraced the impact of the African American on Europe during the first third of the twentieth century. With the range of his vast travels abroad, he came to voice a global vision of African American culture.

W. Jason Miller clarifies that Hughes's imaginary accomplishments were certainly written against the dispiriting backdrop of racial lynching. In addition to seeing photographs and hearing stories of atrocities,

Hughes had read about them in such publications as the *Crisis*, the official publication of the National Association for the Advancement of Colored People (NAACP). The three kinds of lynching so distinct during his lifetime included the *spectacles*, with crowds numbering tens of thousands on courthouse lawns, and *mob* deeds that were more spontaneous. Then, too, there were the *legal* murders, the speedy trials and executions sanctioned by courts with all-white juries. For African Americans, such institutionalized violence was used to mandate social behavior.

David Roessel inquires into the complementary dimensions of history and the writer's voice. Observing that the blues form is largely absent from Hughes's poetry between 1931 and 1939, Roessel attributes this absence to a rise in leftist politics during the Great Depression. There were others who experienced difficulty in adapting poetry to the decade. In surveying that turbulent time in 1941, in fact, writer and critic Malcolm Cowley found vigor in the literary criticism and experimentation in the drama as well as brilliance in the novel but noted a nadir in poetry and in strictly imaginary literature. Hughes himself concentrated on a new and varied poetics during the 1930s, even though the blues had been such fertile ground for his poetry during the 1920s.

Carmaletta Williams probes into Hughes's psyche. While others are often more concerned with the importance of history in his imaginary construction of the world, Williams inquires into the actual construction of his thought itself. For years, she argues, Hughes sought to create and later to simulate a stable family structure. Eventually he decided that the only way to secure such lasting bonds was to advance beyond the dysfunctional family into which he was born. Aware of glaring contradictions between personal (emotional) and public lives, he sought an imaginary space to transcend both and find peace within. Perhaps Hughes was looking for a sympathetic "family" of readers all his life.

Both Christopher C. De Santis and John Edgar Tidwell seek to explain an aesthetic of Hughes's work based on history and culture. A year after the publication of *The Weary Blues* in 1926, according to De Santis, Hughes began to articulate a black aesthetic. In essays such as "The Negro Artist and the Racial Mountain" (1926), "These Bad New Negroes: A Critique on Critics" (1927), and "To Negro Writers" (1935), Hughes reveals himself as a writer committed to revising an aesthetic of Western Europe. While he became an exemplary voice in that regard, the concept had evolved from the poetry of Phillis Wheatley in the late eighteenth century to the prose of W. E. B. Du Bois at the turn of the twentieth. During the New Negro movement, Hughes became at once the inheritor and the innovator of at least three centuries of intellectual history. Tidwell proposes that the connections depend on a folk aesthetic voiced so diversely by Hughes and Sterling A. Brown. Both poets encountered Ma Rainey, the greatest blues singer of the day. While the experience may not have proved decisive regarding the overall quality of their poetry, it could have certainly exerted an impact on their shared aesthetic. Both poets witnessed Rainey's performances, or knew about them, during her prime. In the highly personal medium of the blues, both poets displayed a communal sense of suffering and of release.

It is important to remember that Langston Hughes was a poet of ideas. In his exploration of the vital role of the female figure in Hughes's poetry, R. Baxter Miller recognizes in great detail the decisive source of Mary Langston, the maternal grandmother, in Hughes's literary world. Hughes's rendition of the figure converted his autobiographical experiences into representations of African American spirituality and of indomitable will. On a practical level, the female figure appears in Hughes's poetry of the 1940s as a folk worker or an ingenious trickster who incites comic delight. Later, she nearly disappears from his poetic world during the 1950s and 1960s. Usually her image incarnates the great range of Hughes's imagination and the complex masks through which it appears. Therefore, the black woman is a marker, a litmus test or *lens*, through which to trace the rise and fall of his entire career. Through a detailed comparison of the prose character Simple with his poetic counterpart, Madame Alberta K. Johnson, Donna Akiba Sullivan Harper explains new distinctions about the ways such figures function. While Joyce Lane Semple bears the surname of her male equivalent, she desires a higher place in society. In the concluding years of the Simple stories, she simplifies a distinctly black perspective. For the most part, Hughes shows an impressive understanding of female experience.

Steven C. Tracy and Sharon Jones take varied angles on the moral subject. In focusing on the psychological consequences of the American dream, Tracy explores the assumption of national "normality" in "Blessed Assurance," one of Hughes's final stories. Tracy notes that this concept had become absurd by the time of Edward Albee's production of *The American Dream*, which premiered at the York Playhouse on January 24, 1961, and ran for 370 performances. As a traditional concept, the dream favors white privilege, including the hegemony of heterosexual, middle-class values. Deviation from the norm places the ideal of a nuclear family out of reach. Jones examines whether Hughes locates a moral dilemma within the Christian concept itself. In "On the Road" and "Big Meeting" as well as in "Blessed Assurance," she observes, Hughes tests faith to see whether it functions well. Laurence Prescott explores Hughes's poetry as a source for the Latin American reshaping of the American dream. In particular, Hughes's signature piece, "I, Too," resonated with many of his Latin American peers who discovered in Hughes's poetic world a mirror of themselves.

Several remaining essays prepare for a new African American modernist reading. Leslie Sanders observes numerous forms of dramatic experimentation by Hughes, particularly during the 1930s. Hughes, she says, challenged the demeaning representations of blacks on the stage. Despite the use of the tragic conventions of folk drama, he subverted them. And through the transformation of historical struggle into hope, he earned a "major place in the history of American theater." Hughes was modernist in his stubborn refusal to accept inherent limits of genre, of literary kind. His gospel plays, in the sacred language of faith, encapsulate the soul of a people.

John Lowney concludes the book by testing scholar Michael Hanchard's idea that black modernity "consists of the selective incorporation of technologies, discourses, and institutions of the modern West within the cultural and political practices of African-derived peoples to create a form . . . distinct from its counterparts of Western Europe and North America." African American modernists eventually make the concept their own. Though the idea applies to Hughes's earliest poetics, Lowney's emphasis is on *Montage of a Dream Deferred* (1951) and *Ask Your Mama*, and his essay brings full circle the African American modernist frame with which this text began. Hughes emerges as a writer who speaks to his time and to ours. He represents the citizens around him. His strategy voices a black aesthetic and a global one. It is this breadth that makes his artistry so enduring.

CAREER, LIFE, AND INFLUENCE

On Langston Hughes

R. Baxter Miller

James Langston Hughes—fiction writer, columnist, playwright, and poet—was perhaps the most wide-ranging and persistent African American writer in the twentieth century. Deeply rooted in the Harlem Renaissance of the early 1920s, he exerted a profound influence on American arts and culture well into the last third of the twentieth century. By then he would be nearly an anachronism to modernist purists, except for the experimental work that survives him. But in the early days of the twenty-first century, his reexplored writing often seems more prophetic and avant-garde than his critics and his many admirers ever really knew. Indeed, his novels, dramas, translations, and seminal anthologies of the writings of his contemporaries in America and Europe helped develop a literature of the African diaspora. All the while, Hughes helped endear the American audience to the future of ethnic equality and democracy. In many ways, he crafted the literary vision of an American dream better perhaps than any national poet since Walt Whitman, whom he celebrated but eventually doubted. Then, too, he encapsulated the artistic forms of African American secular music.

Hughes, working to free American literature from the plantation tradition of racial stereotypes, introduced new idioms that reflected personal confidence and racial pride. In addition to the well-designed revelations through his characters, he achieved a deceptive literary craft in the creative works. A product of the Jazz Age in many ways, he helped influence at least five decades of American culture. After the 1920s—into which his musical poetics had emerged—he learned from the Great Depression of the 1930s to represent the class inequities of the nation. By the 1940s, he wrote lyrics that provided temporary relief from the racial murders that had persisted in the country for half a century. Particularly during the McCarthy era, or the Red Scare, Hughes urged the nation to advance toward racial integration. He voiced the necessity of social justice throughout the civil rights movement of that decade. When the momentum toward interracial equity waned, he continued to dream of better days.

By his final decade, he witnessed the integration of restaurants and hotels across the nation. Though he observed a breakdown of the Left in the United States, he and his works remained idealistic. He was, in other words, a rare integrationist who respected the dignity of the racial self. Nearly an incurable optimist, he did not believe in the liberal philosophy completely. An exceptional humorist, he rarely underestimated either the impact of history or the writer's compulsion to rewrite it. While he acknowledged the deterministic forces in the great American story, he charted ways for his fellow citizens to transform them into a great imaginary future.

To appreciate the great diversity and formal range of Hughes's prolific and voluminous career, one must understand its historical backdrop, advancing from *The Weary Blues* (1926), his earliest literary experimentation in African American blues and jazz; to *Fields of Wonder* (1947), the most lyrically finished and yet often overlooked volume of his early maturity; and, finally, to the denouement of *The Panther and the Lash* (1967, published posthumously), his final and perhaps most skeptical volume, except perhaps for the brilliant *Ask Your Mama* (1961). The point here, then, is to represent his oeuvre succinctly rather than exhaustively. To restate the chronology of his life in aesthetic terms, Hughes was initially a late romanticist well on his way to becoming a modernist, then a developing modernist who came to value dramatic situations of the personal moment, then an atypical African American modernist who recognized that even poetic form is subject to politics, and ultimately a consummate African American contemporary who recognized that experimental devices such as stream of consciousness and free association do not absolve the poet of his responsibility to history.

To understand *The Weary Blues* and its impact on American culture, it is necessary to understand the biographical moment of the modernist idea into which it appeared. Hughes returned to the United States from

Europe late in 1923 but was in Paris again by the spring of 1924. Alain Locke, a leader of the Harlem Renaissance and a Howard University professor, visited him there to invite poems for an extraordinary edition of the popular magazine *Survey Graphic*. In entreating Hughes to visit Venice with him, Locke directed a personal excursion during which the professor recounted the history of the great architects involved, observing elegantly the death site of Richard Wagner, the nineteenth-century German composer. Instead of reveling in such wonderful, elitist narratives, Hughes searched for enlightening experiences beyond the famous monuments and artwork detailed in the popular guides. Soon moving away from such carefully managed paths, he was relieved to perceive the poor people of Venice in the back alleys. Returning to New York, he gave a number of his poems to poet Countee Cullen, whose acquaintance he had already made. Together they attended a National Association for the Advancement of Colored People (NAACP) fundraiser, hence meeting Carl Van Vechten, a white bohemian.

In 1924 Hughes met poet Arna Bontemps, beginning what would become a lifelong friendship and collaboration. The two became mutual fans of each other, perhaps because Hughes appreciated his fellow's determination to remain a productive author despite the many demands of domestic life. For Bontemps's part, it must have been equally impressive that Hughes continued to write while maintaining such a nomadic life. Working together so well, the two shared many major projects over the years while Hughes explored the distant world; indeed, Bontemps became an intellectual anchor in Hughes's life.

During the winter of 1925, Hughes began work with Carter G. Woodson at the Association of Negro Life and History in Washington, DC. When the paperwork resulted in tired eyes, he forfeited the presumed middle-class status of professional employment to labor as a busboy for higher wages at the Wardman Park Hotel. One afternoon he encountered Vachel Lindsay, a contemporary poet in the Whitman tradition of the sweeping American vernacular. Hughes placed copies of his own poems, including "The Weary Blues," on the table next to the elder poet's place setting. Newspaper headlines later reported that Lindsay had discovered him, though *Opportunity* and the *Crisis* already had.

In 1925, Hughes achieved first place in a poetry competition funded by *Opportunity*, the publishing forum for the Urban League, and, less well known, by Casper Holstein, a benevolent criminal. While at the awards ceremony, Hughes encountered the white liberal Mary White Ovington and the African American elder poet James Weldon Johnson, as well as Carl Van Vechten. After a renewal of acquaintances, Van Vechten asked if Hughes had sufficient poems for a book. Reading them later, he forwarded the manuscript to the legendary firm Alfred A. Knopf for publication.

Though Hughes's *The Weary Blues* certainly announced a bold new poetics of the New Negro of the 1920s and of the Harlem Renaissance, the jazz era is now somewhat romantic and distant from the contemporary reader. It is certainly the revolutionary zeitgeist that his famous essay "The Negro Writer and the Racial Mountain" (1926) sets the tone for. But the actual history at the Renaissance moment was far more visceral. Roland Hayes, a leading African American tenor of the time, declined to perform a recital on stage at the Lyric Theater in Baltimore. His insistence was that the admission policies of the music hall had to change. Hughes would write Hayes into his poetry as an exemplar of artistic courage during the next two decades. Meanwhile, the historic backdrop of the mid-1920s set the stage for his cultural appreciation and for his audience's enlightenment. In 1926, Woodson earned the much coveted Spingarn Medal for definitive work in the research and publication of records of African American history. [Woodson had been a founder of the Association for the Study of Negro Life and History in 1915 and the quarterly *Journal of Negro History* (now the *Journal of African American History*) in 1916.] During the same year, William Sanders Scarborough, a black classicist who had risen to the presidency of Ohio's Wilberforce University and became the first African American member of the Modern Language Association (MLA), died at the age of seventy-four. Hence, Hughes's literary experimentations of the 1920s and his musical energies over several decades helped expand the creativity and thoughtfulness of a black intelligentsia to which he was only sometimes endeared. In addition, Hughes helped the nation reach for more democratic and modern forms of poetics. He wrote in part to reestablish the popular ideals through which the public voice of Whitman, his favorite white male poet of the nineteenth century and beyond, still appeals to modern readers in a now older and more challenged world.

Hughes was more of a romantic lyricist of nature than a modernist who honed the introspective self. So much of his early poetry is youthfully idealistic, portraying nature, moments of personal wonder, and solitary figures. Such unpretentious poems as "Fantasy in Purple" and "As I Grew Older" capture in turn the cadences of human survival and the African American dream framed at once by shadow and light. Much of Hughes's poetic success derives from a subtle blend of auditory and visual sensation. In "Song for Billie Holiday," what one sees is really what one hears:

> Voice of muted trumpet,
> Cold brass in warm air.
> Bitter television blurred
> By sound that shimmers—
> Where? (lines 16–20)

Nearly all of these poems appeared in *The Weary Blues*, which was published in January 1926. Today such pieces are celebrated primarily as bold experimentations in the poetics of African American music. Perhaps equally important, they helped revolutionize the subject matter of American modernism. Suddenly, the dramatic monologue form, which had served Euro-American poets such as Alfred Tennyson, Robert Browning, and T. S. Eliot so well, was no longer privileged terrain. Finally, the national poetics were headed toward becoming part of a multicultural democracy.

Published in the early years of the next decade, two of Hughes's most accomplished stories encapsulate his significant contributions to American literary history. Such memorable stories as "Home" and "The Blues I'm Playing," first published in *Esquire* and *Scribner's* magazine, respectively, appeared subsequently in the experimental collection *The Ways of White Folks* (1934). In the latter story, Hughes imaginatively revises his emotional divorce from wealthy patron Charlotte Mason into the wonderfully detailed story of Oceola Jones, a Harlem pianist who deviates from favoring the nineteenth-century European classics over contemporary African American jazz. Though the player's patron, the childless widow Dora Ellsworth, proposes a clear superiority for what she values as an elite and detached music, Mason actually preferred "primitive folk art" to modernist innovations. Jones celebrates African American culture encapsulated within the playing. Whether the character involved is the fictive Ellsworth or the historical Mason, the acceptance of the player's jazz aesthetic becomes a critique of the patron's own dispassionate life. The new idea means the final rejection of the Western binaries that force artists to choose such absolute preferences. Absolutism, says Hughes's literary world, is the dictate of small minds. In a sense, the African American protégé in "Blues" represents the vicarious daughter of Ellsworth, while the two characters are divided according to their aesthetic ideologies. Certainly, the player's syncopations subvert Ellsworth's preference for classicism at nearly every turn, finishing in the personal climax, the liberation of the player's newly realized self. Understandable as a true right angle, at an interface point of history and fiction, the jazz player figuratively faces the patron in one direction and the writer in yet another. The intercultural player *is* the vicarious Langston Hughes.

Therefore, one of Hughes's most accomplished stories reveals a tension between tradition and innovation. Just as the pianist performs music representing the modern time, the Persian vases in the patron's vast display area represent a most elegant and traditional space. Once again, Hughes's narrator exists somewhat anxiously at the recurring juncture between Victorian neoclassicism and the modern era. The stock market crash of October 29, 1929, initiating the Great Depression of the 1930s, would raise the question of whether classical or modernist preferences would prevail as the American aesthetics. History itself, of course, had already made the decision. By the year of the story's publication, so many creative performances and productions that had once been funded during the Harlem Renaissance were long gone. But taken as a whole, the narrative favors a diverse modernism in which African American aesthetics achieve a transformative meaning, enriching the nation with new experimentations in culture and literary form.

In retrospect, Hughes was already experimenting with literary strategies that would become the cornerstone of a new African American modernism: the radical binary of classical and innovative forms, the wonderful complement of time and space, the connecting point between history and story, and the compulsion of the modern imagination to rethink all of the binaries. His eventual gift to the nation, of course, was the ability to imagine and therefore reshape a new concept of beauty for all Americans.

"Father and Son," the concluding story of *Ways*, confirms Hughes's high literary status within contemporary American culture. Returning to the Southern plantation of his childhood in the fourth part of the story, Bert Lewis comes home to the white father who has denied Bert the family name of Norwood. Bert remembers a beating he received from his father as a boy, and his father and mother recall the punishment at different points in the story. Hence, the recurrence of the deed in all of their memories serves as a common bond. The storyteller, relating the interwoven destinies of the dysfunctional family, speaks many of the finest words Hughes would ever write. After what would certainly seem to have been military service in the Civil War rather than World War I, the apparent nineteenth-century colonel has lived into the dawn of the twentieth century. Such a modern conflation of time confirms that history has indeed passed him by. Perhaps his literal death at the end of the story only confirms that he was already a ghost of his Confederate history and had to die along with it. Meanwhile, the Ford (probably a Model T) driven by Bert, a revolutionary, is an innovative force as well. The Ford is to the avant-garde technology of the postwar world as Bert is to the antebellum South. They are, in other words, complementary sides of the same modernity. Both encapsulate the intensity and immediacy of a transformative language:

> Bow down and pray in fear and trembling, go way back in the dark afraid; or work harder and harder; or stumble and learn; or raise up your fist and strike—but once the idea comes into your head you'll never be the same again. Oh, test tube of life! Crucible of the South, find the right powder and you'll never be the same again. . . . (*Short Stories* 139)

While one speaker is religiously conservative, another cowers away in alienation. Perhaps it is a union worker who vows to resist the status quo of the 1930s and, by sleight of hand, speaks to new student audiences in the twenty-first century. There are wild leaps of varied thought, dexterous shifts in place and time, that set Hughes on an experimental path toward a progressive literary form.

It is intriguing to reassess the vitality of his literary skills as part of a new African American adaptation of the modern. When his narrator describes patterns of memories among various characters, such as that of the beaten child, he conveys the sense that the historical truths of the nineteenth century repeat themselves well into the twentieth. The past becomes the present, and in a way, Reconstruction still recurs. To Hughes, the images of the son and the car reflect the same modernity. Considered together in their literary effects, the figures confirm Hughes's status as a leading American contemporary.

At midcareer Hughes was developing into more of a modernist who focused his poetry on dramatic situations and objective personal states. The lyrical *Fields of Wonder*, coming not long after Hughes's personal truce with the American war efforts of the 1940s, belied his persistent struggle for civil rights. After all, between 1947 and 1962, as Peter Bergman records in *The Chronological History of the Negro in America* (1969), twelve black Americans were lynched, with three lynchings per year occurring in 1949 and 1955. It was indeed in Hughes's milestone year of 1947 that the African American historian John Hope Franklin published *From Slavery to Freedom*. On April 9, 1947, the Congress of Racial Equality (CORE) dispatched a cohort of student activists to the South to test whether a ban on segregated bus travel along the interstates, as mandated by the Supreme Court on June 3, 1946, was really implemented. Since its earlier founding in 1942, CORE had achieved most of its reputation for planning the first "sit-ins" of racial resistance in segregated restaurants. This impetus for resistance would crest in May of 1961. Perhaps Hughes's greatest lyrical period, based on his careful crafting and focus of intense personal emotion, gave way to the milieu of the civil rights movement, one that he would address directly during the final two decades of his poetry. It is possible that the prose of the Simple tales and of his own political histories served to balance the varying outlets for his social commentary of the times. He still found a way to write the lyrics to Kurt Weil's score for *Street Scene*, which some observers considered to be the first Broadway opera.

In appreciating two of Hughes's finest poems that suspend modernity—the contemporary forces of industry, cultural and political collapse, and even history itself—it is possible to be reinvigorated in recovering his lyrical voice as epitomized in *Fields of Wonder*. "Carolina Cabin" presents a very romantic meeting of a loving couple in a modern and compressed scene. Against a backdrop of hanging moss and straight pine, young lovers laugh aloud, enjoying their red wine as the gloomy world turns. In addition to serving as Hughes's likely unintended completion of the figurative pattern of the Victorian poet Matthew Arnold's "Dover Beach"—two lovers huddled against the world's cold armies beyond—the poem keeps with one of Hughes's most captivating archetypes. Especially during the 1920s and 1930s, and in the middle of his career, he was concerned with the cherished moments in which the literary artist, and indeed the African American historian, could stand apart from the political and cultural moments to which the artist must in time return. But the imagination, which allows the literary artist to stand outside of historical and social time, makes the revolutionary and the lyricist quite special. As Hughes says figuratively, the narrator voices the capacity to *wonder* as the real and practical black man, the alter ego, *wanders* throughout Africa, Europe, and the Americas. Near the end of "Carolina Cabin," the narrator reveals an autobiographical self:

> The winds of winter cold,
> As down the road
> A wandering poet
> Must roam. (14–17)

It is a figure to which Hughes would return years later in his second autobiography, *I Wonder as I Wander* (1956), while recalling the intense memories of France in the early 1920s and of Cuba in the mid-1930s.

The poem from which *Fields of Wonder* derives its title, "Birth," provides a clear illustration of the lyricist's deferment of modernity as well. In celebrating the "fields of wonder," the originating site for the natural bodies of light, stars, moon, and sun, the lyricist creates a simile that is electric:

> Like stroke
> Of lightning
> In the night
> Some mark
> To make
> Some word
> To tell. (6–12)

While the sense of wonder may well be romantic, the technological implication of it is modern.

In the last quarter of his life, Hughes subtly confirmed the fallacy that elite modernism, especially the African American variety of it, was ever free of the political world. His third milestone year of 1953 may not have been a watershed moment in the trajectory of his creative works, but it did highlight a political event that threatened to label him as an extreme leftist. It nearly ruined his reputation as the great American he surely was; fortunately, this political branding failed to taint the final fourteen years of the life. In an initial wave of American intolerance, inflamed in part by the Cold War between the United States and the Soviet Union after World War II, the House Committee on Un-American Activities initiated an inquisition into the patriotism of the nation's citizens. At the time, the popular novelist Ayn Rand, an expatriate from Eastern Europe and ideologue of the Right, testified that there was a pro-Soviet slant in the film *Song of Russia* (1944). Serving as an informer, she was directly responsible for the blacklisting and imprisonment for contempt of Congress of a group of entertainers who became known eventually as the "Hollywood Ten." By the second wave of political intimidation in 1951, the Republican senator Joseph McCarthy led a new charge with his Permanent Subcommittee on Investigations. During the infancy of television, he subpoenaed many of the most accomplished performers and creators of the era, including the representative figures Lucille Ball, Orson Welles, Dashiell Hammett, and Lillian Hellman. Hardly content with exonerating the accused artists as individuals, he insisted that they could only prove their ideological purity by informing on others leftists. Though the committee was, according to the original charge, supposed to investigate American extremism regardless of political persuasion, the final result was actually to neglect the dangers posed by the Ku Klux Klan while emphasizing the presumed infiltration of the Federal Writer's Project by the Communist Party. Almost none of McCarthy's wild claims would ever be substantiated, but his strategy proved effective in defeating progressive policies of all sorts. The committee was also very efficient in weakening the power of the nation's unions. In 1953, Hughes was summoned by the committee to prove that he was not a communist, and his public lectures declined for a while. In a poem entitled "Un-American Investigators," a satiric piece in which the speaker narrates the indignity of being falsely accused, the liberal speaker expresses a patriotic concept that would have made Henry David Thoreau, the nineteenth-century American transcendentalist, proud.

To be sure, it was certainly Langston Hughes who in 1953 emerged on the right side of history. After all, it was the dimension of modernist poetics that was real. The same year, President Dwight Eisenhower's administration brought to an end the segregation of schools and of the civilian employees of the navy working on military bases. In addition, the government terminated the separatist policy in the hospitals of the Veterans Health Administration. Segregation was abolished in many district agencies, but the policy persisted in the area of recreation as well as in the welfare division and the fire department. In keeping with its plans to abolish all racial discrimination by 1963, the NAACP initiated in 1953 a ten-year plan to fulfill the American dream of economic and social equality.

Hughes's experimental *Ask Your Mama: 12 Moods for Jazz*, appearing in 1961, only six years before his death, tests the formal limits of twentieth-century poetics as even the great midcentury black modernists Robert Hayden, Melvin Tolson, and Gwendolyn Brooks had not done. In the volume Hughes blends allusions and indirect references, in a streaming consciousness of political history and African American survival across several centuries. His captivating tone, as much a celebration of survival as an accusation, encapsulates the rising anger of the 1960s. His work demonstrates brilliantly the innovations that infuse jazz tones with a pervasive sense of history. Situated once in the child's mind, his historical storyteller shifts adeptly into the adult's without missing a beat. Indeed, given the undisputed importance of *The Weary Blues* to the African American literary canon, critics have often overlooked the enormous contribution of *Ask Your Mama* to American poetry. In intellectual as well as sheer artistic force, the latter volume expresses the deepest concerns of modernity: dissipating humanism, threats to free speech (such as the McCarthyism of the previous decade), racism, human decline, assimilation, racial integration, poverty, and nationalism. Despite Hughes's concern for the United States in particular, the book sets a tone in general for a new Pan-African poetics. While such writing was concerned with a personal integrity of celebrating the national experience, it helped clear a path across international boundaries. It assisted, in other words, in establishing future criteria for poets of the modern and, eventually, postmodern world.

One of his most brilliant expressions of the modern idiom appears in his depiction of the nineteenth-century abolitionist Sojourner Truth, a folk prophet whose brilliant leadership and guidance of slaves from South to North helped reshape African American destiny. Beyond the development of many new telescopes since the Copernican seventeenth century, romanticism had not dissipated, as confirmed by the durative verb "be." "Be there before the root man comes," the black folk said once of John Henry, the emblem of their hope. "Be there now. Be there when he's gone." Hence, Langston Hughes re-creates an African American modernism, a vernacular that maintains a fluent and unfinished racial identity. As Truth says to the modern reader in "mood" 10 of *Ask Your Mama*, "Bird in Orbit":

> I LOOK AT THE STARS
> AND THEY [the children] LOOK AT THE STARS
> AND THEY WONDER WHERE I BE
> AND I WONDER WHERE THEY BE (53–56)

She offers a double image that exists both now and then. Indeed, this is the greatness of Langston Hughes's legacy. By the time of *Ask Your Mama*'s publication in 1961, Hughes had lived from one celebrated moment of African American culture in the twentieth century, the Harlem Renaissance of the 1920s, to the next remarkable one, the black arts movement of the 1960s and early 1970s. Indeed, his very life exemplified the African American arts of the century.

"Not What Was" proves to be the last great poem translating Hughes's romantic impulse into modern idiom. Unrecognized now by readers for at least two generations, the neglected masterpiece articulates the "wondrous" juncture of romanticism and modernity. As the poet commences the story of his creative writing in the present tense, reflecting nevertheless on his personal odyssey—"By then the poetry is written" (1)— he emphasizes that the subjective (personal) and modern (objective) moments must be synchronized as flowers that bloom at the same time. Indeed, it is the proper juncture of the historical moment with personal experience that allows such an instant to spiral beyond its time. If a literary moment, or age, represents its own time well, only then will it be able so paradoxically to outlive it:

> to fill the vase unfilled
> or spread in lines
> upon another page—
> that anyhow was never written
> because the thought could not escape
> the place in which it bloomed
> before the rose had gone. (15–21)

Hence, the greatness of the modern poet means maintaining the imaginary fields of poetic wonder until nearly the last third of the twentieth century. Yet, as became apparent in *Ask Your Mama*, Hughes personally adapted his early romantic poetics to modern expression. By the 1960s, his transition between literary modes and temperaments was complete.

At the time of his death on May 22, 1967, Hughes was admired for his repudiation of both the liberal and reactionary views of race. Often he was lauded for his optimism as well as his experimentations in the poetics of blues and jazz. In addition to his great humanistic faith, his personal generosity became legendary. Even modernism, the self-preoccupation with the text and aesthetic form, could not account for his personal demise, his sudden disappearance from history. By the year of his death in Harlem's Polyclinic Hospital, America had changed. In the Midwest, the Chrysler Corporation, Michigan Bell Telephone Company, and Ford Motor Corporation were all making efforts to create jobs in Detroit in order to employ more African Americans. In fact, Ford publicized many opportunities and then dispatched recruiters into black communities to hire the chronically unemployed. During February of that year, President Lyndon Johnson proposed that Congress pass civil rights legislation to prevent racial discrimination as part of public opportunities and the selection of juries. In 1967, Martin Luther King Jr. informed the nation that he had come to oppose the Vietnam War, a fiscal impediment to civil rights and quite an unacceptable expense in American blood and treasure, in his view (Bergman 425–27, 514–15, 601–02). Hughes would end his posthumous volume with "Daybreak in Alabama," a figurative representation of the national landscape of the sort that had distinguished his poetry of 1947.

Hughes's gift for inspired hope survived even the white backlash against American diversity. According to his life's trajectory, he advanced from the experimental forms of African American music of the 1920s to the sarcastic cadences of the late 1960s. In between, he accounted for the political unrest and economic needs of the proletariat during the 1930s. In the aftermath of World War II, he kept lyricism in the foreground of his poetic representations. His volumes became an artistic and moral narrative of the nation's commitment to African American freedom and therefore of the American creed.

Langston Hughes has so rightfully become a central figure in African American modernism. He was born near the turn of the twentieth century, and his fiction, plays, public discourse, and poetry coexisted with, and even advanced, the modern temper in democratic ways. It is clear now that he restored to American literature a vital concern for social justice—a secret but forbidden politics—without forfeiting the beautiful qualities of irony and complexity. He was deceptively thoughtful without elitist pretense. Especially for the middle third of the twentieth century, he achieved a balanced concept of literary artistry. He distinguished himself as a black modernist more than just a modernist. In the process, he exposed assumptions that, according to critic Steve Giles, underlie both modernism and postmodernism: the industrialism of modern times, the capitalist system of commodities, the devices of surveillance and administration, and the systematic control of the tools of violence (181). Langston Hughes championed American democracy. As was true with the more experimental and radical voices of his century, he recognized a bond between political reality and cultural representation. If the purpose of high modernism were to *separate* place and feeling, his mission was rather to recalibrate the natural bond between literature and history. He represented the American masses far more than he proposed to be self-reflexive and self-important. As Walt Whitman noted in the nineteenth century, the public masses *were* the American self. Often Hughes accepted the premise that the modern writer had to break entirely with the formal and linguistic conventions inherited from the British writers of the mid-nineteenth century. Though he demonstrated the modernist imperative of effective contradiction, of paradox, he resolved the hidden tension between politics and culture. He did not pretend there was no disparity, no difference.

 So Langston Hughes positioned himself within the public history of modernity, yet beyond the most elitist, modernist forms of it. It was not his way to support the formal criterion of a textual difficulty that distinguished the critical reception of modernists James Joyce, Gertrude Stein, Marianne Moore, T. S. Eliot, Ezra Pound, William Faulkner, and Virginia Woolf. An African American independent, he wrote outside of a modernist insistence on obscurity because, as an original thinker, he saw beyond the academic world. Perhaps his greatest legacy is that his artistry helped make America more diverse.

The 1980s saw a sensible resurgence in Hughes's national recognition. In March 1981, a conference held in his hometown of Joplin, Missouri, led to the establishment of the Langston Hughes Society, formed in Baltimore, Maryland, in June of the same year. By April 1982, the society met jointly with the College Language Association, and in 1984, it became the first group focused on a black author to become an affiliate of the MLA. Still later, in 1988, poet and educator Raymond R. Patterson directed "Langston Hughes: An International Interdisciplinary Conference" at the City College of the City University of New York, a pioneering honor to the writer. Soon a public television release reaffirmed the high status of Hughes among the most recognized American poets. At the time, many distinguished authors revaluated his contributions to the reshaping of the American literary imagination. Diverse audiences celebrated his legacy at the many conferences honoring the centennial of his birth in 2002, especially those held at the Case Western Reserve Society in Ohio, California State University, and the University of Kansas. By the beginning of the twenty-first century, Langston Hughes was widely recognized as one of the greatest American writers.

Works Cited

Bergman, Peter. *The Chronological History of the Negro in America*. New York: Harper, 1969.

Giles, Steve. *Theorizing Modernism: Essays in Critical Theory*. New York: Routledge, 1993.

Hughes, Langston. *The Collected Poems*. Ed. Arnold Rampersad and David Roessel. New York: Knopf, 1995.

_____. *The Short Stories*. Ed. R. Baxter Miller. Columbia: U of Missouri P, 2002. Vol. 15 of The Collected Works of Langston Hughes. 16 vols. 2001–03.

Biography of Langston Hughes
Donna Akiba Sullivan Harper

Langston Hughes is often remembered as a Harlem Renaissance poet, but he wrote much more than poetry. As the sixteen-volume *Collected Works of Langston Hughes* (2001–03) verifies, Hughes wrote novels, newspaper columns, essays, plays, short stories, histories, autobiographies, and children's books in addition to his well-known verse. Moreover, while Hughes rose to international attention during the Harlem Renaissance, publishing his first two volumes of poetry during the 1920s, he continued to write and edit volumes of literature until his death in 1967. When he died, he left several projects to be completed, and subsequent volumes of his works and letters continue to be published. It is true that Hughes loved and is associated with Harlem, New York, where a section of East 127th Street is known as Langston Hughes Place in his honor. However, Hughes also traveled internationally and throughout the United States, and his travels significantly influenced his writing. Thus, Hughes was much more than a Harlem Renaissance poet.

James Langston Hughes was born February 1, 1902. His father, James Hughes, abandoned his mother, Carrie Langston Hughes, leaving young Hughes to become what his character Simple terms "a passed-around child." Nevertheless, Hughes absorbed human and cultural lessons from all the places and people he encountered. As Carrie and Homer Clark, her second husband, searched for employment in various cities, young Hughes was left in the care of his maternal grandmother in Lawrence, Kansas. Hughes later lived in other midwestern cities, including Topeka, Kansas, and Lincoln, Illinois.

In libraries and in books, Hughes found the beauty, sufficiency, and stability that eluded him because of his frequent moves and financial marginality. He desired to communicate with others as did those authors he read and loved. Encouraged by teachers and classmates, he earned the title of class poet and wrote short stories while attending Central

High School in Cleveland, Ohio, where he learned to distinguish "reactionary" white schoolmates and neighbors from "decent" white folk.

In 1920, after graduating from high school, Hughes traveled to Mexico to live with his father. Caught in the conflict and hostility between his parents, Hughes exercised his remarkable gift for using writing to cope with internal anguish, transforming it into enduring literature. En route to Mexico, with his mother's anger in his mind, Hughes wrote the brilliant poem "The Negro Speaks of Rivers," which would be published by the *Crisis* in 1921.

In Mexico, Hughes discovered new dimensions of racial and economic class distinctions. His personal appearance and proficiency in Spanish permitted him access to venues that enriched his cultural and personal awareness. Moreover, he discovered how a new language could change Americans' perspectives about race. Hughes produced poems, short stories, and even a children's play, "The Gold Piece," in response to his experiences in Mexico.

After a year, Hughes left Mexico and enrolled in Columbia University, from which his money-focused father expected him to earn an engineering degree. Although neither the school nor the major satisfied Hughes, he did at last see Harlem. Uncertain about his next step but very certain that he would move on from Columbia, Hughes relinquished his father's financial support and left the university in 1922, working a series of jobs that required physical labor. In 1923, he found work on a ship and began a period of travel that would greatly shape his later work.

Unlike many Harlem Renaissance writers who merely idealized Africa, Hughes actually visited several ports along the continent's western coast. Poems and short stories captured Hughes's impressions of the land and the people he met on the ship and in the ports. When he tired of life on the ship, he traveled to Paris and worked as a dishwasher in a cabaret, where he heard much jazz music. The work was hard, but the environment and the people provided him with rich material for his writing. He mailed some of his new poems and prose writings to publications in the United States, and they were published while he was still living abroad. His reputation grew, even in his absence.

Weary of financial difficulties overseas, Hughes moved back to the United States, joining his mother in Washington, DC. He briefly worked as an assistant in the office of the noted historian Carter G. Woodson, but the prestige of his new employer did not override his aversion to the work he was asked to do. Complaining of too much eyestrain and too many detailed assignments, Hughes left Woodson and took a job in a restaurant while continuing to write poetry and prose. *Opportunity* magazine awarded him first prize in a poetry contest in 1925, and writer Carl Van Vechten successfully urged publisher Alfred A. Knopf to offer Hughes a book contract. Although *The Weary Blues* was already under contract with Knopf, Hughes posed for photos and made the news when he was "discovered" as the "busboy poet" by poet Vachel Lindsay at the Wardman Park Hotel in Washington, DC, later that year.

In 1926, the same year that Knopf published *The Weary Blues*, Hughes returned to university. Already recognized as a writer, Hughes enrolled in Pennsylvania's Lincoln University, the oldest historically black college in the United States. His second volume of poetry, *Fine Clothes to the Jew*, was published in 1927. During his matriculation at Lincoln, Hughes worked on his novel *Not without Laughter* (1930), majored in sociology, and joined the Omega Psi Phi fraternity. Hughes frequently traveled to New York City to enjoy theater, music, and the atmosphere of the period later known as the Harlem Renaissance. His education was financially supported by friends, and his literary endeavors were supported and monitored carefully by a wealthy but controlling patron, Charlotte Mason.

Having already collaborated with several young writers and artists to produce the first and only volume of the magazine *Fire!!*, Hughes aligned himself with the rebellious new generation of African Americans who took pride in the language, music, and behavior of common black folk. More conservative and better-educated black critics sometimes condemned Hughes, with one even calling him the "poet low-rate" of Harlem in a review of *Fine Clothes to the Jew*.

Hughes graduated from Lincoln University in 1929. The following year, he broke away from Mason, even though fellow writer Zora Neale Hurston and Howard University professor Alain Locke remained associated with her. Once again, Hughes refused to surrender his personal aesthetic and philosophy for the sake of financial support.

To promote his writing and gain some funds, Hughes heeded the advice of Mary McLeod Bethune—racial leader and founder of Bethune-Cookman College—and took his poetry to the people by touring the South, reading his work, and meeting his fans. He secured an award from the Rosenwald Foundation and sold his works as he traveled. Adoring fans welcomed the young, handsome, and engaging poet, and his audiences and readership grew. Hughes remained aware of political issues as he made his first real tour of the South, focusing in particular on the case of the Scottsboro Boys, a group of young black men accused of raping two white women in Alabama in 1931. Hughes visited the accused men and wrote poems, essays, and plays in response to their plight.

In 1932, Hughes joined a group of African Americans who accepted an invitation to work on a film project in the Soviet Union. The venture failed, but Hughes remained in the region, traveling and observing conditions. He was particularly impressed to see that in Soviet Asia, those with brown skin did not always face discrimination. Unlike many other American writers, who were drawn to purely theoretical concepts of socialism during the 1930s, Hughes appreciated behaviors and attitudes he actually observed in Eastern Europe. He celebrated the absence of Jim Crow segregation practices, the apparent absence of anti-Semitism, and the availability of education and medical care. He recorded impressions of his travels in many poems, in his *Chicago Defender* column, and in his second autobiography, *I Wonder as I Wander* (1956). Before returning to the United States, he also visited China and Japan.

Turning his attention to other genres of literature, Hughes published his first volume of short stories, *The Ways of White Folks*, in 1934. His career as a playwright blossomed when his play *Mulatto* experienced a successful run on Broadway between 1935 and 1936. In addition, Hughes worked in Cleveland, Ohio, with the Karamu House, and in New York he established the Harlem Suitcase Theater. Guggenheim and Rosenwald Fellowships helped to finance and encourage his work in theater. Hughes also turned to journalism and autobiographical writing during this period. In 1937, he reported on the Spanish Civil War for the *Baltimore Afro-American*. He was encouraged by friends and supporters to tell his own life story, the first volume of which was published in 1940 as *The Big Sea*.

Although Hughes was not compelled to serve in the military when the United States entered World War II, he did offer his writing skills to promote nationalism, creating jingles to encourage Americans to buy war bonds. He had also begun writing weekly columns in the *Chicago Defender*. While these columns typically discussed books, food, and travels, they also sometimes urged readers to remain loyal to the United States and the Allied forces—in spite of persistent segregation and discrimination in civilian and military life. His fictional creation Jesse B. Semple, also known as Simple, gave Hughes another voice through which to express frustration about racism in a nation that alleged its advocacy of democracy. From occasional appearances in the *Chicago Defender*, Simple grew to become one of Hughes's most enduring and well-crafted creations. Simon and Schuster published *Simple Speaks His Mind*, the first book-length collection of Simple stories, in 1950.

Although the newspaper columns increased his audience, Hughes's greatest financial success resulted from a theatrical collaboration with Kurt Weill and Elmer Rice. Hughes helped to adapt Rice's play *Street Scene* into a musical, which opened on Broadway in 1947. Its success allowed Hughes to purchase his first and only home, a brownstone in his beloved Harlem.

Clearly, Hughes established himself as a citizen of the world, a creator of many genres of literature, and an artist whose success extended far beyond the Harlem Renaissance. Despite his reputation as a talented and respected American artist, which was underscored by an award granted to him by the American Academy of Arts and Letters in 1945, Hughes became the subject of an investigation by Senator Joseph McCarthy's subcommittee on subversive activities in 1953. Due to his travels in the Soviet Union and association with known members of the Communist Party, Hughes became a target for those who questioned his loyalty to the United States. However, this negative attention did not end his career. Hughes went on to serve as an official US representative to the 1966 First World Festival of Negro Arts in Dakar, Senegal, and travel to other countries on behalf of the US State Department.

Hughes had been determined to make a living as a writer, but he had no idea how much writing he would have to do in order to succeed. In the last fifteen years of his life, he typically worked on multiple book projects and a few plays simultaneously. His correspondence with his close friend and collaborator Arna Bontemps, much of which is collected in *Arna Bontemps–Langston Hughes Letters, 1925–1967* (1980; ed. Charles H. Nichols), clearly reveals how frantically Hughes juggled his multiple assignments. Hughes produced an amazing variety of books, including edited anthologies and collaborations. Among his best-known works are his volumes of Simple stories, including *Simple Takes a Wife* (1953) and *Simple's Uncle Sam* (1965), and a musical play, *Simply Heavenly*, which ran on Broadway in 1957. One of his most innovative poetic volumes, *Ask Your Mama: 12 Moods for Jazz*, was published in 1961, the year Hughes was inducted into the National Institute of Arts and Letters.

Hughes also published a series of histories for young readers, including *Famous American Negroes* and *The First Book of Rhythms* in 1954 and *The First Book of Jazz* and *Famous Negro Music Makers* in 1955. Hughes published the second volume of his autobiography, *I Wonder as I Wander*, in 1956. He published *Fight for Freedom*, the history of the National Association for the Advancement of Colored People (NAACP), in 1962.

His numerous collections include two volumes of short stories, *Laughing to Keep from Crying* (1952) and *Something in Common* (1963); *Selected Poems* (1957), from which he omitted his controversial poems about socialism; and a volume that combines several genres, *The Langston Hughes Reader* (1958).

Hughes worked on a number of collaborations with various writers, editors, and artists in the last fifteen years of his life. With photographer Roy De Carava, he published *The Sweet Flypaper of Life* in 1955, co-editing *A Pictorial History of the Negro in America* with Milton Meltzer the following year. Sometimes referred to as a dean of literature, Hughes also made significant contributions as an editor. In assembling *The Best Short Stories by Negro Writers* (1967), he recognized the talent of Alice Walker, publishing her first short story, "To Hell with Dying." He also edited two volumes of literature from Africa.

After two weeks of treatment at the New York Polyclinic Hospital, Hughes died on May 22, 1967, from complications related to prostate cancer. He retained his own brand of humor to the very end, leaving instructions stipulating that Duke Ellington's "Do Nothing Till You Hear from Me" be played at his memorial service.

Several books and collaborations by Hughes were published posthumously. His final volume of poetry, *The Panther and the Lash* (1967), was already complete at the time of his death. Several collaborations were also under way at the time, including a pictorial study of blacks in entertainment, *Black Magic* (1967; with Meltzer), and a revised edition of *The Poetry of the Negro 1746–1970* (1970; with Bontemps).

Scholars of Hughes have continued to study and edit collections of his work. Faith Berry brings to light many of the socialist works Hughes suppressed after his subpoena to appear before Senator McCarthy in *Good Morning Revolution* (1973). *The Collected Poems of Langston Hughes* (1994), edited by Arnold Rampersad and David Roessel, has eclipsed Hughes's own *Selected Poems*. *The Return of Simple* (1994), edited by Donna Akiba Sullivan Harper, introduces readers to the stories omitted from *The Best of Simple* and even includes some stories never before printed in books. In *Langston Hughes and the Chicago Defender* (1995), Christopher C. De Santis restores to readers many of the nonfiction columns Hughes wrote during his lengthy career as a newspaper columnist.

The centennial of Hughes's birth in 2002 inspired scholarly programs and musical celebrations throughout the United States as well as a commemorative stamp issued by the US Postal Service. Forty years after his death, in 2007, *Foreign Literature Studies* held an international symposium on Hughes at Central China Normal University in Wuhan, China. Representatives of the Langston Hughes Society, organized in 1981, joined scholars from China and other nations to remember the works of Langston Hughes—a citizen of the world, a writer of many genres, and an individual whose works continue to be read and enjoyed.

CRITICAL CONTEXTS

The Critical Reception of
Langston Hughes, 1924–2012

R. Baxter Miller and Dolan Hubbard

In 1926, Langston Hughes's fellow poet Countee Cullen believed that Hughes's long-term reputation would be assessed according to his blues lyrics, which Cullen believed could never be literary art. Though Cullen was certainly right in one sense of measure, the issue was more complex. Hughes's work has indeed been evaluated on those terms, but the result has been more positive than Cullen imagined. While Cullen's own view on poetry was traditional and perhaps even anachronistic, Hughes ventured on the path of bold experimentation in the poetics of popular forms during the 1920s, the proletarian effects and angry moods of the Great Depression during the 1930s, and the modernist devices such as montages and streams of consciousness during the 1940s and 1950s. Eventually, during the 1960s, Hughes wrote the explosive visual and auditory effects of African American history and jazz. Hughes, usually more imaginative that those who wrote about him, portrayed the rich multidimensions of existence in forceful blends of cinematic and political images.

Today the critical trajectory of eighty-eight years of scholarship about Hughes's literature is clear. Cullen was correct in that the critical reviews of Hughes's first volume of poetry, *The Weary Blues* (1926), remain an initial milestone for evaluating Hughes's accomplishments as a writer. What Cullen could not have prophesied during the Harlem Renaissance, however, was that Hughes's oeuvre would be tested against three subsequent landmarks in critical acclaim. By midcareer, marked by the publication of *Fields of Wonder* in 1947, Hughes's reputation would situate him as a postblues lyricist in the postwar world; in 1967, the year of his death in New York, Hughes and his work would be considered a testimony to African American culture and freedom. At the same time, the sudden epiphany by American readers of Hughes's inestimable value at the moment of his passing reinvigorated the recognition of his impact on transatlantic culture and aesthetics. Even so, it has taken until the first decade of the twenty-first century to articulate the critical legacy about his political world, taking into account the social world that produced Langston Hughes and the literary art that transformed it.

During much of the twentieth century, both the popular and scholarly writing on Hughes tended to be rooted in the idiomatic expressions of the Harlem, or New Negro, Renaissance of the 1920s. As time went on, the criticism advanced past the civil rights movement of the late 1950s and 1960s on to the present day's poststructuralism. We inquire now into the critical reception of Hughes's work, which has had an inexorable influence on writers around the world, especially in mid-twentieth-century France and present-day Latin America. In historical order, then, we lay out the significant themes and theories of Hughes's literary reputation, beginning with the Harlem Renaissance and advancing to today. We finish with the scholarly effect that this volume's contributors have had on Hughes's legacy.

The scholarship of the 1920s was particularly concerned with comparing Hughes to his black contemporaries, especially with regard to his innovative usage of music and his literary dialect. James Weldon Johnson, a leader of the old guard and editor of the *Book of American Negro Poetry* (1922), believed that racial dialect must be abandoned because such linguistic experimentation could express only sadness or humor. On the other side of the argument were the "New Negro" writers Zora Neale Hurston, Langston Hughes, and Sterling Brown, all of whom set out to prove that the humanity of blacks, if represented deeply despite such limits, could eventually collapse them. Often, many white traditionalists praised dialect for condescending reasons, while even a few middle-class blacks accepted such expression as authentic examples of culture. The more traditionalist position came from Robert T. Klein and Countee Cullen. In contrast to Herbert Gorman, who claims in a review that Hughes's blues poems represent a "vivid sensation of the Negro spirit" (2; Miller, *Reference* 9[1]), Alain

Locke, a Howard University professor of philosophy, comments about the folk style in a less demeaning way, placing Hughes in the context of Anglo-American modernists. To Locke, Hughes voiced "not the ragged provincialism of a minstrel but the descriptive detachment of a Vachel Lindsay and [Carl] Sandburg" and the "democratic sweep and universality of a [Walt] Whitman" (qtd. in Miller 9–10). Elizabeth Sergeant, somewhat more concerned with Hughes's literary strategies, remarks rather dubiously that Hughes's style was colloquial, casual, and fervent—in the "manner of the race" (371–72; Miller 7–9). Babette Deutsch compliments a folk idiom that transcends the old stereotypes of African Americans (220; Miller 9). Though reviewers such as Kenneth Fearing proposed that Hughes was unfamiliar with Standard English (29), Julia Peterkin accepted Hughes's conversational manner. Without the use of conventional forms, she notes in her review of *Fine Clothes to the Jew* (1927), Hughes created despair in comedy and tragedy. In fact, according to her, Hughes may well have created a literary space beyond the standard genres (44–47; Miller 10).

At the time, the use of African American folk diction often resulted in controversy among literary circles. As Hughes notes in his 1940 autobiography, *The Big Sea*, "Negro" critics such as Benjamin Brawley often assigned black literature the task of "uplifting" the race (265–68). Hence, these critics condemned *Fine Clothes to the Jew*, Hughes's second volume of verse, for its explicit representations of female sensuality. And yet, it was precisely the same volume of poetry that would be celebrated by critical realists a decade later. On balance, Hughes hardly portrayed the racial mask rendered so brilliantly by Paul Laurence Dunbar thirty years before. In his classic poem "We Wear the Mask," Dunbar expresses his regret that so many prejudiced readers refused to perceive a black humanity voiced within and beyond the vernacular. Hughes, on the contrary, recovered vital human qualities that had been so distorted by the minstrel devices of the late nineteenth century. Already, Hughes was on the road toward creating a new African American modernism that would represent the displacement of blacks in historical time and the fragmentation of their lost identity. In the 1920s, hardly anyone really knew what to call this intellectual advance on behalf of black writers. There was, of course, no critical school to proclaim the young Langston Hughes an early deconstructionist who critiqued the values of an old order so as to refashion a more innovative one. Though Hughes's great dramatic monologue "Mother to Son" and T. S. Eliot's long poem *The Waste Land* both appeared in 1922, it would take decades for readers to recognize that African American writers represented a distinct variant of modernism.

If the scholarship of the 1920s situated Hughes clearly in the context of the Harlem Renaissance, the critical reception of the 1930s reflected on this earlier decade, which appeared romantic to those later observers living during the Great Depression. It might have been expected that Johnson, an uplift idealist from the turn of the twentieth century, would have agreed with Cullen, a younger traditionalist who was convinced that Hughes's blues lyrics could never be literary art (Miller 7–8). Indeed, it was Cullen who was wary of Hughes's rebellion against classical form.[2] Hughes, according to Johnson, took poetic subjects from the gutter—in other words, from his sensual acknowledgment of black female bodies (Miller 11–13).

In 1930 J. Saunders Redding, who would become director of the National Endowment of the Humanities in 1966 and the Ernest I. White Professor of American Studies and Humane Letters at Cornell University in 1970, recognized Hughes as the natural counterpart to Cullen (*To Make* 113–17; Miller 13). Indeed, at the time the two poets represented major alternatives in African American aesthetics. In "The Poetry and Argument of Langston Hughes" (1938), Norman MacLeod characterizes Hughes as an honest and sincere man, yet a folk poet who expressed emotion more than cognition (358–59; Miller 16). In the long run, however, Cullen has proved to be the less profound and enduring of the two poets. Though contemporaries often preferred Cullen, Hughes is almost indisputably recognized today as the foremost African American poet to emerge from the Harlem Renaissance.

While the intelligentsia may have preferred Cullen, the adopted son of a Methodist minister, the masses chose Hughes. Redding recognized this authenticity in Hughes's work more than MacLeod did.

As the Great Depression deepened during the decade, much of the scholarship of Hughes struck a proletarian tone. Lydia Filatova characterizes Hughes's work as deviating from that of the bourgeois intellectuals of the time and argues that in breaking with the "old" Negro tradition, Hughes became a social realist, a "revolutionary poet of the Negro proletariat" (103–05; Miller 13) Since Hughes's socialist critics prescribed the devices of poetic polemic and didactic persuasion, popular theorists often began critical analyses of his works by seeking out the political qualities. Bolstered by the widespread public resentment at the failures of the American government in providing adequate employment for most citizens during the Depression, such critics made politics a litmus test for enabling writers to publish work in progressive forums. To the socialists, of course, the public voice in literary works was much more important than the individual one. It was not enough for these well-meaning critics to inquire about Hughes's literary representation or form. After all, they privileged revolutionary documentary over beautiful poems. The literary quality of some of Hughes's finest stories probably disappointed them.

Similar to the reception of Hughes's first novel, the response to his first collection of short stories, *The Ways of White Folks* (1934), evinced critical subjectivity. To Sherwood Anderson, a Chicago realist, Hughes's blacks were "alive and warm" while the whites were "pretentious and fake." Anderson teases in his review, "Mr. Hughes, my hat is off to you in relation to your own race, but not mine" (49–50; Miller 14). Herschel Brickell saw in *Ways* some of the best stories to appear in the country, strengthening Hughes's reputation as a talented black writer (286; Miller 14). Despite a noticeable consciousness of race and class, according to Horace Gregory, the work transcended the traditional separation of propaganda and art (4; Miller 14). Alain Locke recognized the tales as challenging all who wanted to understand race in America. In *Negro Voices in American Fiction* (1948), Hugh M. Gloster recalls Hughes's alliance with the leftists of the 1930s and describes *Ways* as an "outstanding indictment of Nordicism in modern American fiction" (219–22; Miller 22). John W. Parker, a prolific reviewer of works over the next decade, later insisted that Hughes exemplified the era. But Harvey Curtis Webster, a critic who clearly favored an Anglo-American modernism, faulted Hughes for expressing the community more than the individual.

During World War II, critics shifted the focus from Hughes the writer to Hughes the man, affirming a broad humanity on an international scale. Arna Bontemps, a close friend and collaborator of Hughes for many years, describes him as a "great lover of simple people" (i–xvi; Miller 17). Edwin Embree, a white liberal, recognizes him as an individual artist who was free of "any church, even the party's" (96; Miller 19). In *Negro Caravan* (1941), Sterling Brown and Arthur P. Davis, probably the two most accomplished African American anthologists during the first half of the century, describe Hughes as a cosmopolitan who encountered many people in Africa, Asia, Europe, and the Americas. In contrast, Rebecca Chalmers Barton depicts him as an interloper who mingled with elites. At the same time, G. Lewis Chandler appreciates Hughes for viewing the world through a racial lens in order to acquire a more universal outlook (189–91; Miller 23). Hughes's astute perception of global linkages derived from a subconscious agreement with the concept of negritude—the idea that fulfilling the personal self becomes a conduit to a broader humanity. By not accepting an arbitrary binary between races, Chandler distinguishes himself from the vast majority of his critical contemporaries.

Of all the critiques of Hughes's work by fellow writers, Richard Wright's is probably the most salient. Hughes, according to the eventual founder of the Black Chicago Renaissance and master of the protest novel, contributed much to American literature; he freed black writing from intellectual timidity, just as Theodore Dreiser, a twentieth-century naturalist, liberated American letters from Puritanism (600–01; Miller

18). Critics respected Hughes as a reliable voice of African American culture. An anonymous reviewer for the *Nation* recognizes a light tone in *Shakespeare in Harlem* (1942), while M. Column observes Hughes's spiritual power as reconstituted from the spirituals. These observations show a concern for African American cultural tradition that would distinguish works by later critics such as George E. Kent of the University of Chicago. Having pointed out that *Shakespeare* had a superior structure, Owen Dodson, playwright and chair of the theater department at Howard University, labels the volume a careless surface job unworthy of Hughes, "backing into the future, looking at the past" (337–38; Miller 19). Already Hughes was shifting emphasis from poetry to prose, as the popular reviewer Rolfe Humphries helped clarify the subjectivity within Hughes's critical reception. Regarding the poetry, Humphries expresses a preference for complex style and more personal, rather than racial, subject matter (80; Miller 23). As one would theorize, Langston Hughes needed to be a Euro-American modernist.

On the contrary, Hughes's publications displayed a writer well on his way to becoming an African American modernist. Hughes helped fashion a new idiom in which the global strategies of modernism became diversified into innovative expressions of African American experience. Indeed, the variety of Hughes's creative output was startling: *Simple Speaks His Mind* (1950), a collection of comic tales; *Montage of a Dream Deferred* (1951), his first complete book of jazz in mosaic format; *Laughing to Keep from Crying* (1952), the first major book of short fiction by Hughes to appear in eighteen years; *The First Book of Negroes* (1952), a chronology and history; *I Wonder as I Wander* (1956), his second autobiography; *Tambourines to Glory* (1958), a comic novel; and finally *Selected Poems* (1959), the definitive collection of Hughes's poetry for the next thirty-five years. During Hughes's perhaps most productive decade, the 1950s, the major scholars of his creative writing were reviewer Parker and essayist Davis.

Two important contributions by Davis to *Phylon*, the prominent journal on African American culture founded by W. E. B. Du Bois in

1940, sparked an interest that would continue for at least twenty years. Davis explains that Hughes used Harlem both as place and as symbol ("Harlem" 276; Miller 27). By portraying a particular ghetto, Hughes described them all. Later, Davis wrote the definitive article on the function of the tragic mulatto in Hughes's oeuvre. In the advance from his evaluation of *Montage*, Parker critiques *Laughing to Keep from Crying* (1952) while emphasizing Hughes's effectiveness in blending a humor of characterization with a comedy of situation ("Literature" 257–58; Miller 26). In reviewing *The First Book of Jazz*, Parker confirms Hughes's change of emphasis from poetry to prose ("American Jazz" 318–19; Miller 31). In a later review, he discerns a unity of action in *Simple Stakes a Claim* (1957) ("Remarkable" 435–36), thus applying Aristotelian principles of dramatic theory successfully to Hughes's craftsmanship in short fiction.

Certainly Jesse B. Semple, or Simple, whose name is a play on "just be simple," has been one of the most critiqued characters in all of Hughes's works. Through the placement of the Simple figure in the comic tradition of Mr. Dooley, an Irish saloon keeper featured in the writings of newspaper humorist Finley Peter Dunne, Redding provides a useful context of literary history. In accord with this reasoning, Hughes's second novel, *Tambourines to Glory*, was quite humorous in gospel hilarity and might have sustained a larger readership than *Laughing to Keep from Crying* ("What It Means" 13; Miller 24). Perhaps this prediction never really came true because the view underestimated the importance of literary technique and intellectual depth; *Tambourines* was instead perceived as a little superficial. Having noted its simplicity of plot and character, Atlanta University professor Richard Long also perceives in *Tambourines* a mastery of black idiom (192–93; Miller 36). Keith Waterhouse writes that the story proved amusing but incorporated hymns that recurred all too frequently. Few critics admitted that the novel was almost never the best genre for Hughes, certainly less suited to his talent than lyrics and short stories.

And there were, too, the fundamental disagreements between African American artistic and critical generations. James Baldwin's review of *Selected Poems* was somewhat insensitive and arrogant (6; Miller 35). Baldwin was twenty-two years younger than Hughes and a native son of New York who spoke with local authority. While Hughes, a successful migrant from Missouri and Kansas, was a New Yorker by choice rather than by birth, Baldwin expressed a homegrown authenticity. By 1953 Baldwin was the well-known author of the Christian novel *Go Tell It on the Mountain*, and by 1955 he became the accomplished voice of *Notes of a Native Son*, which favored lyricism in fiction over literary protest. By the publication of *The Fire Next Time* (1963), Baldwin changed his mind about literary protest. In time, the common belief in the civil rights movement brought Baldwin and Hughes ideologically closer, but they never reconciled.

By the end of Hughes's life, many other critics came to appreciate his conversion of blues sources into literary expression, and he became a bridge between the Harlem Renaissance of the 1920s and the black arts movement of the 1960s and early 1970s. On May 22, 1967, by all reports, Hughes died of prostate failure and a heart ailment in the Polyclinic Hospital of New York City. In national and international publications such as the *Nation, Newsweek*, the *Crisis, Freedomways, Negro Digest* (later *Black World*), and *Présence Africaine*, his death brought sympathetic responses. Essays portrayed a man of high conscience whom writers fondly remembered. His inspiration of young writers, along with his imaginary portraits of the folk masses, survived. While he was generous to a fault, his work authenticated a black quest for freedom in North America. In the extension of racial sensibility to its universal implications, he demonstrated humanity.

The most thoughtful comments came from fellow black writers. The Pulitzer Prize–winning poet Gwendolyn Brooks described Hughes as an inspiration to aspiring authors who appreciated folk verisimilitude. Poet Mari Evans, whose volume *I Am a Black Woman* (1970) would become a rallying cry of black feminism in the 1970s, called Hughes the "most generous professional I have ever known" (36; Miller 47). Hughes's friend Nicolás Guillén, a legendary Cuban poet, remembered him well, while Bontemps recognized Hughes's fidelity to the African American people and their cause ("He Spoke" 142–43; Miller 50). Loften Mitchell, the brilliant playwright of *Star of the Morning* (1965) and an acquaintance of Hughes, described Hughes as a greater man than Mitchell himself would ever become (77–78; Miller 57). Extensive summaries of Hughes's critical reputation appeared in R. Baxter Miller's *Langston Hughes and Gwendolyn Brooks: A Reference Guide* in 1978. By then most critics agreed that Hughes expressed a continuity of race in the modern world.

If, for Hughes, the 1960s were a decade of recognition, one reason was certainly the emergence of James Emanuel, the first scholar to write a published book about Hughes in the United States. Beginning with an original analysis of Hughes's first short story, Emanuel went on to complete a doctoral dissertation on Hughes at Columbia University. En route he mapped out significant areas of terrain: sixty-five short stories; biography; the theme of negritude; "Body in the Moonlight," Hughes's first short story; and *Panther and the Lash* (1967), the last volume of verse, which was published posthumously. Emanuel's brief biography of Hughes, published in the anthology *Dark Symphony* (1968), demonstrates a great deal of knowledge researched during seven years of publication.

The last decade of Hughes's life highlighted the ongoing debate of whether Hughes was a 1930s radical or a 1940s dreamer. W. Edward Farrison, a doctoral graduate of the Ohio State University during the 1930s and an early president of the College Language Association (CLA) years later, reviewed Hughes's writings several times during the decade. Farrison's productivity ran parallel to the development of the *CLA Journal* (*CLAJ*), founded in 1957. The Farrison School (the CLA contingent of the old guard) argued that Hughes believed in the American dream, but since then commentators such as Faith Berry have reprised the socialist tradition while insisting that Hughes was a popular revolutionary.

Often, Southern white critics such as James Presley agreed with the Farrison group (380–86; Miller 41). In a way, the 1960s actually prepared for the 1970s, since both camps skewed the critical interpretations of Hughes according to personal ideologies. If Berry's collection of Hughes's political poems, *Good Morning Revolution* (1973), shows a Marxist tone, Hughes's fine lyric "Daybreak in Alabama" confirms the importance of the poet's imaginary landscape. Instead of emphasizing violent revolution, Hughes expresses a vision representing both his aesthetic terrain and his political commitment.

The 1970s saw a flowering of Hughes scholarship in an extensive range of studies, with a variety of critiques, pioneering bibliographies, and international studies published during the decade. Donald C. Dickinson's *Bio-Bibliography of Langston Hughes, 1902–1967* (1967) was published in 1972. Critiques by Davis first published in the 1950s were reprinted in Donald B. Gibson's *Five Black Writers* (1970) and Therman B. O'Daniel's *Langston Hughes: Black Genius* (1971). Davis's own *From the Dark Tower* (1974) summarizes many insights about Hughes's work. Emanuel, who had been the definitive critical voice on Hughes during the 1960s, continued to produce original work, exploring Hughes's religious themes in Gibson's *Modern Black Poets: Twentieth Century Views* (1973). Onwuchekwa Jemie's *Langston Hughes: An Introduction to the Poetry* (1976) reprises the theory that political circumstances of the times produced the literary effects of political resistance and change expressed in Hughes's writing, challenging New Critical views that literature is only art for art's sake. In particular, the 1970s helped establish pioneering works in reference and in textual scholarship.

The first wave of research with an international focus appeared during the 1970s. Often this research focused on the comparative biography of black writers in the African diaspora, as its second wave would later emphasize comparative literary patterns and transnational experiences. The basic trend had begun during the 1960s. As early as 1962,

Enrique Noble had completed "Nicolás Guillén y Langston Hughes" for the Spanish-speaking world, and it was followed nearly a decade later by Lemuel A. Johnson's *The Devil, the Gargoyle, and the Buffoon: The Negro as Metaphor in Western Literature* (1971). Similarly, a pioneering contribution in 1977 by Edward J. Mullen, a prolific critic at the University of Missouri at Columbia, set the stage for a focused monograph by Martha K. Cobb, *Harlem, Haiti, and Havana: A Comparative Critical Study of Langston Hughes, Jacques Roumain, Nicolás Guillén* (1979). While Hughes was African American, Roumain was Haitian and Guillén Cuban. Each writer voiced the personal and national variation of racial liberation. So, the Italian *Testo e contesto della poesia di Langston Hughes*, published by Stefania Piccinato in 1979, completed an international pattern initiated in part by the Haitian René Piquion in *Langston Hughes: Un chant nouveau* in 1940 and the intellectual history narrated by François Dodat in *Langston Hughes* (1964). The latter two volumes were published in France. Perhaps the most impeccably detailed and discerning of all European critics was the French scholar Jean Wagner, whose impressive tome *Les poètes nègres des États-Unis* (1962) was translated into English by Kenneth Douglas for the University of Illinois Press in 1973.

In the 1970s, R. Baxter Miller began to set a tone of inquiry into the aesthetic and political strategies of Langston Hughes's writings in various genres. Miller recognizes the lyric "Daybreak in Alabama" as a delightful closure to Hughes's vision, opening inquiry into the writer's use of poetic landscape. Trying to combine the folk aesthetic of Kent with the reader's response criticism of Davis, Miller grounds critical insights in facts reported by literary historians such as Farrison in earlier reviews and by Richard K. Barksdale in *Langston Hughes: The Poet and His Critics* (1977).[3] In addition, Miller extends a literary sophistication of interpretation to matters of literary structure, metrics, imagery, and myth. What was left for Miller to realize, of course, was that such aesthetic qualities are invariably linked to the process of storytelling itself, especially in the autobiographies; to Hughes's voice within the stories; to the political circumstances that produce the aesthetic responses in readers; and to the African American and human communities that bind text and reader.

As much as in any decade, the 1980s helped establish the study of Hughes as a global interest. O'Daniel, the founder and original editor of the *CLA Journal* for the years 1957 and 1958 and, like Hughes, an alumnus of Lincoln University in Pennsylvania, was a good friend to Hughes for many years. Shortly after Hughes's death in 1967, O'Daniel directed the publication of six essays paying homage to the writer in the June 1968 issue of *CLAJ*. Coupled with five additional papers, the original collection became the core of the groundbreaking *Langston Hughes: Black Genius* (1971). By 1981, O'Daniel became the founding editor of the *Langston Hughes Review*, which began to publish fine articles on Hughes's legacy, including studies of his textual and formal influence on later writers. Almost immediately the new publication developed into the official publication of the Langston Hughes Society, the first association established to honor an African American writer. In 1981 the society took shape as an international association of scholars, performing and creative artists, students, and public admirers. In part, it was the product of a successful conference on Langston Hughes held in Joplin, Missouri, the city of his birth, on March 13 and 14, 1981. The meeting, sponsored by Missouri Southern State College and funded by the Missouri Committee for the Humanities, confirmed Hughes's distinction within modern American literature.

Supported initially by Brown University, the journal later moved to the Institute of African American Studies and the Department of English at the University of Georgia. Editors have been, in turn, George Bass, professor of African American studies, English, and theater at Brown and former executive secretary to Langston Hughes; Thadious M. Davis; Dolan Hubbard; Valerie Babb; and Miller. With a limited membership of about fifty subscribers, the circulation came to include nearly two hundred supporters. In addition to scholarly articles, the journal publishes book reviews and announcements. Among its varied interests are the African diaspora and therefore the critical receptions of Hughes's writings in Haiti, Cuba, France, Colombia, and Japan; the subject of black women as agents of racial culture; and the critical narratives about definitive artists, writers, and scholars such as Bass, Darwin Turner, Frank Marshall Davis, Hughes, and Dorothy West. In complement to the *CLA Journal*, which features scholarship by many of the leading African American and literary historians of the previous thirty years, the *Review* developed into a forum for critical voices across generations. It has especially sought to publish work and provide forums of leadership for the ablest young scholars of African American literature and diaspora studies.

The 1980s also saw the publication of Berry's fascinating narrative *Langston Hughes: Before and Beyond Harlem* (1983) and the definitive two-volume work *The Life of Langston Hughes* (1986, 1988), researched and written by Arnold Rampersad. *Langston Hughes and the Blues* (1988), by Steven C. Tracy, considers the impact of black performers such as Ma Rainey, Bessie Smith, and Blind Lemon Jefferson on Hughes. In *The Art and Imagination of Langston Hughes* (1988), Miller reminds readers that the aesthetic universe of the blues still allowed for innovative experimentations in Hughes's personal imagination.

In many ways, the final decade of the twentieth century was appropriately a time for the fruition of earlier promise. In *Langston Hughes: A Bio-Bibliography* (1990), Thomas A. Mikolyzk helps complete the pioneering work by Donald Dickinson in 1967 and the follow-up by Miller in 1978, presenting the first fully annotated bibliography on Hughes and a concise biography of the author. By 1992, Sharynn O. Etheridge updated a bibliography produced by Blyden Jackson, the first senior African American scholar of English hired by a major white research university in the South. With *Langston Hughes: The Contemporary Reviews* (1997) and *Langston Hughes: The Man, His Art, and His Continuing Influence* (1995), Tish Dace and C. James Trotman, respectively, bring to closure the bibliographical and critical work begun during the final third of the twentieth century. Rampersad's impeccably researched biography of Hughes for the *Oxford Companion to African American Literature* (1997) continues the tradition of fine biographical essays such as those by Arthur Davis in the *Dictionary of American Negro Biography* (1982) and Miller in the *Dictionary of Literary Biography* (1987). The publication of many of Barksdale's papers was delayed until the release of his collected essays, published by the University of Illinois Press in 1992. These essays include "The Humanistic Techniques Employed in Hughes's Poetry" (1981), "Langston Hughes and James Baldwin: Some Observations on a Literary Relationship" (1988), and "The Poet, the Preacher, and the Dream" (1988), the latter of which draws analogies between the poetic representation of freedom by Hughes and the political narrative by Martin Luther King Jr. The next year, Hans Ostrom published *Langston Hughes: A Study of the Short Fiction* (1993), the first book devoted to the subject.

Michel Fabre, owing to the immense success of his biography of Richard Wright published in 1973, probably replaced Wagner as the finest scholar of African American literature not only in France, but indeed in all of Europe. In *From Harlem to Paris: Black American Writers in France, 1840–1980* (1991), Fabre reports that historical circumstances altered the temper of African American expectations across the Atlantic. Paris, he argues, became a site of "aesthetic enjoyment" (71). A leading scholar of the current generation, Tyler Stovall explains in *Paris Noir: African Americans in the City of Light* (1996) that Hughes discovered in the city an African American community freed of the racial limitations of the United States. In "Local Color, Global 'Color'" (1993), testing the assimilation premise discussed by Paul Gilroy in *The Black Atlantic: Modernity and Double Consciousness* (1992), David Moore situates Hughes within the global context of a borderless world, especially Soviet Central Asia in 1932.

The 1990s marked a decade in which criticism of Langston Hughes's theatrical works came of age. In *Langston Hughes: Folk Dramatist in the Protest Tradition, 1921–1943* (1997), Joseph McLaren responds to a scholarly request made by Jackson in *Black American Writers:*

Bibliographic Essays in 1978. By the late 1990s, many of Hughes's plays had not been critiqued for at least thirty years. Darwin T. Turner examines the functions of characterization and practical context in "Hughes as Playwright" (1968), but a systematic inquiry of the kind had to await the theatrical history by Leslie Sanders entitled *The Development of Black Theater in America* (1988).

This development happened in many complementary venues on many creative fronts. By 1997 the *Langston Hughes Review* had printed a special issue on Hughes's plays, including a bibliographical appendix compiled by McLaren. On the performance front, Brian D. Bethune observes in "Langston Hughes's Lost Translation of Federico García Lorca's *Blood Wedding*" (1997) an effective expression rooted in Spanish soul. Bethune reaffirms excitement expressed by David Ignatow in "Memories of Langston Hughes" (1995) regarding Hughes's 1951 translation of García Lorca's *Gypsy Ballads* (1928). In the 1991 introduction to the three-act folk comedy *Mule Bone*, coauthored by Langston Hughes and Zora Neale Hurston in 1931, Henry Louis Gates Jr. reports on one of the most heated disputes in African American literary history. The play was belatedly produced at Lincoln Center in New York City that year.

Perhaps the most significant critical voices on Langston Hughes to emerge since 1990 are those of Donna Akiba Sullivan Harper and Christopher C. De Santis. Through the publication of *Not So Simple: The "Simple" Stories by Langston Hughes* (1995), Harper, the fourth president of the Langston Hughes Society, became the definitive scholar on both a subject and a character. In a detailed analysis, she explores the development of Hughes's bar buddy and street philosopher from Simple's initial appearance in the African American newspaper the *Chicago Defender* in 1943 to his farewell in the *New York Post* in 1965. Simple, of course, had been a transitional medium through which Hughes moved deftly between popular fiction and political commentary. As part of a larger trend that has continued unabated for twenty years, De Santis places these writings in a historical context with *Langston Hughes and the Chicago Defender: Essays on Race, Politics, and Culture, 1942–62* (1995). Largely through the excavation of lost primary materials, De Santis uses the techniques of New Historicism to reveal the ways in which recovered documents influence imaginary writing. At the same time, the method occasionally returns readers to the earlier days of historical context before critical insights by Emanuel and subsequent new, discerning analyses of artistry began to revolutionize the close reading and aesthetic theory of Hughes's works. Though *The Political Plays of Langston Hughes*, by Susan Duffy, was published in 2000, the historical positioning belongs naturally to the 1990s. Meanwhile, James Smethurst's *New Red Negro: The Literary Left and African American Poetry, 1930–1946* (1999) has emerged as one of the superbly researched New Historicist books explaining the ways in which ideologies of the Left influenced African American poetry between the Great Depression and World War II.

The scholarship of sexual orientation became more pronounced in the 1990s and early 2000s. An article by Charles Nero about homophobia in Rampersad's *Life of Langston Hughes* and a book by Siobhan B. Somerville entitled *Queering the Color Line: Race and the Invention of Homosexuality in American Culture* (2000) take bold new angles on Hughes's sexuality. In *The Scene of Harlem Cabaret: Race, Sexuality, Performance* (2009), Shane Vogel inquires into the formal poetics of queerness as well. While such observations belong technically to the new century, they actually complete pioneering research led by Gregory Woods in "Gay Re-Readings of the Harlem Renaissance Poets" (1993).

The scholarship of the early twenty-first century shows recurrences in subject matter and critical voices. In 2001, thirty-four years after Hughes's death and a year before the centennial celebration of his birth in states as varied as Ohio, New York, and Kansas, the University of Missouri Press commenced publication of Hughes's *Collected Works*. Because most future criticism of Hughes's life and writing will now have the benefit of being based on extensive primary materials, the event marked a watershed moment in Hughes scholarship. *Remember*

Me to Harlem: The Letters of Langston Hughes and Carl Van Vechten, 1925–1964, edited by Emily Bernard, reprises much historical information and provides the most exciting access to Hughes's epistles since the publication of the *Arna Bontemps–Langston Hughes Letters, 1925–1967* (1980), edited by Charles H. Nichols. Hans Ostrom's *Langston Hughes Encyclopedia* appeared in 2001. New critical momentum has resulted from fresh research into the correspondence between Bessie Head, an African writer of mixed blood, and Hughes, as demonstrated by Regennia N. Williams in 2007. Alfred Guillaume's 2007 analysis of Hughes's translations of francophone poetry considers international texts other than published letters.

In many ways, this volume demonstrates a historical unity in Hughes studies over the last forty years. In her comparison of Hughes's comic figures in poetry and fiction, Donna Akiba Sullivan Harper completes much of the inquiry that intrigued readers of her definitive book on Simple. David Roessel's analysis of the proletarian poetry by Hughes in the 1930s proves inventive, completing in part an interest that concerned Roessel during the coediting, with Rampersad, of the *Collected Poems*. Joseph McLaren, who has written pioneering work about the protest drama (1997), later extended insight of Hughes's trans-Atlantic connections to Africa (2000). It is his useful recovery of historical details that enriches his critical editions of the autobiographies in the *Collected Works*. Such critical recurrences allow for seamless transitions to the twenty-first century. R. Baxter Miller, editor of the short story volume in the *Collected Works*, has rounded out new interpretations initiated in "Café de la Paix: Mapping the Harlem Renaissance" (2000), "Remembering Hughes and His Art" (2004), and "Reinvention and Globalization in Hughes's Stories" (2005), articles revised for his *Literary Criticism of Five Generations of African American Writing: The Artistry of Memory* (2008). Several of his insights appear in the introduction to the 2006 paperback edition of his 1989 book. Steven C. Tracy featured many of the most accomplished Hughes scholars to appear since the 1980s in his critical volume *A Historical Guide to*

Langston Hughes (2004), including James Smethurst and Tracy himself. Indeed, it is fitting that Tracy, who served with Dolan Hubbard on the centennial board for the *Collected Works*, invited the latter to write the splendid bibliographical essay that concludes the *Historical Guide*. In addition, John Lowney's excellent article in this volume represents a fine issue of the *Langston Hughes Review* (2009), edited by Matthew Hofer, a collection derived from panels that took place at the annual meetings of the American Literature Association for 2007 and 2008. Impressed by the intellectual and cultural impact of Hughes on Latin Americans, Laurence Prescott explores further the originality of inquiry that he began in the *Langston Hughes Review* (2006) and the *Afro-Hispanic Review* (2006). While Hughes's global reach into the francophone world was well acclaimed by the mid-twentieth century, the trans-American connection has earned new emphasis during the last fifteen years. John Edgar Tidwell, who with Cheryl R. Ragar edited *Montage of a Dream Deferred: The Art and Life of Langston Hughes* (2007), and W. Jason Miller[4], who wrote *Langston Hughes and American Lynching Culture* (2011), inspire a new fervor for the historical and political contexts of Hughes's life and work.

Therefore, the critical reception of Langston Hughes reveals the history and literary history of the Harlem Renaissance and the Great Depression; the radicalism and artistry that emerged from the New York and Chicago popular fronts; the conscientious and ethical resistance to Anglo-American aesthetics as an exclusive standard for valuing texts by blacks and other communities of color in Africa, Europe, the Caribbean, and the Americas; and the organic nature and inseparability of the racial person from universal culture and literary art and the eventual reshaping of a new black aesthetic. It further reveals the experimentations in the narrative devices of stream of consciousness and the interiority of lyric or emotional expression; the often-overlooked explorations into African American modernist forms of the lyric and the dramatic monologue; the later literary devices of pictorial and media representation; the bonds of friendship and the political struggle of the 1940s, 1950s, and 1960s; and an emergent African American modernism. For the most part, the themes appear as developed across five decades in Hughes's rich variety of writing; they reveal his profound sense of African American resistance to an unjust order. It is a vital wisdom that the most gifted readers appreciate about Hughes, and they have done so now for nearly a century.

Notes
1. Unless otherwise noted, parenthetical references to Miller correspond to pages in R. Baxter Miller's *Langston Hughes and Gwendolyn Brooks: A Reference Guide*.
2. Cullen's own aesthetic model was the British romantic John Keats.
3. Barksdale was the graduate dean at North Carolina Central University before he moved to Atlanta University and then the University of Illinois.
4. At Washington State University, he wrote a doctoral dissertation on the subject of lynching in the lives and works of Langston Hughes and Elizabeth Bishop.

Works Cited
Anderson, Sherwood. "Paying for Old Sins." *Nation* 139 (1934): 49–50.
Baldwin, James. "Sermons and Blues." Rev. of *The Selected Poems of Langston Hughes*, by Langston Hughes. *New York Times Book Review* 29 March 1959: 6.
Barksdale, Richard K. "Langston Hughes: His Times and His Humanistic Techniques." *Black American Literature and Humanism*. Ed. R. Baxter Miller. Lexington: UP of Kentucky, 1981. 11–26.
_____. *Langston Hughes: The Poet and His Critics*. Chicago: ALA, 1977.
Berry, Faith. *Langston Hughes: Before and Beyond Harlem*. Westport: Hill, 1983.
Bontemps, Arna. Introduction. *Langston Hughes: Un chant nouveau*. By René Piquion. Port-au-Prince: Imprimérie de l'État, 1940. i–xvi.
_____. "Langston Hughes: He Spoke of Rivers." *Freedomways* 8 (1968): 140–43.
Brickell, Herschel. "The Literary Landscape." *North American Review* 238 (1934): 286.
Brown, Sterling. *The Negro in American Fiction*. Washington: Associates in Negro Education, 1937.
Calverton, V. F. *The Liberation of American Literature*. New York: Scribner's, 1932.
Chandler, G. Lewis. "Selfsameness and a Promise." *Phylon* 10 (1949): 189–91.
Cobb, Martha. *Harlem, Haiti, and Havana: A Comparative Critical Study of Langston Hughes, Jacques Roumain, Nicolás Guillén*. Washington: Three Continents, 1979.

Dace, Tish. *Langston Hughes: The Contemporary Reviews*. New York: Cambridge UP, 1997. Amer. Critical Archives 10.

Davis, Arthur P. *From the Dark Tower: Afro-American Writers, 1900–1960*. Washington: Howard UP, 1974.

———. "The Harlem of Langston Hughes's Poetry." *Phylon* 13 (1952): 276–83.

———. "Langston Hughes: Cool Poet." *CLA Journal* 11 (1968): 280–96.

Deutsch, Babette. "Four Poets." *Bookman* 65 (1926): 220–21.

Dickinson, Donald C. *A Bio-Bibliography of Langston Hughes, 1902–1967*. Hamden: Archon, 1967.

Dodson, Owen. "Shakespeare in Harlem." *Phylon* 11 (1942): 337–38.

Du Bois, W. E. B., and Alain Locke. "The Younger Literary Movement." *Crisis* 27 (1924): 161–63.

Duffy, Susan, ed. *The Political Plays of Langston Hughes*. Carbondale: Southern Illinois UP, 2000.

Emanuel, James A. *Langston Hughes*. New York: Twayne Publishers, 1967. Twayne's US Authors Ser. 123.

Embree, Edwin R. "A Poet's Story." *Survey Graphic* 30 (1941): 96.

Evans, Mari. "I Remember Langston." *Negro Digest* Sept. 1967: 36.

Fabre, Michel. *From Harlem to Paris: Black American Writers in France, 1840–1980*. Urbana: U of Chicago P, 1991.

Fearing, Kenneth. "Limiting Devices." *New Masses* 3 (1927): 29.

Filatova, Lydia. "Langston Hughes: American Writer." *International Literature* 11 (1933): 103–05.

Gibson, Donald. "The Good Black Poet and the Good Gray Poet." *Langston Hughes: Black Genius*. Ed. Therman B. O'Daniel. New York: Morrow, 1971. 65–80.

Gloster, Hugh M. *Negro Voices in American Fiction*. Chapel Hill: U of North Carolina P, 1948.

Gorman, Herbert, S. "Tradition and Experiment in Modern Poetry." *New York Times Book Review* 27 March 1967: 2.

Gregory, Horace. "Genius of Langston Hughes." *New York Herald Tribune Books* 1 July 1934: 4.

Guillaume, Alfred, Jr. "And Bid Him Translate: Langston Hughes's Translation of Poetry from French." *Langston Hughes Review* 4 (1985): 1–8.

Harper, Donna Akiba Sullivan. *Not So Simple: The "Simple" Stories by Langston Hughes*. Columbia: U of Missouri P, 1995.

Hofer, Matthew, ed. Spec. issue of *Langston Hughes Review* 15 (2009).

Hubbard, Dolan. "Bibliographical Essay." *A Historical Guide to Langston Hughes*. Ed. Steven C. Tracy. London: Oxford UP, 2004. 197–234.

———. "Call and Response: Intertextuality in the Poetry of Langston Hughes and Margaret Walker." *Langston Hughes Review* 7.1 (1988): 22–30.

———. "Langston Hughes Society." *Organizing Black America: An Encyclopedia of African American Associations*. Ed. Nina Mjagkij. New York: Garland, 2001. 299–300.

Hudson, Theodore. "Langston Hughes's Last Volume of Verse." *CLA Journal* 11 (1968): 345–48.

Huggins, Nathan. *Harlem Renaissance*. New York: Oxford UP, 1971.
Hughes, Langston. *The Big Sea*. New York: Hill, 1940.
_____. *The Collected Poems of Langston Hughes*. Ed. Arnold Rampersad and David E. Roessel. New York: Vintage, 1994.
_____. *The Collected Works of Langston Hughes*. Ed. Arnold Rampersad et al. 16 vols. Columbia: U of Missouri P, 2001–03.
Hughes, Langston, and Arna Bontemps. *Arna Bontemps–Langston Hughes Letters, 1925-1967*. Ed. Charles H. Nichols. New York: Dodd, 1980.
Hughes, Langston, and Carl Van Vechten. *Remember Me to Harlem: The Letters of Langston Hughes and Carl Van Vechten, 1925-1964*. Ed. Emily Bernard. New York: Knopf, 2001.
Humphries, Rolfe. "Verse Chronicle." *Nation* 168 (1949): 80.
Jackson, Blyden. "A Word about Simple." *CLA Journal* (1968): 310–18.
Jemie, Onwuchekwa. *Langston Hughes: An Introduction to the Poetry*. New York: Columbia UP, 1976. Columbia Introd. to Twentieth-Century Amer. Poetry.
Johnson, James Weldon, ed. *The Book of American Negro Poetry*. New York: Harcourt, 1922.
Kent, George E. "Langston Hughes and the Afro-American Folk and Cultural Tradition." *Langston Hughes: Black Genius*. Ed. Therman B. O'Daniel. New York: Morrow, 1971. 183–210.
Kinnamon, Keneth. "The Man Who Created 'Simple.'" *Nation* 205 (1967): 599–601.
Lewis, David Levering. *When Harlem Was in Vogue*. New York: Knopf, 1981.
Locke, Alain. "The Negro Poets of the United States." *Anthology of Magazine Verse for 1926 and Yearbook of American Poetry*. Ed. William Stanley Braithwaite. Boston: Brimmer, 1927. 143–51.
_____, ed. *The New Negro*. 1925. New York: Atheneum, 1968.
Long, Richard A. Rev. of *Tambourines to Glory*, by Langston Hughes. *CLA Journal* 2 (1958): 192–93.
MacLeod, Norman. "The Poetry and Argument of Langston Hughes." *Crisis* 45 (1938): 358–59.
McLaren, Joseph. "Langston Hughes and Africa: From the Harlem Renaissance to the 1960s." *Juxtapositions: The Harlem Renaissance and the Lost Generation*. Ed. Loes Nas and Lesley Marx. Cape Town: U of Cape Town, 2000. 77–94.
_____. *Langston Hughes: Folk Dramatist in the Protest Tradition, 1921–1943*. Westport: Greenwood, 1997. Contributions in Afro-Amer. and African Studies 181.
Mikolyzk, Thomas A. *Langston Hughes: A Bio-Bibliography*. New York: Greenwood, 1990. Bio-Bibliog. in Afro-Amer. and African Studies 2.
Miller, R. Baxter. *The Art and Imagination of Langston Hughes*. 1989. Lexington: UP of Kentucky, 2006.
_____. "Café de la Paix: Mapping the Harlem Renaissance." *South Atlantic Review* 65.2 (2000): 73–94.
_____. "Framing and Framed Languages in Hughes's *Ask Your Mama: 12 Moods for Jazz*." *MELUS* 17.4 (1991–92): 3–13.
_____. "Langston Hughes, 1902–1967." *A Historical Guide to Langston Hughes*. Ed. Steven C. Tracy. New York: Oxford UP, 2004. 23–62.

———. *Langston Hughes and Gwendolyn Brooks: A Reference Guide*. Boston: Hall, 1978. Ref. Pub. in Lit.
———. *On the Ruins of Modernity: New Chicago Renaissance from Wright to Kent*. Champaign: Common Ground, 2011.
———. "Reinvention and Globalization in Hughes's Stories." *MELUS* 30 (2005): 69–83.
Mitchell, Loften. "That Other Man." *Crisis* (1979): 77–78.
Mullen, Edward J. *Critical Essays on Langston Hughes*. Boston: Hall, 1986. Critical Essays on Amer. Lit.
———. *Langston Hughes in the Hispanic World and Haiti*. Hamden: Archon, 1977.
Noble, Enrique. "Nicolás Guillén y Langston Hughes." *Nueva Revista Cabana* (1961–62): 41–84.
O'Daniel, Therman B., ed. *Langston Hughes: Black Genius*. New York: Morrow, 1971.
Ostrom, Hans. *A Langston Hughes Encyclopedia*. Westport: Greenwood, 2002.
———. *Langston Hughes: A Study of the Short Fiction*. New York: Twayne, 1993.
Parker, John W. "American Jazz: Composite of Many Influences." *Phylon* (1955): 318–19.
———. "Literature of the Negro Ghetto." *Phylon* 13 (1952): 257–58.
———. "The Remarkable Mr. Simple Again." *Phylon* 18 (1957): 435–36.
Patterson, Louise. "With Langston Hughes in the USSR." *Freedomways* 8 (1968): 511–17.
Peterkin, Julia. "Negro Blue and Gold." *Poetry* 31 (1927–28): 44–47.
Presley, James. "The American Dream of Langston Hughes." *Southwest Review* 48 (1963): 380–86.
Rampersad, Arnold. *The Life of Langston Hughes*. 2 vols. New York: Oxford UP, 1986–88.
Redding, J. Saunders. *To Make a Poet Black*. Chapel Hill: U of North Carolina P, 1939.
———. "What It Means to Be Colored." *New York Herald Tribune Book Review* June 1950: 13.
Roessel, David. "'A Racial Act': The Letters of Langston Hughes and Ezra Pound." *Paideuma* 29.1–2 (2000): 207–42.
Sanders, Leslie Catherine. "'Also Own the Theater': Representations in the Comedies of Langston Hughes." *Langston Hughes Review* 11.1 (1992): 6–13.
Schatt, Stanley. "Langston Hughes: The Minstrel as Artificer." *Journal of Modern Literature* 4 (1974): 115–20.
Sergeant, Elizabeth. "The New Negro." *New Republic* 12 May 1926: 371–72.
Sheffey, Ruthe T. "Zora Neale Hurston and Langston Hughes's 'Mule Bone': An Authentic Folk Comedy and the Compromised Tradition." *Trajectory: Fueling the Future and Preserving the African American Literary Past*. Ed. Sheffey. Baltimore: Morgan State UP, 1989. 211–31.
Smethurst, James Edward. *The New Red Negro: The Literary Left and African American Poetry, 1930–1946*. New York: Oxford UP, 1999.

Stovall, Tyler. *Paris Noir: African Americans in the City of Light*. Boston: Houghton, 1996.

Tracy, Steven C. Introduction. *A Historical Guide to Langston Hughes*. Ed. Tracy. London: Oxford UP, 2004. 3–22.

_____. *Langston Hughes and the Blues*. Urbana: U of Illinois P, 1988.

Trotman, C. James. *Langston Hughes: The Man, His Art, and His Continuing Influence*. New York: Routledge, 1995.

Turner, Darwin T. "Langston Hughes as Playwright." *CLA Journal* 11 (1968): 297–309.

Wagner, Jean. *Black Poets of the United States: From Paul Laurence Dunbar to Langston Hughes*. 1962. Urbana: U of Illinois P, 1973.

Walker, Margaret. "New Poets." *Phylon* 11 (1950): 345–54.

Ward, Jerry W. "Langston Hughes/Blues Griot." *Langston Hughes Review* 12.2 (1993): 27.

Woods, Gregory. "Gay Re-Readings of the Harlem Renaissance Poets." *Critical Essays: Gay and Lesbian Writers of Color*. Ed. Emmanuel S. Nelson. New York: Haworth, 1993. 127–42.

Wright, Richard. "Forerunner and Ambassador." *New Republic* (1940): 600–01.

The "Diamond Stair" Within: Black Female Inspiration in Hughes's Poetry_____

R. Baxter Miller

Langston Hughes's comic detachment in poetry may well depend upon a deceptive artistry in locating his female personae in the historical moment, the postwar world, yet achieving a balanced viewpoint well beyond American history. It is especially the last of these that he rarely underestimated. It is possible to consider this female figure as a remarkable lens through which to perceive some of his most lasting poetry, from the early origins of his texts to the final resolutions of the spirit encapsulated within his poetic form. Indeed, through an inquiry into the formal and archetypal reach of his artistry, one can infer Hughes's transformative perception of the United States across the twentieth century.

He empowers his various renditions of the black woman with a double-edged vision. At once it heroically faces the racial segregation of the early part of the twentieth century, taking in some comic detachment as well, and shows blacks transcending the social limitations some whites would impose upon them. What Hughes sensed in the folk source of woman was the dynamic will to epic heroism in both the physical and spiritual dimensions. While the compulsion reveals itself in varying forms—the disciplined application to labor, the folk trickery that allows comic wit to circumvent defeat, the direct act of social defiance—black woman incarnates the complex imagination and the masks through which it appears.

Though it was appropriate to Hughes's largesse, as an ethical writer, to restore a complex humanity to the African American woman in particular and woman in general, he had to replace the great void she had once occupied as an idol and type. Then he would have to look at her as the well-rounded human being she was. Even in the great lyrics "The Negro Speaks of Rivers" (1921) and "Daybreak in Alabama" (1940), in which the black woman disappears as a persona, her symbolic yet invisible presence pervades Hughes's metaphors of the fertility of the earth, the waters, and the rebirth of the morning (Miller, "Mere" 30). To trace the complex and rich design of her in Hughes's world means to understand her symbolic advances across his entire career, with varying degrees of free play from the great lyrics and monologues ("Mother to Son," 1922), on through his melodramas ("Father and Son," 1934). Perhaps it would be useful to have a working definition of terms. While *lyrics* are poems of intense personal passion in this instance, *monologues* suggest the modern forms in which the poem's listener is only implied. *Melodrama*, rather, indicates the literary form that sets up Good and Evil as binaries, stark contrasts.

The poems on women help to establish an overview for all his succeeding genres. They lead from his lighter humor and cryptic "warning" to white America in 1951 to the brilliant and underestimated stream of consciousness of *Ask Your Mama* (1961), subsuming yet transcending them all. For Hughes, the metaphor of woman marks the rise from the historical source, the folk expression of his grandmother in 1910, to the civil rights movement and the white backlash in late 1967. The black woman in particular signifies the cycle through which the poetic imagination emerges from history and transcends it, but, as in the Simple story "Fancy Free," then falls back to earth or history. Maud Baudkin, a pioneering critic of feminist introspection during Hughes's time, explains:

> Following the associations of the figure of the muse as communicated in Milton's poetry, we have reached a representation of yet wider significance—the figure of the divine mother appearing in varied forms, as Thetis mourning for Achilles, or Ishtar mourning and seeking for Tammuz. In the mother and child pattern the figure of the child, or youth, is not distinctively of either sex, though the male youth appears the older form. In historical times, the pattern as it enters poetry may be present, either as beautiful boy or warrior—Adonis, Achilles—or as maiden—Prosperine, Kore—an embodiment of youth's bloom and transient splendor. In either

case, the figure appears as the type-object of a distinctive emotion—a complex emotion within which we may recognize something of fear, pity and tender admiration, such as a parent may feel, but "distanced," as by relation to an object universal, an event inevitable. (165)

Such a figure appears not only in "Mother to Son" and "The Negro Mother" (1931), possibly the two most famous of Hughes's matriarchal verses, but also in some of his less well-known poems. The overall effect is ultimately to reveal the idea of religious belief and deliverance in our national narrative. As James Emanuel suggests, "Mother to Son" initiates the definitive representation of women in Hughes's literary world.

In a dramatic monologue of twenty lines, the mother clarifies to her son the inevitable suffering inherent in African American life, revealing the hidden paradox of the mythmakers who assert the equality of all citizens. The figure then represents herself as an ascendant light in her advance. Through the inflections of black colloquialisms, the individual lines skillfully blend anapestic, iambic, and trochaic cadences. Structurally, the poem provides the folk diction and rhythm that make the woman real.

> But all the time
> I'se been a-climbin' on,
> And reachin' landin's,
> And turnin' corners,
> And sometimes goin' in the dark
> Where there ain't been no light. (lines 8–13)

Varied in syllabic length, the lines have ten, nine, eight, and seven cadences; others have four, three, and one.

> So boy, don't you turn back.
> Don't you set down on the steps

>	'Cause you finds it's kinder hard.
>	Don't you fall now—
>	For I'se still goin', honey,
>	I'se still climbin',
>	And life for me ain't been no crystal stair. (14–20)

While the final line keeps an iambic rhythm, the cadence suggests folk expression. Here is the imaging of Christian myth that renders the spiritual attributes of the black figure so concretely. Resembling the messianic type of the New Testament or the poet guide Virgil in Dante's *Divine Comedy*, the black woman lacks the righteous authority of the Bible and the literary power of the Western classic. Nevertheless, her decisive closure—"And life for me ain't been no crystal stair"— reinforces her second line. Through the unfaltering power of her indomitable will, her transcendent imagination endows the world far more richly than society ever afforded opportunities for her advancement. Yet, her inner light—the tangible expression of her remarkable spirit— remains undimmed. While the social world has hardly encouraged her, she ennobles it. The quality of her spiritual grandeur marks the depth of our common humanity. She cautions her son, "Don't you fall now." In associating her quest with divine vision, the artistic detachment implies a fallen world, a descent from heavenly grace. Christian myth proves central to the tightness of the poetic meanings in the text as the work implies the interwoven actions of quest and self-realization. "Be" becomes the lasting verb that indicates present perfect time: "I'se been a-climbin' on." Shrouded in religious myth, the African American female confronts secular reality, revealing the anxiety inherent in racial struggle. In the literal climb up the ascendant path, she represents an intangible faith in the cosmic order of things. Dilapidated boards and bare feet imply deprivation or poverty in the symbolic house, the figurative home of the nation and race. Because the mother lives literally in an edifice, surrounded by loose metal and woodwork throughout her life, she risks literal infection from the body politic, yet she withstands fatal injury to the communal soul. Her internal light illuminates the nation and the outer world. She is the figure of American possibility.

"The Negro Mother" resembles "Mother to Son" in its maternal theme but is written in Standard English. Of considerable intrigue are the voice and tone that remain in the vernacular despite traditional expression:

> Children, I come back today
> To tell you the story of the long dark way
> That I had to climb, that I had to know
> In order that the race might live and grow.
> Look at my face—dark as the night—
> Yet shining like the sun with love's true light. (1–6)

Here tetrameter and pentameter lines provide a formal consistency. The length of the poem facilitates its division into a well-unified structure of three parts. In the first part, the reader encounters the spiritual figure that enacts or performs the spirituality, enabling the female body to survive. Ultimately the black woman achieves an aesthetic distance from her own monologue, hence creating a romantic wonder of herself in modern time. Romanticism means imaginative hope, but modernity means dislocation:

> I couldn't read then. I couldn't write.
> I had nothing, back there in the night.
> Sometimes, the valley was filled with tears,
> But I kept trudging on through the lonely years. (23–26)

In spirit, the figure merges with her children to guarantee continued racial success. Her advance in the second part prepares artistically for the third, in which she transitions from introspection to self-articulation. Finally, she cautions the listener, in other words the undramatized chorus, to speak at the interface of poetic vision and social resistance:

"Remember how the strong in struggle and strife / still bar you the way..." (46–47).

In this instance, myth is a spirituality that informs the communal monologue. Indeed, the woman's story sets into stark relief the historical tension between the American ideal and the real. In the second part, she turns the emphasis from her own suffering to the moral imperative of those who must complete her moral reach.

"But God put a song and a prayer in my mouth. / God put a dream like steel in my soul"—through the folk voice, Hughes's female narrator expresses a distinct identity quite her own (18–19). In contrast, several of the more personal poems such as "Who but the Lord?" articulate his own humanism much more directly. Of a deeper religiosity, the mother's early faith prepares for the dynamic will that completes the third part of her story: "Oh, my dark children, may my dream and my prayers / Impel you forever up the great stairs" (50–51). Christian images help to reveal the heroic sacrifice. In the concluding sections, the "valley" to be crossed finishes with the journey's "road." Subsequently, the poetic narrative presents the goals that she urges her symbolic children—the race—to pursue. When she tells the allegorical children to "look ever upward," she speaks of the African American experience. The voyage expressed in the poem serves as a double metaphor, referencing movement within both the horizontal space of civil rights history and the vertical space of the African American soul. As in "Mother to Son," such spaces merge in the metaphor of sacred passage. Like the lighted figure in "Mother to Son," the "Negro Mother" sets into relief social restrictions that limit but do not define the black figure. During the three centuries of African American suffering, the communal historian forged a "dream like steel" in her soul; consequently, this aspiration inspired her to survive a valley "filled with tears," and a road "hot with sun." Despite racial discrimination, she encourages her posterity to persevere now in the communal story. The steel bars in the third part of the poem persist, as does her spirit for all who inherit it. The constraints are limited by time, but the imagination of social change is not. Posterity can triumph over the currently unforeseen hurdles of the future, just as the black mother once overcame her own illiteracy. Time is therefore the great ally of social transformation. By the third part of her poetic memory—the poem is actually the shape of it—she transcends the physical impediments of slavery.

Often, of course, literary criticism of such poems may be reduced to a deadening analysis of individual lines. In looking at the broader pattern of the poem's deceptive beauty, however, so much more emerges. While the physical pain inherent in the figure's historical suffering is certain, it gives way to a communal story that endures. And while the greater spiritual narrative may well have been grounded once in folk illiteracy, the current voice is literate, yet less intense and therefore less articulate. Eloquence means ultimately the measure and depth of rhythmic authenticity that strikes the indigenous tone, rather than the linguistic precision of speaking Standard English. Hence, Hughes challenges the very assumption of polished grammar as an ethical measure of humanity.

So much of nature revolves around the central icon of the black woman. Both light and fertility mark her personal attributes. Hughes distributes five such images in the first part of the poem, three others in the second, and three in the third. The "long dark way" of the outset prepares for the black woman who has nearly finished her journey, though not *the* journey to be completed by posterity, by the conclusion. Therefore, the ultimate unity belongs less to her than to the generations that follow her. She is a historical sign that actually points to the future. By the end of her poetic story, she has evolved into a multivoiced woman who reflects on the Atlantic slave trade of the past. Yet, the indisputable bleakness of her journeyed way—the very *blackness* of it—and the transcendent figure representing all sufferers who must explore anguish across time and space marks even the New Negro moment in literary history. Indeed, the spiritual journey turns figuratively from night to day. The diurnal cycle, in this instance, represents a spiraled instant of history remembered again, a turn that is not only cyclical but upward in the advance of civil rights. The woman "had nothing, back there in the night." Her banner that is lifted from the "dust" becomes a fiery emblem, a "torch for tomorrow," enlightening readers about the secret of African American art, the transmutation of suffering into elation. It is the literary form of blues, of jazz. Therefore, the black woman emerges as a figured light whose spiritual force, while rooted in global fertility, resists historical misery. She signifies a trajectory of faith. Indeed, her journey is conveyed in present tense because her struggle becomes a metaphor that is not so easily reduced to historical time.

Hughes wrote several other poems about women at various points in his poetic career. It is possible to discern at least twelve often inseparable functions of the spiritual figure that operate in such poems: the black woman signals stories about her yesterdays; she survives adversity; she reminisces humorously about the splendor of youth that has vanished; she celebrates a folk life of vibrant color; she at times encounters so much trouble that she cannot transcend adversity; she converts her personal suffering into lyrical form; she signifies the heavy yet affirmative tone through which humanity sublimates suffering into such lyrical art; she clarifies a secular person's comic, yet serious, confrontation with death; she suspends human demise, if not desire, through her story; she sets her poem against the backdrop of history; she invokes her female-led black family; and she incarnates heroic determination.

The poems illustrate the different functions quite well. In "Aunt Sue's Stories" (1921), Aunt Sue situates the story of her life within the historical landscape while revealing it to the black boy. Her story is really the communal narrative of the race. While only the boy's imagination seems to confirm the authenticity of her tale, history verifies the story rendered by her, at least to the extent that historical and literary worlds are ever parallel.

The boy's silent history makes for a revealing angle on the aunt's credible tale and on the historical truth the two family members share. While aunt and nephew may indeed represent varied places in the historical continuum of the race, they exhibit common signs of diverse generations. The realistic boy mediates between the aunt's imaginary recollection and his own historical world. In other words, the aunt is both cultural historian and poet; she *is* the vicarious Langston Hughes.

Obviously, the biographical source is Hughes's maternal grandmother, Mary Langston, who set the tone for his spiritual persistence by the time he was eight and living with her in Lawrence, Kansas. Though she was an engaging artist in her folk way, she was very much the tragedian who hardened him to future pain. She exemplified both a love of her work and a stubborn resistance to life's unfairness; she expressed, too, a human bleakness without the debilitating emotion of it. If the first stage of her blues meant to accept a nearly overwhelming despondency of existence, the second phase encapsulated within her the very jazz of the African American soul—the transformative power so celebrated in Hughes's "Trumpet Player" (1949). Mary Langston *was* jazz. The transmutation of suffering into art, the vindication of the cultured spirit, is indeed a redemptive gift; it is in part the torch that other African American writers such as Ralph Ellison, James Baldwin, and Toni Morrison would take up during Hughes's middle and final years and, indeed, even after his death. Mary Langston's engagement with historical suffering prepared for Hughes's written triumphs years later. She led him on the visionary path he was to follow, and he did not depart from it very often. For most of the remaining way, he would prove more hopeful:

> Through my grandmother's stories always life moved, moved heroically toward an end. Nobody ever cried in my grandmother's stories. They worked, or schemed, or fought. But no crying. When my grandmother died, I didn't cry, either. Something about my grandmother's stories (without her ever having said so) taught me the uselessness of crying about anything. (*BS* 17)

Hughes laughed to keep from crying and, better yet, gave voice to countless black women who did the same.

The female figure in "Mexican Market Woman" (1922) possesses an interracial wisdom similar to that of the mother figures. What most of the women figures in Hughes's literary world have is indisputable agency—self-proclaimed control over their own destinies—even though the narrators do not always recognize their power. Though the storytellers certainly appear to possess a distinctiveness of voice, their male counterparts often speak for them—yet certainly not in the great maternal poems and the Madam verses.

> This ancient hag
> Who sits upon the ground
> Selling her scanty wares
> Day in, day round,
> Has known high wind-swept mountains,
> And the sun has made
> Her skin so brown.

Though the female figure in "Troubled Woman" (1925), a short lyric of sorrow constructed around two brilliant similes, is less transcendent than Aunt Sue, the narrator achieves a success in poetic representation. Almost a catechism, a holy recital, the tone of the poem achieves a sermonic cadence:

> Bowed by
> Weariness and pain
> Like an
> Autumn flower
> In the frozen rain,
> Like a
> Wind-blown autumn flower
> That never lifts its head
> Again. (4–12)

At first the persona in "Strange Hurt" (1926) seems masochistic. Some man has deserted a woman:

> In months of snowy winter
> When cozy houses hold,
> She'd break down doors
> To wander naked
> In the cold. (11–15)

In a sense, Hughes creates poems in which the seeking individual, or poet, vacates a secure place in life in order to explore the personal space of something more. While such compulsion is necessary for self-completion, it is risky as well. Though the paradox is not completely logical, it marks the very heart of creative activity. The woman who has lost love becomes indifferent to what happens to her body.

In one reading, "Cora" (1927) renders the racial dilemma allegorically:

> I broke my heart this mornin',
> Ain't got no heart no more.
> Next time a man comes near me
> Gonna shut an' lock my door
> Cause they treat me mean—
> The ones I love.
> They always treat me mean.

This serves as an understated analogy between the personal story and the communal legacy. Because a man has broken her heart, Cora swears off *all* men. Hence, the individual, like the race, risks vulnerability yet seeks the promise of human communication. The lover's dilemma is both the black race's choice and the nation's trial. While the race pouts, it tires of the irreparable hurt imposed by history, the weight of traversing a gap in human empathy that it never created.

Over time Hughes diversified the design of the Divine Mother into broader treatments that are heroic, comic, or despairing. As the years wore on, he worked to free the image from religious myth. In part, the change is due to his diminishing optimism. In poems such as "Southern Mammy Sings" (1941) and "Down Where I Am" (1950), the speaker has lapsed from energetic hope into fatigue a generation later. Tone and sense reverse themselves rather drastically in "Down Where I Am":

> Too many years
> Climbin' that hill
> 'Bout out of breath
> I got my fill.
>
> I'm gonna plant my feet
> On solid ground.
> If you want to see me,
> *Come down.* (9–16)

With a bang far more than a whimper, Hughes brings to a close a lifelong preoccupation with the myth of the transcendent woman. "Southern Mammy Sings" marks a turning point because her figure encapsulates spiritual as well as physical exhaustion. Indeed, she despairs because whites have hanged a "colored boy" whose only crime was saying people should be free. The "southern mammy" is an allegorical foil to the "Miss Gardner," "Miss Yardman," and "Miss Michaelmas," each of whom personifies a place in a way that Mammy does not. With no real location for her in the country or world, the alienated servant, having seen the death of her sons, anticipates only world war.

The Madam poems illuminate the ideas of nation and doubt. "Madam and the Fortune Teller" (1944), for example, is a particularly skillful poem of far more realistic representation. The teller imparts self-determination to the customer, but the latter, unwilling to accept the humanistic burden of being her own person, continues to press for divine intervention. When the teller refuses to assure her that anything of the kind really occurs, the customer shifts the ground impatiently to seek a man as external support. While she must accept the responsibility of her own life, she is unwilling. Now aware that the customer declines to apprehend the truth, the teller asks for another dollar and a half before proceeding to read the customer's other palm. As the folk ballad goes, the teller "picked poor robin clean"—but only because "robin," the black female customer, refuses to live without illusion.

What Langston Hughes dramatizes so brilliantly in the fortune teller's customer he must have discerned finally about himself and humanity. In the pursuit of some outside decision, the seeker overlooks her responsibility on earth. She always needs the sign of something beyond, the ideal of which the present realism reminds her only indirectly. Though Hughes's early poems sometimes mark dramatically an ascent from earth to heaven, the later ones often embody not only a return to earth but a closure of the mother's diamond stairway. The vertical route that had never existed for woman or anyone else in physical space now recedes from the external world in its return to the mind of the poet. In the process, Hughes recasts his fictional self as the perky persona of Madam. Though the customer can read in her cards the obvious fortune of what the teller narrates forthrightly, the teller reads a deeper irony of the human self, ever in struggle with history. What separates the two women is Madam's most human imagination.

Hughes's female figure is an emblem of hope possessing spiritual imagination. At once she is an icon that engages historical suffering yet transcends personal pain. The black woman refuses to express naïveté regarding either. What empowers her creative energy is surely the diamond will within her. Almost paradoxically she is, to keep Hughes's metaphor, a beautiful gemstone polished in the cauldron of historical suffering. She is not always well rounded or even professional, but she is Madam as much as Madonna. She remains one of the foremost testimonies to Hughes's literary and spiritual legacy—a lens through which his creative universe can be understood.

Notes
This chapter is rewritten from "'No Crystal Stair': Unity, Archetype, and Symbol in Langston Hughes's Poems on Women," published in the *Negro American Literature Forum* (now *African American Review*) and *The Art and Imagination of Langston Hughes* (UP of Kentucky, 1989, 2006).

Works Cited
Bodkin, Maud. *Archetypal Patterns in Poetry*. New York: Oxford UP, 1934.
Emanuel, James. *Langston Hughes*. New York: Twayne, 1967.
Gibson, Donald. "The Good Black Poet and the Good Gray Poet." *Langston Hughes: Black Genius*. Ed. Therman B. O'Daniel. New York: Morrow, 1971. 65–80.
Henderson, Stephen. *Understanding the New Black Poetry*. New York: Morrow, 1973.
Hughes, Langston. *The Best of Simple*. New York: Hill, 1961.
_____. *The Big Sea*. London: Hutchinson, 1940.
_____. *The Collected Poems of Langston Hughes*. Ed. Arnold Rampersad and David Roessel. New York: Random, 1995.
_____. "Fancy Free." *Simple Takes a Wife*. New York: Simon, 1953. 80–84.
_____. *One-Way Ticket*. New York: Knopf, 1949.
_____. *The Ways of White Folks*. New York: Allen, 1934.
Miller, R. Baxter. *The Art and Imagination of Langston Hughes*. 1989. Lexington: UP of Kentucky, 2006.
_____. "'A Mere Poem,' 'Daybreak in Alabama.'" *Obsidian* (1976): 30–37.

History and Historicity in the Work of Langston Hughes

Hans Ostrom

"The Negro Speaks of Rivers," which the *Crisis* published in June 1921, when Hughes was just nineteen (Rampersad 2: 17), uses the simple but elegant devices of speaking through a first-person collective persona and linking notable rivers to historical epochs. In just thirteen lines focusing on the African diaspora, Hughes presents a historical sketch from the cradle of civilization to Central Africa, on to Egypt, and thence to North America, including the history of enslavement. Even when still in his teens, then, Hughes possessed a historical imagination and knew how to evoke different perspectives on the past (Osborne, "Collective Persona"). The poem links him to a view of history that has been variously identified as internationalist or Pan-African, in the English speaking world, or as negritude, in the francophone one. Hughes's sketch of the diaspora ties African American history to the African origins that have had a significant impact on the whole Western Hemisphere, owing chiefly to the institutions of slavery and colonialism.

Probably the last poem Hughes submitted for publication before his death is "The Backlash Blues," which, fittingly, *Crisis* published in June 1967 (Ostrom 16). Returning to the vernacular form and idiom of the blues, Hughes uses the poem to call attention to the American resistance not only to Black Power and the implementation of the *Brown v. Board of Education* Supreme Court decisions (Haltom), the social devices for racial integration, but also to the hard-won but still insufficient gains in civil liberties and economic opportunity since the 1930s (Gilmore). That "Rivers" and "Backlash" concern history and historicity so transparently is no mere coincidence. Rather, it is a fitting reflection of Hughes's work, not just in poetry but across genres such as fiction, drama, comic tales, criticism, autobiography, biography, translation, and children's literature. Probably no American literary writer from the modernist period was more consistently attuned to history and current events than Hughes. The two poems reflect on the one hand a calm, long view of events, and on the other, an immediate response to the urgent moment. Whereas "history" usually refers to the past itself or to an account about events, places, and people in the past, "historicity" often refers to historical qualities in art or other endeavors, and it can refer as well to the nature of particular historical perspectives; thus, these two poems reflect two different types of historicity in Hughes's writing.

By now Hughes has become many different things to many different people. For some he is a blues poet, an unofficial poet laureate of African Americans, and an unpretentious counterpoint to imperial high modernists such as T. S. Eliot, Ezra Pound, James Joyce, and Wallace Stevens (Osborne, "Modernism"). For others he is fierce writer who maintained extraordinary senses of wit and humor and whose mysterious sexuality would be researched decades after his death. For some he remains a heterosexual writer who maintained a private sexuality, but others view him as a gay or queer, bisexual, or even asexual writer (Julien; Ponce; Rampersad; Vogel).

A favorite of teachers at all educational levels, Hughes's voice remains popular far beyond the academy. To some he is or was radical, to others progressive, and to some in the 1950s, a communist who deserved to be investigated by his government (Osborne, "McCarthyism"). As racial labels changed in the twentieth and twenty-first centuries, Hughes has been in turn known as a Negro, black, and African American writer. His relatively plain-spoken poetry and affinity for working people have induced some to place him in an American poetic tradition of Walt Whitman, Carl Sandburg, and William Carlos Williams.

According to perplexing binaries and potentially false dichotomies, Hughes's literary voice is either an international one or a home-grown, provincial one from Harlem. Some readers remember his as an uncompromising voice of the American proletariat in the 1930s, while others emphasize his dazzling versatility and sophistication; for instance, his words have been set to blues music, folk music, art songs, opera, jazz, and Broadway scores (Osborne, "Songs").

For developing readers who cherish in literature a sense of history and social change, Hughes's opus is exemplary. Therefore, this essay explores "the historical Hughes," beginning with a clearly discernible first phase of his career, moving to an equally clear politically radical period, and concluding with his literary negotiations during the civil rights movement of the 1950s and 1960s until his death on May 22, 1967.

Hughes of the Harlem Renaissance

Hughes went to New York in 1921 to attend Columbia University, but he fell permanently in love with Harlem, which had become a "Negro" city of two hundred thousand residents. When he was not absent from Harlem, he was squarely in the midst of the artistic and social fray later called the Harlem Renaissance or New Negro Renaissance. Actually, the impetus of the movement extended southward into the northeastern corridor of Washington, DC, a city associated with Renaissance writers Jean Toomer, Georgia Douglas Johnson, and Sterling Brown, among others. The Renaissance reached even farther south—as far as Atlanta, where Walter White, a writer and eventual leader of the National Association for the Advancement of Colored People (NAACP), lived. Though agreement about the start and end dates of the Renaissance is difficult to come by, a relatively expansive chronology might begin in 1919, the year that African American soldiers returned from distinguished service in World War I to a celebratory parade that began in Manhattan and ended in Harlem. Such a chronology might end with the onslaught of the Great Depression in the early 1930s, but that actually began with the crash of the stock market in 1929. In other words, the phenomenon of the Renaissance belongs primarily to the 1920s (Hughes, *Big Sea*; Lewis, *When Harlem*).

The Renaissance cultivated the careers of writers now considered to be central to African American and American literary history. Countee

Cullen, Rudolph Fisher, Zora Neale Hurston, Georgia Douglas Johnson, Claude McKay, and Wallace Thurman are among these. The period also quickly became a site of disagreement concerning the most appropriate path for the advancement of African Americans. Although he would become more radical later, writer and activist W. E. B. Du Bois favored a politically centrist position in which a "talented tenth" of African Americans composed of well-educated artists, professionals, and public figures would, he and others hoped, lead the rest of the black population into fully assimilated citizenship (Du Bois, "Returning Soldiers"; Woodson, "The Migration"). Du Bois and others characterized this position as being much more progressive than that of Booker T. Washington and his admirers, who favored achieving some measure of economic success but not attacking frontally the question of full civil rights. A more radical, Marxist-influenced position was taken up by A. Philip Randolph, a labor organizer and an editor of the journal the *Messenger* (Briley).

Hughes became an "official" member of the Harlem Renaissance with the publication of "The Negro Speaks of Rivers" in the *Crisis*, the literary voice of the NAACP and therefore of Du Bois, who edited the magazine. The well-received publication of his first collection of poetry, *The Weary Blues*, by the major publisher Alfred A. Knopf in 1926 solidified Hughes's role in the Renaissance, as did the publication of his landmark critical essay "The Negro Artist and the Racial Mountain" in the *Nation* that same year.

The collection and the essay link Hughes, with regard to a historical and political ethos, to Du Bois, who called upon African American artists to deploy "propaganda" on behalf of "the race." What Du Bois meant by the term is close to what is commonly considered "advocacy" now and distant from what political scientists such as Jacques Ellul consider propaganda—the state-run, total control of ideas and images. Du Bois also urged writers and other artists to write about "the race" and racial issues rather than representing more presumably universal themes and experiences.

In "The Negro Artist and the Racial Mountain," Hughes supports and extends these notions. He urges black writers never to shy away from their experiences and those of other African Americans. He also advocates using African American modes of expression, including vernacular ones such as the blues. And indeed, *The Weary Blues* includes many poems based on the lyric form and written in the style.

Consequently, in the context of the Renaissance, we may see Hughes as generally in the "camp" of Du Bois, James Weldon Johnson, and others. In other words, his position is not significantly different from that of the NAACP. Moreover, he became a close, lifelong friend of Carl Van Vechten, one of the Renaissance's primary white patrons and supporters. In fact, Hughes even wrote blues lyrics for Van Vechten's controversial novel with the incendiary title *Nigger Heaven* (1926). In many ways, Van Vechten represented classic northern liberal views—again, not at all at odds with the NAACP, in which white liberals had participated from the beginning (Hughes and Van Vechten, passim). Van Vechten was sympathetic to the plight of African Americans but more interested in experiencing "Negro" culture and society, especially the Harlem nightlife. Though Hughes's poem "Northern Liberal" does not concern Van Vechten, it does suggest that such bohemians like to keep a safe distance from political struggle, are not radical or militant, and may be fair-weather friends who are more curious than committed (Ostrom 276).

Where Hughes did diverge from Du Bois's views was in his devotion to vernacular idioms and forms and in his interest in an unvarnished celebration of working-class African American life. Variously Hughes's poems did not represent the kind of "propaganda" or advocacy Du Bois had in mind, and from the Du Boisian perspective, they ran the risk of reinforcing white stereotypes of African American behavior. From Hughes's point of view, such works were valid because they represented authentic African American experience. As expressed in "The Negro Artist and the Racial Mountain," an unashamed expression of one's experience not only trumped the kind of advocacy Du Bois had in mind but amounted indirectly to an advocacy of its own, for it helped establish a black writer's right (even duty) to represent a full range of experience. Though middle-class himself, more because of his education and profession than because of his family's often precarious economic status, Hughes felt an affinity for the black and white working class. By contrast, Du Bois was solidly bourgeois.

Nonetheless, in the midst of the Renaissance and in spite of differences with intellectual leaders such as Du Bois and Alain Locke, Hughes had not yet become a political radical, even as he demonstrated an early interest in the lives and material conditions of ordinary folks, of those African Americans struggling desperately to find a niche in the political economy. In this regard, the historicity of Hughes may be most significant in its depiction of what the Great Northern Migration of African Americans was like in particular cases. Many poems in *The Weary Blues* constitute an informal ethnography of the historical moment in which vast numbers of African Americans decided to leave the South.

Just as Hughes was precociously alert to the shape of the African diaspora, so was he conscious of new challenges that greeted African Americans in urban centers they were encountering for the first time. *The Weary Blues* seizes the historical moment artistically. "The Negro Artist and the Racial Mountain" recognizes similarly a turning point in African American literary history when black writers could deploy vernacular forms for their own purposes. Certainly it was time to end the caricaturing of the vernacular specifically for white audiences in the manner of some poems by Paul Laurence Dunbar. In this way, *The Weary Blues* is a deceptively modernist work, for although many of its poems seem relatively simple and straightforward and therefore not deliberately difficult or overwrought in the manner of the high modernism of Eliot, Joyce, and Pound, the collection instinctively follows Pound's edict to "make [art] new," not for the sake of newness itself but in response to overwhelming social changes. Hughes's "new" remains influential; one may draw a line from his experimentation with the vernacular in the 1920s to the black arts movement of the 1960s and the rise of hip hop and rap in the 1980s.

Radical, Ironic Hughes in the 1930s and 1940s

After the Great Depression began in 1929 and 1930 (Osborne; Miller, "Langston Hughes" 805), Hughes explored a wide variety of genres beyond poetry, including the novel, short fiction, drama, autobiography, and journalism. Throughout most of the Harlem Renaissance his political stance was progressive, keeping with the carefully measured advances in racial equality. His posture in the 1930s became radical with the times.

Few decades in world history have seen as much turmoil and change as the 1930s and 1940s. The Bolshevik Revolution had transformed Russia from a feudal state to a communist one; in the 1920s and 1930s, before the rise of Stalin, communism in particular and socialism in general seemed to be viable modes for solving the implacable problems created by the Great Depression. Of course, the 1930s also saw the rise of fascism, which led directly to World War II and caused many radicals to adjust their views accordingly. Often the goals of fascism seemed more menacing than those of capitalism. Trade unions, along with a worldwide struggle for workers' rights and "universal" suffrage, were crucial to the period.

Hughes was extremely intrigued by the possibilities Marxism might offer. He covered the Spanish Civil War, which pitted republicans against fascists, for a black newspaper. About the same time he became fully involved in the Scottsboro Boys controversy (Haltom, "Scottsboro Boys"). The 1930s and 1940s were simultaneously volatile at home and abroad. The world was embroiled in turmoil, and Langston Hughes artistically embraced it.

Certainly the times did provide him with opportunities to explore political nuances beyond the lyric form. Another reason for Hughes's broadening of his literary concerns was practical. He was determined to make his living as a writer, not as an author who was also a professor.

Then, too, there was his temperament. His attitude toward writing ran counter to the nineteenth-century romantic notion of the inspired genius and was closer to the temper of the late eighteenth and nineteenth centuries in England and the United States. His flexible practicality toward writing led him to explore a wide variety of genres. In turn, the multiple genres provided more outlets for his often-radical interest in current events. In poems such as "A Christian Country," "Christ in Alabama," and "Goodbye, Christ," Hughes explicitly attacks the efficacy of Christianity in solving social problems. In fact, the latter two poems were regarded as so incendiary that protesters who showed up at readings for *The Saturday Evening Post* attacked him in print. In such works, then, the historicity of Hughes's writing is plainly influenced by Marxism's critique of religion. Multiple works attack institutional racism, including "Advertisement for the Waldorf Astoria," which points out that the hotel would not accept black customers; "The Colored Soldier," which calls attention to the segregation of the US armed forces; and "Ph.D." and "Letter to the Academy," which challenge the social quietism of the academy. Such works display the political advocacy that Du Bois likened to protest but are more literary. The historicity of the works shows urgency.

Indeed, Hughes's poems encapsulated the great domestic and international movements of his time, including the unjust 1931 arrest and trial of the Scottsboro Boys in Alabama; the more just society that Hughes believed was emerging in Russia during the 1930s, having traveled there in 1931; the Italian invasion of Ethiopia in 1935; the social upheaval in China in 1937; and the Spanish Civil War of the same year. No matter how urgent issues in the United States became, Hughes maintained a global view of emerging history.

Other poems speak strongly in favor not just of strong labor unions but of a comprehensive, militant labor movement in the United States; others, including "Ballad of Roosevelt" and "Dear Mr. President," characterize the administration of President Franklin Delano Roosevelt, which many other observers thought to be excessively leftist, as too sluggish in addressing consequences of the Great Depression as well as the Jim Crow laws.

The picture of Hughes that emerges from his political poems, as well as from the works of this period in other genres, is of a writer fully engaged with domestic and international events during two decades that changed the world forever. The economic and sociopolitical maps of the early twenty-first century, in other words, may still be traced back to the history of the 1930s and 1940s. Hughes seems to have understood how high the historical stakes were in these decades.

Rather than retreating from history or using art to refine responses to national and global crises, Hughes took his writing to several different fronts and enlisted it in many battles. To some degree, the radical shift in his historicity is a logical extension of his stance in "The Negro Artist and the Racial Mountain." Here, as we have seen, he urged "Negro" artists to embrace the experiences they knew and to represent black experience unabashedly. Although the focus is almost exclusively on African American culture, the broader and implicit philosophy is to respond artistically to what is happening in the world—and not only in one's personal world.

Consequently, once the Great Depression hit, dashing the optimism of the Renaissance and the Great Northern Migration, and once the Marxism and socialism of the time appeared to offer concrete solutions to the plight of oppressed persons worldwide, Hughes forcefully responded in his writing. Of course, from a twenty-first-century perspective, seeing clearly through the lenses of communist totalitarianism and Stalinism, one may be apt to regard Hughes's political and artistic choices as naïve and misguided. But as Gilmore points out, socialist ideas and the Communist Party in particular were actually vital to the civil rights movements, especially in the South during the 1930s and 1940s, and helped set the stage for the more celebrated movements of the 1950s and 1960s. Hughes was pragmatic in the Jamesian sense; he was vitally interested in questions of difference and power (James 20). What difference would one's art and ideology make in shifting the terms and consequences of each? Such pragmatism led to ideological flexibility in Hughes's case, too. Initially he was opposed to US involvement in the war in Europe because, like many, he reasoned that the United States needed to fight reactionary racial supremacy, as exemplified by the Ku Klux Klan, first. He began to change his mind when fascist Italy invaded Africa and fully changed it when the extent of Hitler's white supremacy emerged. After the United States entered World War II, he even published poems advocating the purchase of war bonds to support the American military (Ostrom 54).

How many different literary forms did Hughes's historicity inform in these decades? It is hard not to be still astonished at his versatility. He wrote experimental plays in response to lynching and to the Scottsboro Boys' plight (Osborne, "Drama," "Harlem Suitcase Theater"); covered the Spanish Civil War for the *Baltimore Afro-American* newspaper, establishing himself as a viable journalist; and gathered short stories in a tour de force first collection, *The Ways of White Folks* (1934). Indeed, his groundbreaking edition in the short story form serves as a postmortem on the Harlem Renaissance, treats northern liberal white society's short-lived fascination with blacks with irony and satire in "Slave on the Block" and "The Blues I'm Playing," challenges the hypocrisy of white, middle-class Christian values in "Berry" and "Cora Unashamed," and treats the legacy of slavery and white supremacy with fully realized tragedy in "Father and Son," which alludes to the Scottsboro Boys.

His play *Mulatto*, which works with the same material and character types as "Father and Son," was produced on Broadway. In a column for the *Chicago Defender*, he began his long-running series of short tales featuring Jesse B. Semple (or Simple) and the comic straight man Boyd. These tales often allowed Hughes to address topical issues (Hughes, *Chicago Defender*; Harper; Osborne, "Jesse B. Semple"). Hughes also began to carry out operatic collaborations that were pointedly historical. *Troubled Island* is based on the revolution in Haiti (Ostrom 401–02). Meanwhile, Hughes published *The Big Sea*, the first of his two autobiographies, adding directly to his first historical responses to the Harlem Renaissance, when, as he puts it in one chapter title, "the Negro" was suddenly, but only temporarily, "in vogue."

Some traditional readers may be tempted to prefer the Hughes of the Harlem Renaissance and the early blues poetry, or even the slightly mellower Hughes of the 1950s, to the radical writer of the 1930s. Owing partly to the continuing influence of New Criticism, which advocated separating a literary work from biography and history and analyzing it as a "verbal icon" (Wimsatt), all of us may be tempted at times to react negatively to the literature that responds forcefully to history and to immediate social and political circumstance—literature that blends advocacy and art and seemingly thrusts itself into the fray of events. But the widely varied works Hughes produced during the 1930s and 1940s possess great power; many of them experiment boldly with form and idiom, and almost all of them reflect a protean energy of an author fully immersed in his times. Indeed, he grounds himself well in the plight of the oppressed, in the conditions of working people globally, and in the struggle of his race. Moreover, every age has produced political literature and protest literature, and it is important to remember that some of the most firmly canonized writers wrote in this vein: Geoffrey Chaucer, Ben Johnson, Andrew Marvell, John Milton, and Jonathan Swift as well as William Blake, Percy Bysshe Shelley, Lord Byron, Charles Dickens, Leo Tolstoy, Oscar Wilde, William Butler Yeats, Pablo Neruda, Frank Norris, Sinclair Lewis, Richard Wright, Albert Camus, Federico García Lorca, James Baldwin, Amiri Baraka, and Robert Bly.

New Criticism in particular and a longstanding desire, in general, to maintain a firewall between politics and literature lead many readers to label all politically charged writing as "propaganda." But as noted earlier, propaganda more properly means a total manipulation of media by a state or by a political group or party that controls the state (Ellul). Hughes articulated advocacy and protest rather than propaganda, except to say the "honest" propaganda, as W. E. B. Du Bois had called the strategy during the Renaissance. Of course, readers still have the right to react negatively to advocacy and protest in literature, but clarifying the terms of the debate, especially in the context of historicity, is crucial. Moreover, the "debate" may tempt us to forget that for Hughes, literary advocacy did not preclude less politically sharp, more traditional products; for him, the situation was one not of either/or but of both/and. He did not abandon literature that takes a more indirect approach to social issues and represents complementary angles to political struggle.

For him, the 1930s had begun with the publication of his first novel, *Not without Laughter* (1930). His work on the novel helped to foment the bitter break with his patron, Charlotte Osgood Mason, and the split led to friction between Hughes and Zora Neale Hurston, as well as providing material that allowed him to critique the relationship of the patron and the patronized in "The Blues I'm Playing," an autobiographical story in *The Ways of White Folks*. Following his early two decades of writing, during the 1940s Hughes produced the humorous, beloved "Madam" poems, which touched on social issues but focused on the witty representation of his resilient figure Madam Alberta K. Johnson. Another circumstance brings complexity to the picture of "radical Hughes" in the 1930s and 1940s. He was at once a "home-boy" at ease in Harlem and a compulsive traveler. The latter trait, especially, played a significant role in his sense of history.

Travel not only generated material for his many genres and projects but also made history concrete. Though his initial opinions about Western and Eastern nations, the independent Caribbean, and colonial Africa took root in the United States, they were refined and often deepened particularly through international journeys. For whatever reasons, Hughes was driven to see things for himself. Travel energized him, and it grounded global culture in immediate experience.

As noted earlier, Hughes spent part of the Harlem Renaissance abroad, famously throwing some books from his Columbia studies into New York's harbor from the deck of a freighter, the *West Hessel-*

tine—an archetypal, youthful gesture signaling a quest to learn from the world rather than from academia. Shipping out multiple times allowed him to see Africa for the first time and live in Paris for a while. In 1932 he traveled to Russia with a group of friends, where they participated in an ill-fated film project about race relations in the United States. For Hughes, however, the trip was so satisfying that he kept going, traveling by train through China and ending up in Japan. The next year found him on the West Coast, staying with his friend Noël in Carmel, publishing poems in the *Carmel Pine Cone* newspaper, and sipping cocktails with poet Robinson Jeffers and his wife, Una (Haltom; Rampersad, passim).

Other private and professional journeys took him to Mexico, Spain, Haiti and Cuba, the American South, and again to Africa. Earlier, during his formative years, he had traveled with his mother throughout the Midwest and West, attending grammar school in Lawrence, Kansas, and high school in Cleveland, Ohio.

Therefore, when experience derived from travel finds its way into his writing, it tends to make his literary take on history, culture, and politics more particular and less purely ideological. A few sections in *The Big Sea* and later essays on Russia represent concrete observations about the way healthcare worked there in 1932 and 1933 and about the treatment of women, so that his writing is sharply different from a mere rehearsal of socialist principles during the 1930s (Ostrom 373–74). Similarly, his coverage of the Spanish Civil War in 1937 allowed him to explore the unusual position into which Moorish Spaniards were placed—pressed into fighting for the fascists even though the republicans arguably represented Moor interests better. Travel, as a potent source for Hughes's personal construction of history, is palpable and robust.

The Hughes of the 1930s and 1940s is indisputably radical, then, in his literary representation of politics and society. In the introduction to *The Collected Poems of Langston Hughes*, Arnold Rampersad and David Roessel write,

In the 1930s especially, in response to the Great Depression, certain features of his verse were altered as he began to emphasize the need for radical political action. Hughes then wrote some of the most radical poems ever published by an American, as well as some of the most poignant lamentations of the chasm that often exists between American social ideals and American social reality, as in his 1935 anthem, "Let American Be America Again." Some of his radical poems, especially "Goodbye Christ," would haunt Hughes's career for the rest of his life, with conservative political and religious groups citing them as evidence of his alleged communist beliefs and associations. Under such pressure, Hughes himself eventually repudiated "Goodbye, Christ" and in general suppressed the bulk of his radical socialist poetry. (4)

If by "suppressed" one means that Hughes included few explicitly radical poems in his *Selected Poems*, then the word succeeds, but a more complete assessment might include the observation that many of the poems from the 1930s and 1940s responded to specific events (the invasion of Ethiopia, for example) and might therefore require the kind of contextualization not customary for public readings. It is perhaps tempting to make too much, then, of Hughes's choices with regard to *Selected Poems*. And although Hughes certainly distanced himself from one poem, "Goodbye Christ," he never distanced himself from his central critique of Christianity *as it is often practiced* in the United States: that it was hypocritical and had done little, if anything, to change the conditions of African Americans and working people. Nor did he "repudiate" other works from the 1930s and 1940s. Lost in the extravagant, provocative rhetoric of "Goodbye Christ" is the more basic point that *because* Christianity has failed the oppressed, Marxism becomes at least one possible solution to explore.

Rampersad and Roessel observe that Hughes "returned as a poet to older themes—or, as he put it ironically, to 'Negroes, nature, and love'" (4). "Ironically" is the crucial word here, for in fact, Hughes had never abandoned "Negroes, nature, and love" in the 1930s and 1940s.

Especially with regard to "Negroes," he did not suppress the political realities of African American life. In "Prelude to Our Age: A Negro History Poem," Hughes notes that blacks had to go "to the United States Supreme Court— / For the right to get a meal on a train" (lines 190–91). Advocacy and hard irony persist here. This is not the poetry or rhetoric of a writer who has repudiated his essential sense of history and politics. Times and circumstances had changed. By then Stalin was revealed to be a totalitarian, murderous thug, and Hitler obviously had to be stopped. But this is not to say that Langston Hughes changed essentially with regard to his fundamental commitment to justice, working people's rights, and the plight of African Americans.

1950s and 1960s

Langston Hughes literally became a historian in the 1950s when he wrote a series of books for a younger audience. These include the *First Book of Negroes, Famous American Negroes, The First Book of Rhythms, The First Book of Jazz, Famous Negro Music Makers, The First Book of the West Indies,* and, with Milton Meltzer, *A Pictorial History of the Negro in America.* Like many other Americans, he had to experience Senator Joseph McCarthy's interrogation of his patriotism because of his earlier socialist and Marxist leanings. Hughes chose to appear before McCarthy's committee, knowing, as Rampersad writes, that he would "draw the disapproval, even contempt, of the white left, but keep more or less intact the special place he had painstakingly carved out within the black community" (2: 219; Osborne, "McCarthyism"). Hughes did not discuss other persons or "name names"; rather, his statement explained why socialist and Marxist ideas appealed to him in the 1930s and 1940s. His clarification was a "rhetorical tour de force," in Rampersad's opinion, and Hughes had the last word by publishing in *The Panther and the Lash* (1967) the poem "Un-American Investigators," in which the committee members are described as "shivering" in their own "manure." The Hughes of the 1950s and 1960s, occasionally with a greater aesthetic distance, hardly took a less interested approach to history and politics in his writing. *Montage of a Dream Deferred* (1952) presents multiple and varied narrations of Harlem, including one of his most famous poems in its title. Hughes published a history of the NAACP, *Fight for Freedom* (1961), and edited *Poems from Black Africa*, demonstrating that he was as interested in the diaspora at age fifty-nine as he had been at nineteen. Nor did a mellower Hughes mature excessively. His edgy, politically alert play *Jericho-Jim Crow* was produced in Greenwich Village in 1964, and in the year of his death, Knopf published *The Panther and the Lash: Poems of Our Times*, which included selected earlier poems as well as new ones such as "The Backlash Blues" and "Black Panther." In a selection entitled "The Face of War," the Vietnam War does not come off very well, given the history of global colonialism. "Christ in Alabama," once presumably banned from *Selected Poems* in 1959, almost magically reappears. Perhaps the Hughes at the end was never less radical at all.

Conclusion

Thus Hughes remained to the end of his life a poet and writer fully engaged with history, his times, and the sociopolitical milieu in the United States and around the world. History and historicity help reveal the man and the work, and if indeed, as R. Baxter Miller asserts, Hughes "voiced a celebration of survival and beauty that outlived his century," and if Hughes's "writings are for all time" (808), then Hughes's stature owes much to how consistently and energetically he remained alert to the emerging history of his own century and beyond.

Notes

Additional politically radical poems not mentioned in the body of the essay include "Good Morning Revolution," "A New Song," "One More 'S' in the U.S.A.," "Revolution," "Roar China!", and "Song of the Revolution." *Good Morning Revolution*, a selection of Hughes's poetry and other work edited by Faith Berry, is a good source for Hughes's more radical writings.

In the interest of accessibility, this essay uses *The Collected Poems of Langston Hughes* as the source for Hughes's poetry, but readers should be aware that the standard edition of Hughes's works, including the poetry and all other individual works mentioned in this essay, is *The Collected Works of Langston Hughes*, the sixteen-volume edition published by the University of Missouri Press between 2001 and 2003. All works mentioned in this essay also have individual entries in *A Langston Hughes Encyclopedia*, edited by Hans Ostrom.

Works Cited

Bernard, Emily. "The Harlem Renaissance." Ostrom and Macey 718–25.
Briley, Ron. "Asa Philip Randolph." Ostrom and Macey 1362–64.
Du Bois, W. E. B. "Criteria of Negro Art." Lewis, *Portable* 100–05.
_____."Returning Soldiers." Lewis, *Portable* 3–5.
Ellul, Jacque. *Propaganda: The Formation of Men's Attitudes*. New York: Vintage, 1973.
Gilmore, Glenda Elizabeth. *Defying Dixie: The Radical Roots of Civil Rights, 1919–1950*. New York: Norton, 2008.
Haltom, William. "*Brown v. Board of Education*." Ostrom 61–62.
_____. "Robinson and Una Jeffers." Ostrom 181–82.
_____. "The Scottsboro Boys." Ostrom 343–44.
Harper, Donna Akiba Sullivan. *Not So Simple: The "Simple" Stories by Langston Hughes*. New York: Columbia UP, 1995.
Hughes, Langston. *The Big Sea*. New York: Knopf, 1940.
_____. *The Collected Poems of Langston Hughes*. Ed. Arnold Rampersad and David Roessel. New York: Knopf, 1994.
_____. *Fight For Freedom: The Story of the NAACP*. New York: Berkeley, 1962.
_____. *The First Book of Jazz*. New York: Franklin, 1955.
_____. *The First Book of Negroes*. New York: Franklin, 1952.
_____. *The First Book of Rhythms*. New York: Franklin, 1954.
_____. *The First Book of the West Indies*. New York: Franklin, 1956.
_____. *Good Morning Revolution: Uncollected Writing of Social Protest*. Ed. Faith Berry. New York: Carol, 1992.
_____. *Langston Hughes and the Chicago Defender: Essays on Race, Politics, and Culture, 1942–1962*. Ed. Christopher C. De Santis. Urbana: U of Illinois P, 1995.
_____. "The Negro Artist and the Racial Mountain." Lewis, *Portable* 91–95.

_____. *The Panther and the Lash: Poems of Our Times*. 1967. New York: Vintage, 1992.

_____. *The Return of Simple*. Ed. Donna Akiba Sullivan Harper. New York: Hill, 1994.

_____. *The Ways of White Folks*. New York: Knopf, 1934.

_____. *The Weary Blues*. New York: Knopf, 1926.

Hughes, Langston, and Carl Van Vechten. *Remember Me to Harlem: The Letters of Langston Hughes and Carl Van Vechten*. Ed. Emily Bernard. New York: Vintage, 2002.

Hughes, Langston, and Milton Meltzer. *A Pictorial History of the Negro in America*. New York: Crown, 1956.

James, William. *Pragmatism and Other Writings*. New York: Penguin, 2002.

Julien, Isaac, dir. *Looking for Langston*. 1989. Strand, 2007. DVD.

Lewis, David Levering, ed. *The Portable Harlem Renaissance Reader*. New York: Viking, 1994.

_____. *When Harlem Was in Vogue*. New York: Vintage, 1997.

Miller, R. Baxter. "Langston Hughes." Ostrom and Macey 802–10.

_____.. "Remembering Hughes and His Art." *A Literary Criticism of Five Generations of African American Writing: The Artistry of Memory*. Lewiston: Mellen, 2008. 69–106.

Osborne, Elizabeth. "Collective Persona." Ostrom 77–78.

_____. "Drama." Ostrom 104.

_____. "Great Depression." Ostrom and Macey 655–59.

_____. "Harlem Suitcase Theatre." Ostrom 154.

_____. "Jesse B. Semple Stories." Ostrom 184–85.

_____. "McCarthyism." Ostrom 239–40.

_____. "Marxism." Ostrom 233–234.

_____. "Modernism and Hughes." Ostrom 250–53.

_____. "Songs." Ostrom 366–69.

Ostrom, Hans, ed. *A Langston Hughes Encyclopedia*. Westport: Greenwood, 2002.

Ostrom, Hans, and J. David Macey, eds. *The Greenwood Encyclopedia of African American Literature*. 5 vols. Westport: Greenwood, 2005.

Ponce, Martin Joseph. "Langston Hughes's Queer Blues." *Modern Language Quarterly* 66.4 (2005): 505–38.

Rampersad, Arnold. *The Life of Langston Hughes*. 2 vols. New York: Oxford UP, 1986–88.

Van Vechten, Carl. *Nigger Heaven*. 1926. Urbana: U of Illinois P, 1999.

Vogel, Shane. *The Scene of Harlem Cabaret: Race, Sexuality, Performance*. Chicago: U of Chicago P, 2009.

Wimsatt, W. K. *The Verbal Icon: Studies in the Meaning of Poetry*. Lexington: UP of Kentucky, 1954.

Woodson, Carter G. "The Migration of the Talented Tenth." Lewis, *Portable* 6–7.

In the Shadow of the Blues:
Aesthetic Discoveries by Ma Rainey,
Langston Hughes, and Sterling A. Brown

John Edgar Tidwell

As used here, the shadow that appears in this essay's title is not literally the liminal space between dark and light; however, as metaphor, it does suggest something murky, cloudy, misty, foggy, or dim. These descriptors aptly apply to the background in which Ma Rainey, Langston Hughes, and Sterling A. Brown engaged a form of music that profoundly shaped and ordered their individual aesthetic visions. Since the emphasis here is on discovery, my discussion centers on inchoate stirrings and deepening intimacies. At stake is an understanding of a "conversation" that can be inferred from their initial engagements with the music. Ma Rainey (1886–1939), older than the others and therefore more familiar with the blues, functions here as a guiding light, leading Hughes (1902–66) and Brown (1901–89) toward inspiration, vision, and aesthetic practice. I wish to argue that their emergent knowledge of the blues forces them to engage Ma Rainey's well-known reputation and perhaps her model of the classic blues. Because the extant evidence begs precision and cogency, the argument might be considered a bit shadowy. But given the blues context of the era, it is safe to conclude that Hughes and Brown encountered the greatest blues singer of their day. While it does not place them entirely within the long shadow of Rainey's influence, Hughes and Brown reflect enough of her aesthetic to confirm the likelihood of her effect on them.

With the possible exception of Sandra R. Lieb's *Mother of the Blues* (1981), studies of Rainey have yet to examine her life with the breadth and depth accorded the excellent biographies of Langston Hughes and Zora Neale Hurston; nevertheless, several versions reveal a consensus about the details of her personal history. There is general agreement that Gertrude Melissa Pridgett's early performances in church launched her trajectory into a stage career as Ma Rainey, winning for her the sobriquet "Mother of the Blues." At about fourteen, she embarked upon a performative course that took her into the hearts and souls of the people Hughes reverently referred to as the "low down" folks. En route, she developed an uncanny but intimate perspective on their lives, loves, heartaches, disappointment, joys, abuses, successes, failures, and more. The consciousness or "mind" of the folk she accessed distinguishes the inherent complexity of their lives from the simplicity with which it was represented in the proliferation of black racial stereotypes in American literature and popular culture. Her performances in minstrel shows, tent shows, vaudeville, and "opera houses" not only brought her into close proximity with adoring fans but also introduced her to the music for which she became famous.

The music of minstrelsy and vaudeville certainly struck a popular note with fans at the turn of the twentieth century. But the year 1902 is significant, not just because it was the year of Langston Hughes's birth, but also because it is generally believed to date Ma Rainey's discovery of the blues. Musicologist John W. Work documents this story:

> "Ma" Rainey heard [the blues] in 1902 in a small town in Missouri where she was appearing with a show under a tent. She tells of a girl from the town who came to the tent one morning and began to sing about the "man" who had left her. The song was so strange and poignant that it attracted much attention. "Ma" Rainey became so interested that she learned the song from the visitor, and used it soon afterwards in her "act" as an encore. (32)

While Work's revelation certainly has biographical significance, it also provides a larger context in which to view Ma Rainey's blues.

For instance, he also records that Ma Rainey had been asked several times to identify the kind of music to which this song belonged. According to Work, her reply was uttered in a moment of inspiration: "the blues." It is unclear whether Work's interview with Ma Rainey declares her as naming this "weird music." After all, the foundation had already been laid by then; the well-known field hollers, work songs, and other antecedents from slavery had already coalesced into this unnamed music by the end of the nineteenth century. But certainly it was a music in search of definition, and it would, arguably, become formalized in 1903 when W. C. Handy, the putative "Father of the Blues," first heard the melodies and began composing them.[1]

What can be said with greater assurance is that Ma Rainey's touring with different bands, including her own, more likely made her part of what Jürgen Grandt identifies as "territory bands." These groups wound their way through Oklahoma, Kansas, Missouri, Texas, and the South, playing a "kind of black music, weaving fluidly and daringly between different styles and genres, *yet always grounded in the blues*" (121, emphasis added). Steven C. Tracy further validates this claim when he argues that the blues Ma Rainey discovered indicates the form was quite well known in these areas. It probably inhered in the ragtime, jazz, and orchestral music found pervasively in Kansas City (106).

Beyond the questions of naming and definition, then, lie the contextual concerns of Ma Rainey's regional and emergent national reputation and what they might have meant for Langston Hughes and Sterling Brown. Until 1923, Ma Rainey found herself tracing and retracing the South and Southwest, endearing herself to appreciative crowds with her diverse musical styles, including the classic blues. But a contract she signed with Paramount Records greatly enhanced her reputation by taking her voice to places she had not been. Between 1923 and 1928, she recorded, according to one source, at least ninety-two songs for Paramount (Lieb 48). The widespread notoriety she thus enjoyed catapulted her onto an even larger stage. Eventually, changing times and economic decline finally caught up with her. The onset of the Depression, the increased popularity of her protégé Bessie Smith, and the emergence of swing music, which eroded the financial stability of recorded race music, forced her to return to touring. Throughout a career that was nothing short of remarkable, Rainey gave the music world the best of the classic blues. As will be shown, her sense of art proved to be significant for both Hughes and Brown.

Langston Hughes's well-known use of the blues in his early collection *The Weary Blues* (1926) and his first novel, *Not without Laughter* (1930), demonstrates how an informal, experiential engagement culminated in an enviable proficiency with the art form. His discovery of the blues, as he recounts, occurred when, as a six-year-old visiting his uncle in Kansas City, he heard a verse that haunted him until years later, when he wrote a poem incorporating it. In "I Remember the Blues," Hughes recalls being "on a Charlotte Street corner near [his] uncle's barber shop" and hearing "a blind guitar player moaning to the long eerie sliding notes of his guitar" (152). He reiterates the remembered lines in *The Big Sea*: "I got de weary blues / And I can't be satisfied. . . . / I ain't happy no mo' / And I wish that I had died" (215). The precise location is undoubtedly less important than the fact that it places Hughes firmly in the region at a time when different kinds of music were playing against each other, seeking definition. As Grandt writes, quoting Sidney Bechet, "Jazz in the Jazz Age was indeed still 'waiting to be music.'" It was a music "that was only just beginning to gel from the collision of myriad styles, genres, and regional influences" (47). At the epicenter of the aesthetic ferment was the blues, a form the young Hughes would retain in his inchoate memory until years later, when he transformed it into meaningful poetry and fiction. From this rather inauspicious beginning emerged a lifelong engagement with the form.

Aside from his actual experiments with blues form and spirit that find their way into his impressive body of creative work, Hughes, for about forty years, consistently reworked definitions of the blues, which ultimately became variations on a theme. In *Fine Clothes to the Jew* (1927), his "A Note on the Blues" provides an attentive audience with a brief description of poetic pattern ("one long line repeated and a third line to rhyme with the first two") and a statement about its mood ("almost always despondency, but when they are sung people laugh") (*Collected Works* 1: 73). In *The Dream Keeper and Other Poems* (1932), his collection for younger readers, he provides, in addition to the previous background, a distinction between the blues (sung by individuals) and spirituals (sung by groups): "Whereas the Spirituals are often songs about escaping from trouble, going to heaven and living happily ever after, the Blues are songs about being in the midst of trouble, friendless, hungry, disappointed in love, right here on earth" (*CW* 11: 59).

Perhaps Hughes was untroubled by these easy distinctions of blues and spirituals because children were his audience for the poems. His definitions clearly simplify a much more complicated set of claims. But he does seem to redeem himself. Over the years, he would continue to educate readers about the nature of the blues and its significance to his own aesthetic development in brief autobiographical reminiscences such as "Songs Called the Blues" (1940), "Jazz as Communication" (1958), and "I Remember the Blues" (1964).[2] Finally, he also uses an installment of the ongoing Jesse B. Semple (or Simple) narrative to remind observers of his own engagement with the music through a remarkably succinct history. Framed around the idea of memory, the colloquy between Simple and his rather droll friend Boyd debates the relative merits of Bessie, Clara, and Mamie Smith, while pondering whose recollection of the singers is greater. In an ultimate coup, Boyd invokes the name Ma Rainey. Simple's reply echoes the high esteem Hughes no doubt held of her: "Great day in the morning! Ma! That woman could sing some blues! I loved Ma Rainey. . . . Yes, I heard her! I am proud of hearing her! To tell the truth, if I stop and listen, I can still hear her" ("Shadow of the Blues," *CW* 7: 325). The recollections of street-smart Simple testify to the enduring power of Rainey's vocal talent as well as her songs. In comparing her body of work to that of three other obviously sterling performers, Simple credits Rainey as being their superior. Thus the brief reference not only distills Rainey's continuing historical resonance but also restates Hughes's idea of her place in the pantheon of blues queens. Rainey, therefore, is not just a memory; she is *memorable*.

An interesting way of considering Sterling A. Brown's initial engagement with the blues is to examine briefly how he resolved the dilemma of double consciousness. His birth into the rather genteel circumstances of the Washington, DC, upper-middle class fostered a sensibility that naturally clashed with the goals and expectations of the black working class. Easily, he could have gone the way of the bourgeois elite, with its classism and ethos of racial uplift. His very fair skin color presented him with the opportunity to escape all responsibilities to assist black people by passing for white. But he was dissuaded from engaging in acts of class and racial escapism. He cultivated a life of embracing and celebrating black people, especially the people furthest down. Brown parlayed his graduation in 1918 from the prestigious Dunbar High School into a "minority set-aside" fellowship at Williams College, where, among several other life-affirming educational experiences, he discovered the blues.

Brown recalls with considerable clarity the moment he engaged the song "The Crazy Blues" (1920), inspired by vaudeville and Tin Pan Alley and recorded by Mamie Smith. To the two or three other black students at Williams, the song simultaneously attracted and repulsed them. Trapped by the desire to hear the song but embarrassed by the reminder of its origins in slavery and of the lives of those socioeconomically beneath them, they forced Brown to provide a "safe" way of listening to the music. As he recounts: "They wanted to hear it but they didn't want the white boys in the neighboring room to know what they were listening to, so it was that kind of phoniness. They wanted to hear 'The Crazy Blues,' but in a kind of a secret. So I would play 'em and I was glad to have it" (Jones 29). To appease his racially conflicted, embarrassed classmates, Brown closed the slats on the Victrola and draped a towel over it too. With the sound muffled from the hearing of their white classmates, they listened as he played the record over and over again. In effect, the towel and the lowered slats functioned as a veil—not only over the pseudoblues but over the whole of black vernacular culture. For Brown, pulling back the towel was akin to pulling back the veil that shrouded African American cultural history. The gesture represents an inchoate movement, but one signifying the beginning of a lifelong exploration into African American authenticity.

Later, the more culturally aware Brown would come to recognize the shortcomings of "The Crazy Blues." The white actress Sophie Tucker, for instance, the original singer scheduled to record the song, did strive for her own version of authentic blackness. But her efforts fell considerably short in that she appeared in blackface and found black cultural expression in a misguided amalgam of burlesque, vaudeville, coon-shouting, and minstrelsy. She even hired Mamie Smith and Ethel Waters to give her singing lessons and black composers to write songs for her act. But while she was widely popular in the white imagination, she was simply a pretender to members of the black audience. It was almost fortuitous that a sudden illness prevented her from recording "The Crazy Blues" and launching Okeh Records' foray into the burgeoning cottage industry of race records. Her substitute, Mamie Smith, went on to enjoy the fame that accrued to the recording. The initial sales of seventy-five hundred disks per week broke all sales records and prompted, according to musicologist Eileen Southern, such entrepreneurial ingenuity as the hiring of Negro talent scouts to locate the best singers and musicians (398).

Commercialism, a by-product of sales, points to "Crazy Blues" as having little or no relation to actual black life, rather something closer to the fakery of Tin Pan Alley.[3] Brown came to perceive the sound of "Crazy Blues" as simply "tinny": "I can't sleep at night. / I can't eat a bite— / 'cause the [man/gal] I love— / [he/she] don't treat me right." The "sound" of the lines follows a nearly formulaic pattern that historian Philip Furia describes as the AABA sequence of rhyme, often short or confining lines, forced rhythm, and lyrics that were generally unpoetic. Lyric writing, that is, setting words to music, was often considered more difficult than writing poetry, according to Furia (5–14). Brown, of course, took umbrage with the Tin Pan Alley versions of the blues. He found them filled with clichés, inconsecutiveness, false rhymes, crudities, incongruities, and moods that shifted inconsistently from tragedy to cheap farce ("Folk Poetry" 337, 339). As he says on distinguishing the authentic from the imitative: "One critic, even though appreciating the work of Berlin and Kern, says that the fundamental difference between Negro folk-blues and tin-pan alley blues is that in the tin-pan alley blues the grief is feigned, but in the Negro folk-blues the *gaiety* is feigned" ("Blues, Ballads" 17).

Brown's intuited sense of feigned grief and gaiety resulted, in part, from his acquaintance with the itinerant worker and bluesman Calvin "Big Boy" Davis. At Virginia Seminary and College, the young graduate of Williams College and Harvard University taught English to seminary students who were about his age. As he says, they "were old to be in school, and I was young to be out of school" (Rowell 305). By way of introducing him to qualities of black folk culture, they brought Big Boy to his faculty apartment, where the exceedingly talented musician and storyteller taught him stories of John Henry, played the blues, and gave him guitar lessons. Brown preserved their special relationship in three memorable poems: "Odyssey of Big Boy," "When the Saints Go Ma'chin' Home," and "Long Gone."

In an interview in which he reflects again on his relationship to the blues, Brown recalls the conversation that he and the musicologist John Work had with Ma Rainey:

> That night when we saw her, she was having boy trouble. You see, she liked these young musicians, and in comes John Work and I—we were young to her. We were something sent down, and she didn't know which one to choose. Each of us knew we were not choosing her! We just wanted to talk, but she was interested in other things. She was that direct. She was the tops for my money. She was all right. (qtd. in Stewart-Baxter 42)

In one of his finest portrait poems, simply titled "Ma Rainey," Brown captures her essence, her meaning of the blues, and her capacity to represent the emotional range of her adoring fans. Both Hughes and

Brown, then, encountered Rainey in her prime. In retrospect, Hughes recalls that "in Chicago in my teens, all up and down State Street there were blues, indoors and out, at the Grand and the old Monogram theaters where Ma Rainey sang, in the night clubs, in the dance halls, on phonographs" ("I Remember" 153). In the mid-1920s, when Hughes had embarked upon his experiments with the blues and jazz as poetic forms, Ma Rainey's reputation as the consummate blues singer was probably at its peak. While the aesthetic tie that might bind Hughes and Ma Rainey is a bit thin, Tracy writes that Hughes did invoke her name in the contexts of "a mixture of folk blues and a more sophisticated blues" and vaudeville (108).[4] He is on much surer turf when he astutely comments on Hughes's experiments with stanzaic form: "In some of his best 'experimental' blues poems, Hughes used varied stanzas, line placement, and typography to convey both the spirit of the oral performance and a psychological or sociological complexity that stood up to such literary treatment on the page" (144). In so doing, Hughes extended his aesthetic practice beyond Ma Rainey's classic blues form—generally three lines rhyming AAB. He also departed from her usual Southern subject matter by inscribing his blues poems with urban themes and motifs.

In the course of his efforts to find his blues-based voice and thus forge new directions in poetic practice, Hughes encountered severe criticism from fellow poet Countee Cullen. Simply put, Cullen accused Hughes of violating the precepts of good poetry. In a review of *The Weary Blues*, Cullen is especially judgmental:

> Never having been one to think all subjects and forms proper for poetic consideration, I regard these jazz poems as interlopers in the company of the truly beautiful poems in other sections of the book. They move along with the frenzy and electric heat of a Methodist or Baptist revival meeting, and affect me in much the same manner.... I wonder if the quiet way of communing is not more spiritual for the God-seeking heart; and in the

light of reflection I wonder if jazz poems really belong to that dignified company, that select and austere circle of high literary expression which we call poetry. (3–4)

Clearly, Cullen's review betrays the same middle-class ambivalence toward the black vernacular that Brown encountered at Williams. Try as he might, Cullen seems unable or unwilling to see aesthetic possibilities in black folk forms and cultural distinctiveness. It is safe to say that he is spiritually and intellectually divorced from the wonderful possibilities, even the necessity, of founding what Hughes, throughout his well-known "The Negro Artist and the Racial Mountain," calls a "racial art." If this is true, Cullen is incapable of paying homage to Ma Rainey for her contribution to American popular music.

Unlike Rainey's ties with Hughes, the aesthetic lines connecting Brown with Ma Rainey are more clearly delineated. In "Ma Rainey," one of his most memorable poems, he creates an homage to her that is simply uncanny in representing what she means to the folk who come from "Miles aroun'" "to hear / Ma do her stuff" and to the tradition of blues culture (line 4, 7–8). In this marvelous portrait, Brown focuses on the transaction between singer and audience. Unlike the spirituals, which are intended for communal singing, the blues places the burden for song on the individual singer. The success of the strategy depends on the singer's ability to relate to the audience so genuinely that the listeners *feel* the voicing of their own troubles onstage. Ma Rainey had the gift for eliciting that emotional response. As Brown observes:

> Ma Rainey was a tremendous figure. She wouldn't have to sing any words; she would moan, and the audience would moan with her. She had them in the palm of her hand. I heard Bessie Smith also, but Ma Rainey was the greatest mistress of an audience. Bessie was the greater blues singer, but Ma really *knew* these people; she was a person of the folk; she was very simple and direct. (quo. in Stewart-Baxter 42)

Brown nicely rearticulates in poetry what he boldly asserted in prose. Rainey's power hinges on the dynamic strength of three key lines. First, as if invoking a life force or the spirit of a secular savior, the group entreats Ma Rainey to "Git way inside us, / Keep us strong" (31–32). After reestablishing an unconditional trust with their patron saint, the group prepares itself for a communion reserved only for believers. Because she knows their hard luck and the loneliness in their lives, she prepares to sing a cathartic song to release them of their miseries.

The speaker, an outsider, then inquires of a Ma Rainey devotee about the source and meaning of her magical powers. The response takes the speaker and the reader into the very heart of the blues: "She jes' catch hold of us, somekindaway" (40). As if searching for an adequate explanation, the devotee resorts to social history. He points to the blues she sang to exorcise the demons conjured up by the Mississippi River flood of 1927. With farmers displaced, property destroyed, and hope turned into hopelessness, Ma Rainey sang a song that delivered them emotionally from victimization and defeat. Her catharsis inspired those in the audience to reclaim their determination and encouraged them to persevere. She restored their faith in possibilities. With renewed strength and the willingness to give life one more try, the auditor turns to the outsider and delivers a coda to the answer just provided: "She jes' gits hold of us dataway" (52).

The confluence of Rainey, Hughes, and Brown may be justifiably considered a conversation about aesthetics. As different as the three voices appear to be, they share a vision concerning the nature of art. The blues is a highly personal medium of expression. And yet, it also reflects and reveals an often common problem experienced by members of the same group. The axiom "the personal is political" describes the group dynamic or the artist-audience transaction I have developed here. In that same vein, there seems to be a consensus that most blues songs contain an element of protest.

Take, for instance, Angela Davis's rigorous inquiry into feminism and the blues. She argues that an integral part of the form is its "protest consciousness." Her conceptual understanding results from a sustained interrogation into the ideological formation of the blues created by Ma Rainey, among others. Davis concludes that Rainey's legacy "constituted an aesthetically mediated community-building and assisted in developing a specifically African American social consciousness" (92).

Tony Bolden, in an insightful meditation titled *Afro-Blue: Improvisations in African American Poetry and Culture*, deepens Davis's concept by exploring what he calls "resistance poetry." He proposes that a productive way of examining the nexus of black vernacular poetry and the resulting political ferment out of which it grew is to consider its roots in the blues tradition. It is here that he locates poets engaging "in expressive acts of cultural resistance" (37). Somewhere between "protest consciousness" and "resistance," the conversation about blues that Rainey, Hughes, and Brown engaged in coalesced into an early, socially aware aesthetic—one concerned with the material conditions of the lives of the "low down" folks, issues of gender, personal engagements, and the community.

Consider, say, the example of community. Ma Rainey's concern for the folk was not that of a figure who set out merely to entertain her audience. As Brown notes, she "*knew* these people." The quality of her knowledge extended so deeply into their lives that she bonded with them. That is, she knew their lives so intimately that when she sang she revealed their innermost thoughts and feelings. Listeners heard themselves in her songs. Her popularity resulted from her ability to represent their individual concerns as communal consciousness. In turn, the group felt healed or relieved by her music. Rainey was therefore a source of restoration.

It is this crucial concern for building community that lies at the root of the Hughes-Cullen debate about the efficacy of vernacular art. Cullen's reliance on the studied use of Western poetic forms provided him an escape from a racially derived aesthetic. For him, the designation "Negro poet" signified a separate, less rigorous standard of evaluation and therefore a mark of inferiority. He positioned himself as an individual who had no allegiance or affinity to the traditions of black culture. Hughes, on the other hand, believed that his own identity as an individual artist was inextricably intertwined with the lives of the "low down" folks. His raison d'être was bound up in their very being. When he inscribed their lives in memorable poetry and fiction, he solidified an already strong personal and cultural connection. His art became a testament to the community of which he was a part.

Brown too made his blues poetry into an expression of resistance. As much as he was preoccupied with representational issues and racial authenticity, he was more concerned that African American literary art reveal the humanity of black folks. The very struggle to affirm black life required him to be true to their modes of expression. While literary criticism proved to be the proper venue for him to protest or refute racial misrepresentation, poetry was, for him, the site of racial *affirmation*. It is true that his blues form and spirit were *implicit* protests against injustice, lost love, natural disaster, and more. But, all told, they were narrative renditions of stoicism, determination, love, persistence, and so much more that testified to the essential character and the indomitable strength of a people.

In this cultural conversation, then, Ma Rainey's classic blues became a beacon that signaled her own indebtedness and responsibility to the "low down" folks. Hughes's and Brown's artful use of a form made famous by the Mother of the Blues made a powerful dialogic. Both of them "talked back" to her *and* "spoke" to the same people who found reassurance in her music during stressful times. If we stop and listen, as Simple did, we can still hear the resonance of their extended conversation—as it takes place in the shadow of the blues.

Notes

1. Sterling A. Brown provides a spirited defense of Jelly Roll Morton as a better blues and jazz man than W. C. Handy. Morton claimed that Handy even plagiarized some of Morton's own lines. In his autobiography, *Father of the Blues*, Handy ignored the charges. Brown addresses the issue rather forthrightly: "There

is no question that the title of the autobiography is a misnomer; as Handy's own comments establish, the blues go back much, much further than 1912. . . . There is also no question that Handy did not feel the blues as deeply, or play them as convincingly as Jelly Roll Morton. Handy admits that he 'took up with low folk forms hesitantly. I approached them with fear and trembling'" ("Portrait" 39).

2. The following represents a partial listing of reminiscences:
   - "Songs." *Phylon* 2 (1941): 143–45. Rpt. in *The Langston Hughes Reader*. New York: Braziller, 1958. 159–61.
   - "Jazz as Communication." *The Langston Hughes Reader*. New York: Braziller, 1958. 492–94. Rpt. of "Jazz: Its Yesterday, Today and Its Potential Tomorrow." *Chicago Defender* 28 July 1956.
   - See an expanded list of titles in Tracy (138).

3. Despite changes in location, the name Tin Pan Alley remained a consistent descriptor of a kind of music that, when applied to the blues, was regarded as cheaply made, inartistic, and inauthentic. The name came from Monroe H. Rosenfeld, a songwriter who was commissioned by *The New York Herald* in 1900 to do a story on the emerging sheet music publishing industry. He found himself between Broadway and Sixth Avenue on West Twenty-Eighth Street in New York City. To describe the din and racket of upright pianos, he coined the adjective "tinny." Later, when the location changed to Broadway between Forty-Second and Fiftieth, the din continued and the negative connotation for many critics remained the same. See Philip Furia's *The Poets of Tin Pan Alley* for a fuller history, one that attempts to rescue the concept from its poor history and redeem its place in popular culture.

4. He goes on to suggest that Hughes was probably more familiar with Ma Rainey's recordings than with her personally.

Works Cited

Bolden, Tony. *Afro-Blue: Improvisations in African American Poetry and Culture*. Urbana: U of Illinois P, 2004.

Brown, Sterling A. "The Blues as Folk Poetry." *Folk-Say: A Regional Miscellany*. Ed. Benjamin A. Botkin. Norman: U of Oklahoma P, 1930. 324–39.

_____. "Blues, Ballads and Social Songs." *Seventy-Five Years of Freedom*. DC: LC, 1940. 17–25.

_____. "Portrait of a Jazz Giant: 'Jelly Roll' Morton (1885?–1941)." *Black World* 23.4 (1974): 28–48.

Cullen, Countee. "The Weary Blues: A Review." 1926. *Langston Hughes: Critical Perspectives Past and Present*. Eds. Henry Louis Gates and K. A. Appiah. New York: Amistad, 1993. 3–5.

Davis, Angela. *Blues Legacies and Black Feminism*. New York: Pantheon, 1998.

Furia, Philip. *The Poets of Tin Pan Alley*. New York: Oxford UP, 1990.

Grandt, Jürgen. *Kinds of Blue: The Jazz Aesthetic in African American Narrative*. Columbus: Ohio State UP, 2004.

Hughes, Langston. *The Big Sea*. 1940. New York: Hill, 1993.

———. *The Collected Works of Langston Hughes*. Ed. Arnold Rampersad et al. 16 vols. Columbia: U of Missouri P, 2001–03.

———. "I Remember the Blues." 1963. *Missouri Reader*. Ed. Frank Luther Mott. Columbia: U of Missouri P, 1964. 152–55.

———. *The Langston Hughes Reader*. New York: Braziller, 1958.

Jones, Steven. "Interview with Sterling A. Brown." 14 May 1973. Du Sable Museum.

Lieb, Sandra R. *Mother of the Blues: A Study of Ma Rainey*. Amherst: U of Massachusetts P, 1981.

Rowell, Charles Henry. "Let Me Be with Old Jazzbo: An Interview with Sterling A. Brown." *After Winter: The Art and Life of Sterling A. Brown*. Eds. John Edgar Tidwell and Steven C. Tracy. New York: Oxford UP, 2009. 287–309.

Schuller, Gunther. *Swing Era: The Development of Jazz, 1930–1945*. New York: Oxford UP, 1989.

Southern, Eileen. *The Music of Black Americans: A History*. New York: Norton, 1971.

Stewart-Baxter, Derrick. *Ma Rainey and the Classic Blues Singers*. London: Studio Vista, 1970.

Tracy, Steven C. *Langston Hughes and the Blues*. Urbana: U of Illinois P, 1988.

Work, John W. *American Negro Songs and Spirituals*. New York: Crown, 1940.

CRITICAL READINGS

Reassessing Langston Hughes and the Harlem Renaissance: Toward an African American Aesthetic

Christopher C. De Santis

> To create a Negro culture in America—a real, solid, sane, racial something growing out of the folk life, not copied from another, even though surrounding, race.
> —Langston Hughes, unpublished journal entry, August 1, 1929

Langston Hughes's reputation among contemporary students and scholars as the preeminent poet of the Harlem Renaissance was intimated by the publication of "The Negro Speaks of Rivers" in 1921 and secured by his prize-winning poem "The Weary Blues" in 1925. With its Whitmanesque blend of self-revelation and historical consciousness, "Rivers" announces to the world a young poet for whom language serves, paradoxically, to express both the *raceless*—a soul grown deep like the rivers "ancient as the world and older than the flow of human blood in human veins" (line 2)—and the deeply *racialized*, the Negro "I" speaking. In "The Weary Blues," Hughes mutes the paradox, merging blues lyrics he remembers from childhood with a syncopated narrative that captures the actions and emotions of a black musician. With this infectious lyricism, Hughes seems to be doing something never before attempted in poetry—convincingly representing in print the rhythm, tone, and emotive qualities of jazz and blues. As significant, the poet declares an unabashed love for African American culture and demonstrates a level of fearlessness in representing aspects of that culture—historically marginalized, maligned, or outright ignored—in his writing. A year after the publication of "The Weary Blues," Hughes would begin to articulate in nonfictional prose what he was experimenting with in poetry: the creation of a racial art—a black aesthetic proud and bold—and the emergence of a black writer unashamed to embrace the culture of the African American working-class masses.

In essays such as "The Negro Artist and the Racial Mountain" (1926), "These Bad New Negroes: A Critique on Critics" (1927), and "To Negro Writers" (1935) as well as in unpublished journal entries, letters to editors of newspapers, and personal correspondence, Hughes reveals himself to be a young writer deeply committed both to creating art and to theorizing the means by which art might merge with race to challenge and revise dominant conceptions of both. In this respect, Hughes's significance to the Harlem Renaissance must be understood not only in terms of his inventiveness in the genres of poetry and fiction, but also in the context of broader, nonfictional articulations of the nature and purpose of a *racial* art. Equally important to students of the Harlem Renaissance is an informed acknowledgment that Hughes's contributions to the concept of racial art and his articulation of a distinct aesthetic did not spring full-blown in the vacuum of 1920s-era Harlem. Hughes's brilliance in respect to these ideas grew from strong roots established by his literary ancestors. To contextualize the evolution of Langston Hughes's African American aesthetic, I shall trace the historical roots initially from the poetry of Phillis Wheatley in the late eighteenth century to the prose of W. E. B. Du Bois at the turn of the twentieth. Then I shall consider the original impact of Hughes's revolutionary transformation of the concept during the Harlem Renaissance of the 1920s. En route it will become quite clear that Hughes was at once the inheritor and artistic innovator of three centuries of intellectual and artistic tradition.

The tradition of African American writers theorizing about art dates back at least to the late eighteenth century, when Phillis Wheatley used her poems as a platform from which to explore various aspects of the creative process. One common thread in these early poems is a subtle critique of those who would impede the development of the black artist and the potential audience for her literary creations. In "To Maecenas" (1773), Wheatley appeals to the Muses—goddesses from Greek mythology who inspire artistic creation—and questions why a single writer, the ancient playwright Terence, was alone granted "partial grace" to represent "*Afric's* sable race" in history's roll call of celebrated artists (39–40). The poetic persona here expresses confidence that in the near future her creative talents might rival those of the poet Virgil and others, but unhappiness becomes a barrier to full artistic expression; the poet "cannot raise the song, / The fault'ring music dies upon my tongue" (35–36). Who, or what, kills the poet's voice, the vehicle for her music? In the poem "On Imagination" (1773), Wheatley's poetic persona suggests a possible source for the unhappiness alluded to in "To Maecenas": "*Winter* austere forbids me to aspire, / And northern tempests damp the rising fire" (50–51). Wheatley's personification of "Winter" as the force that forbids poetic aspiration and "northern tempests" as the killing source of artistic creation is not unlike Langston Hughes's figurative construction of the "racial mountain" that, over one hundred and fifty years after Wheatley composed her poems, stood in the way of the creation of a true racial art in America. While Hughes, in the 1920s, believed himself to be working against an undertow of creativity-dampening criticism from some blacks, who wished he would be more "respectable" in his literary creations, and some whites, who desired stereotypical representations of black life in his art, Wheatley was, in the early 1770s, still a slave and very much subject to the racist ideologies that held dominance in her society. The literary historian Russell Reising suggests that Wheatley's personified "Winter" is the "poetic embodiment of slaveholding Boston's northern climate and oppressive social regime . . . not merely 'austere' but tyrannical in its denial of imaginative reconfiguration" (99).

If Wheatley's poems suggest a foundational moment in the self-reflexive exploration among African American writers of the creative process, five significant African American writers of the late nineteenth and early twentieth centuries—Frances Ellen Watkins Harper, Charles Waddell Chesnutt, Anna Julia Cooper, Victoria Earle Matthews, and W. E. B. Du Bois—more directly anticipate Langston Hughes's concerns during the Harlem Renaissance with literature reflective of the lives of the black working masses and the creation of a distinct racial art. Harper, best known for *Iola Leroy* (1892), a novel of racial uplift set predominantly during the Reconstruction era, was an outspoken antislavery activist and, after Emancipation, lectured widely on women's rights. In one of a series of brief fictional sketches published as "Fancy Etchings" in the African Methodist Episcopal Church's *Christian Recorder*, her fictional persona, Jenny—a character likely based on Harper herself—announces to her aunt a desire to serve her people by becoming a poet. As the skeptical elder gently questions the recent college graduate about her career choice and its relevance to the black working-class masses, Jenny asserts the primacy of art in teaching "men and women to love noble deeds," confident that "poetry is one of the great agents of culture, civilization and refinement" (225). Implicit in Harper's sketch is the belief that art can be both a vehicle for racial uplift and a conduit through which dominant racial attitudes and stereotypes might be revised, ideas made more explicit in Charles W. Chesnutt's self-conscious conviction that the pathway of the African American writer can also be that of the savant with the capability of morally elevating color-conscious readers.

Like Harper, Chesnutt achieved some recognition as a novelist, though it was his dialect stories, published in books such as *The Conjure Woman* (1899), that brought him relative fame as a writer. At the age of twenty-two—nearly a decade before the publication of his first short story in *The Atlantic Monthly*—Chesnutt recorded in his personal journal literary aspirations not unlike those of Harper's fictional Jenny, though prose rather than poetry would be his chosen medium. In a journal entry dated May 29, 1880, Chesnutt declares his need to write a book and, with a degree of sophistication and seriousness belying his youth, states his intention of participating in a "moral revolution" through the creation of literature that would serve the dual purpose of preparing black Americans for social recognition and equality while also—somewhat subversively—acclimating white Americans to the reality of intelligent, cultured black citizens. Chesnutt acknowledges that literature may serve to entertain the racially prejudiced, but it should also "lead them on imperceptibly, unconsciously step by step to the desired state of feeling" (140). Anticipating Langston Hughes's challenge to black writers during the 1920s to look within African American culture for artistic source material, the youthful Chesnutt believed that the artist could find among black, Southern communities "a fund of experience, a supply of material, which a skillful person could work up with tremendous effect" toward the "high, holy purpose" of enacting change in dominant, prejudicial attitudes about black life and culture (139).

These seminal, bold articulations of a racial literature by writers such as Harper and Chesnutt were followed in the last decade of the nineteenth century and the start of the twentieth century by cautiously optimistic statements by prominent African American intellectuals who affirmed the need for a distinct, racial art while also alluding to social, economic, and political conditions in the United States that hindered the full realization of that art in the medium of literature. Anna Julia Cooper, the brilliant educator who published a series of essays on gender, race, and literature in her 1892 book, *A Voice from the South*, believed that early black vernacular productions—the slave songs, chants, and folk tales, for example, that many scholars now consider foundational to the African American literary tradition—might one day, given an artist or writer talented and sensitive enough to recognize their value, contribute to the creation of a racial literature that would rival the early poetic genius of Caedmon or Homer (178–80). Given the racial violence, political intimidation, and de facto segregation that African Americans faced in the years following Emancipation and leading up to the publication of *A Voice from the South*, however, Cooper believed that black writers had not yet achieved the "sense of freedom *in mind*," though free in body, to create a literary aesthetic that rose above "the eloquence and fire of oratory" (223–24, emphasis added). More critical of early literary efforts by African Americans than Cooper, Victoria Earle Matthews—a former slave who, by the last decade of the nineteenth century, had established a formidable reputation as a writer and lecturer on literature, civil rights, and the role of African American women in racial uplift and empowerment—suggests in an 1895 speech that "nothing distinctive" had yet been produced by black writers in the United States (131). Matthews was nevertheless confident, however, that talented African American writers would soon emerge to create a "Race Literature" that would "stand out preeminent" among all the great literatures of the world (130). "Our history and individuality as a people," Matthews suggests, "not only provides material for masterly treatment; but would seem to make a Race Literature a necessity as an outlet for the unnaturally suppressed inner lives which our people have been compelled to lead" (131).

For W. E. B. Du Bois, the "unnaturally suppressed inner lives" that Matthews predicted would find an outlet in race literature were also a manifestation of the "souls of black folk," souls that, Du Bois firmly believed, had already produced in the form of Negro folk-songs "the sole American music . . . the most beautiful expression of human experience born this side of the seas" (*Souls* 251). In his 1903 masterpiece *The Souls of Black Folk*, Du Bois characterizes these early musical forms—which he terms "the sorrow songs"—as the articulate means by which slaves expressed sorrow, disappointment, longing, and above all, a hope for justice. By 1913, as he was taking stock of the first hundred and fifty years or so of African American art and literature for the scholarly *Annals of the American Academy of Political and Social Sciences*, Du Bois's understanding of the songs had expanded: they not only contained "much primitive poetry" but also constituted a significant part of the "mass of material"—the very foundation of a great art and literature—of which African American writers were only beginning to become conscious ("The Negro" 235, 237).

Writing in 1913 of the possibilities yet to be explored in African American art and literature, Du Bois could not have anticipated the literary rise of Langston Hughes, though the eleven-year-old Hughes certainly knew of Du Bois—Du Bois's eloquent words of strength, protest, and defiance in *The Souls of Black Folk* were among the earliest Hughes remembered from his childhood (Hughes, *CW* 9: 197). Du Bois soon became aware of Hughes and his promising talent when the young poet published "The Negro Speaks of Rivers" in the June 1921 issue of the *Crisis*, the magazine Du Bois had founded in 1910 as the official publication of the National Association for the Advancement of Colored People (NAACP) and for which he served as editor in chief. Only a few years after the publication of "Rivers," Hughes became a well-known and highly regarded personage among NAACP dignitaries, especially those who were part of the burgeoning literary and artistic community at the center of the Harlem Renaissance. Indeed, his arrival at an NAACP-sponsored benefit dance in 1924 after a long stay in Africa and Europe was nearly a cause célèbre, attracting the attention of Walter White, the assistant secretary of the NAACP, and Mary White Ovington, one of the founders of the organization. There, Hughes brushed elbows with Du Bois and was introduced to James Weldon Johnson, the executive secretary of the NAACP and a fellow writer whom Hughes greatly admired (Rampersad 96–97; Berry 56).

While the youthful Hughes gloried in the praise and attention he received from older writers, artists, and intellectuals during the peak years of the Harlem Renaissance, he was also developing a political consciousness that led him to be increasingly critical of white desires for minstrel-show caricatures and black desires for middle-class respectability, both of which he believed could hinder the progress of black artists in the United States. Particularly galling was the tendency of some intellectuals to dismiss racial differences under the guise of American standardization—a manifestation of the popular "melting pot" theory in which cultural differences were absorbed into a homogeneous, national culture—the falsity of which struck Hughes as obvious on at least two counts. First, the jazz, blues, and gospel music being created by black musicians in the 1920s was certainly affecting US culture broadly, but it remained, Hughes would insist, an original art emanating from black America. Second, the nation's insistence on racial segregation—legalized by the 1896 US Supreme Court ruling in the case of *Plessy v. Ferguson*—ensured that any talk of American standardization would inherently involve power imbalances and would, more often than not, articulate a "standard" that was lily-white.

Only six months after the January 1926 publication of Hughes's first book, *The Weary Blues*, in which the young poet draws from African American musical forms to begin the creation of a racial aesthetic in literature, the iconoclastic black journalist George S. Schuyler, a columnist for the *Pittsburgh Courier*, published an essay in the *Nation* attacking the foundation of the aesthetic Hughes was in the process of developing. Schuyler's "The Negro-Art Hokum" challenges the very premise that art produced in the United States is in any way influenced by race. In the wake of the intense excitement surrounding the publication of Alain Locke's anthology *The New Negro* (1925), which heralded an awakening in African American visual arts, literature, music, and scholarship, Schuyler registers strong and bitingly sarcastic skepticism that the movement later known as the Harlem Renaissance was anything more than racial propaganda and the self-promotion of an elite few:

> Negro art "made in America" is as non-existent as the widely advertised profundity of Cal Coolidge, the "seven years of progress" of Mayor Hylan, or the reported sophistication of New Yorkers. Negro art there has been, is, and will be among the numerous black nations of Africa; but to suggest the possibility of any such development among the ten million colored people in this republic is self-evident foolishness. Eager apostles from Greenwich Village, Harlem, and environs proclaim a great renaissance of Negro art just around the corner waiting to be ushered on the scene by those whose hobby is taking races, nations, peoples and movements under their wing. New art forms expressing the "peculiar" psychology of the Negro were about to flood the market. In short, the art of Homo Africanus was about to electrify the waiting world. Skeptics patiently waited. They still wait. (662)

Central to Schuyler's essay—at once brilliant in some of its insights and infuriating in some of its unexplored assumptions—is the idea that race is a cultural construct rather than a biological determinant, a product of socioeconomic class and physical environment. Alluding to the pseudoscientific beliefs of Madison Grant and Lothrop Stoddard, both of whom published influential, strongly racist books in the early twentieth century, Schuyler correctly notes that the concept of fundamental differences among the races was historically used in the United States and elsewhere to support a white supremacist ideology that cast blacks as inherently inferior to whites. The broad cultural effect of such an ideology was most noticeable in US society, Schuyler suggests, in the popular, grotesque stereotypes of black Americans that were as prevalent in advertisements for household products, food, and tobacco as they were on the minstrel-show stage: "The mere mention of the word 'Negro' conjures up in the average white American's mind a composite stereotype of Bert Williams, Aunt Jemima, Uncle Tom, Jack Johnson, Florian Slappey, and the various monstrosities scrawled by the cartoonists" (662). Schuyler insists that celebrations such as those taking place in 1920s Harlem of a distinct African American art—which might be translated by whites as a "peculiar art"—could only serve to legitimize racist ideology and its attendant stereotypes (663). It would be far more preferable for intelligent, reasonable human beings to dismiss such "hokum" as a racial art, Schuyler implies, and to acknowledge that "Negroes and whites from the same localities in this country talk, think, and act about the same" (662).

Hughes understood the merits of Schuyler's argument about racist assumptions of "fundamental differences" among peoples and qualifiedly agreed that blacks were no different from whites with respect to desiring similar opportunities and privileges that the United States provided to its citizens. Hughes was angered, however, by Schuyler's suggestion that "the Aframerican is merely a lampblacked Anglo-Saxon" (662). In a letter to the editor of the *Nation* that appeared shortly after Schuyler's essay was published, Hughes makes his own position clear:

"For Mr. Schuyler to say that 'the Negro masses . . . are no different from the white masses' in America seems to me obviously absurd. Fundamentally, perhaps, all peoples are the same. But as long as the Negro remains a segregated group in this country he must reflect certain racial and environmental differences which are his own." In this important letter, Hughes begins to articulate ideas about the distinctiveness of African American art that would remain central to his writings throughout the Harlem Renaissance and, in most respects, to much of his post-Renaissance creative work as well. While Hughes did not attempt to define "race" as a concept, he was convinced that racial difference, at least in the United States, *must* have an impact on artistic and cultural productions. Acknowledging that racial amalgamation might be desirable for blacks in economic and sociological terms, Hughes nevertheless argues that "until America has completely absorbed the Negro and until segregation and racial self-consciousness have entirely disappeared, *the true work of art from the Negro artist* is bound, if it have any color and distinctiveness at all, to reflect his racial background and his racial environment" ("American Art" 151, emphasis added).

Hughes's fullest articulation of a racial art—indeed, a *black aesthetic*—appears in one of his finest essays, "The Negro Artist and the Racial Mountain," a bold piece of nonfictional prose that would resonate deeply with the younger generation of artists and writers of the Harlem Renaissance. Hughes offers in the essay a voice charged with the idealism of youth—proud, independent, and unencumbered by the constraints of polite society. At the heart of this impassioned, often polemical essay is a pointed critique of the tendency Hughes believed to be endemic among black artists toward seeking aesthetic validation in white cultural productions and the dismissal of black vernacular culture in the United States by the African American middle classes and intelligentsia. Relying on general anecdotes of personal experience to support his argument, Hughes cites a "prominent Negro clubwoman in Philadelphia" who gladly paid top dollar to hear an internationally famous Spanish singer perform but would not even consider patronizing

Clara Smith, the great blues singer billed as the "Queen of the Moaners"; upper-class black churchgoers who preferred the "drab melodies in white folks' hymnbooks" to the Negro spirituals; and black actors and writers who were ignored by black high society until they gained recognition from white audiences. In multiple ways, Hughes suggests, middle- and upper-class blacks enforce among themselves a color line not unlike the line that separates them from whites on a national scale: "In the North they go to white theaters and white movies. And in the South they have at least two cars and a house 'like white folks.' Nordic manners, Nordic faces, Nordic hair, Nordic art (if any), and an Episcopal heaven" ("Negro Artist" 693).

Such examples seem to illustrate at least two points of conflict that could hinder the creation of a true racial art, one rather obvious and the other less so. First, these examples suggest the prevalence in middle- and upper-class black society of "color consciousness," a term popularized a few years after the publication of "The Negro Artist and the Racial Mountain" by Hughes's close friend Wallace Thurman in his novel *The Blacker the Berry* (1929). Like Hughes's "Negro clubwoman" and upper-class black churchgoers, Thurman's protagonist is a victim of a society that has elevated "whiteness" to nearly divine status, a young woman who rejects black culture and dismisses the possibility of black beauty even when doing so threatens her physical and emotional health and destroys her personal relationships with other African Americans. Second, Hughes's examples may also imply that many African Americans internalized broader historical arguments suggesting that the Middle Passage and slavery had obliterated any unique cultural practices and productions among blacks in the United States. This argument, implicit in George Schuyler's "The Negro-Art Hokum," suggests that *Africanisms*—the term later made prominent by the influential anthropologist Melville Herskovits in his 1941 book, *The Myth of the Negro Past*, to describe African cultural forms and traditions that survived the Middle Passage and slavery and continued to shape African American culture—were an impossibility in black American culture. More explicitly, Schuyler suggests that

> if the European immigrant after two or three generations of exposure to our schools, politics, advertising, moral crusades, and restaurants becomes indistinguishable from the mass of Americans of the older stock . . . how much truer must it be of the sons of Ham who have been subjected to what the uplifters call Americanism for the last three hundred years. Aside from his color, which ranges from very dark brown to pink, your American Negro is just plain American. (662)

Hughes firmly rejects this argument in "The Negro Artist and the Racial Mountain," though he understood how powerful its hold was in a nation in which millions of people were reminded daily that blackness was a marker of inferiority, a curse, while whiteness came to represent a powerful symbol of all that was virtuous and beautiful. In the racially segregated United States of the 1920s, a nation half a century removed from the violent end of slavery, *whiteness*, unspoken and unanalyzed, stood for the norm—stood for, in the words of the cultural historian Grace Hale, "the deepest sense of what it means to be an American" (xi). For Hughes, this silent, powerful, strangely racialized sense of national identity presented a daunting barrier to the black artist: "But this is the mountain standing in the way of any true Negro art in America—this urge within the race toward whiteness, the desire to pour racial individuality into the mold of American standardization, and to be as little Negro and as much American as possible" ("Negro Artist" 692). This formidable mountain, Hughes suggests, wreaked havoc in middle- and upper-class black communities, leading to a kind of racial self-loathing, a deep dislike of lower-class blacks, intraracial prejudice and discrimination, and a general desire for all things white.

In "The Negro Artist and the Racial Mountain," Hughes challenges black artists and writers to reject this bland, monolithic "Americanism" and seek within the black communities of the United States the unique aesthetic possibilities and artistic inspiration that might lead to new art, new literature, and a new source of pride for African Americans. To create a truly racial art, Hughes believed, the black artist could not be swayed by critiques of his or her subject matter or techniques, nor could fears of revealing aspects of black life that dominant standard-bearers of propriety frowned upon stand in the way of artistic inspiration. "An artist must be free to choose what he does," Hughes insists, "but he must also never be afraid to do what he might choose" (694). In this respect, Hughes believed that a vast storehouse of largely untapped artistic material resided within the culture of the African American working masses. Jazz, the spirituals, and the blues offered the artist a wealth of resources for the creation of a distinct black aesthetic, and the often-conflicted relations between black and white people in the United States furnished "an inexhaustible supply of themes" for the writer and dramatist (693). In utilizing these resources, the black artist could—indeed, *must*—begin to challenge and overturn dominant white standards of beauty that limited the representation of blackness to minstrel-show stereotypes. Hughes dismisses Schuyler's argument that environment and economics had transformed African Americans into darker Anglo-Saxons, issuing in its place a code of responsibility to the artists of his generation: "[I]t is the duty of the younger Negro artist, if he accepts any duties at all from outsiders, to change through the force of his art that old whispering 'I want to be white,' hidden in the aspirations of his people, to 'Why should I want to be white? I am a Negro—and beautiful!'" (694).

"The Negro Artist and the Racial Mountain" articulated some of the most salient themes that would motivate and distinguish Hughes's long writing career, anticipating his dedication to revealing and critiquing through art the racist and prejudicial ideas, institutions, and practices that hindered black individuals and communities from full enjoyment of the nation's resources and the freedoms it promised its citizens. The essay also set the stage for Hughes's more specific critiques of the ways in which power and prejudice among individuals in middle- and upper-class black communities could serve to reinforce the same racist attitudes that they themselves battled on a national scale. Hughes chastises "the best Negroes" in his essay "These Bad New Negroes: A Critique on Critics" (1927) for rejecting the work of writers such as Jean Toomer due to his representations of conflict and violence within African American communities. He also defended Carl Van Vechten's controversial novel *Nigger Heaven* (1926), describing the book, which shocked the black literati with its stereotypical and sensationalistic depictions of Harlem society, as "true to the life it pictures" (*CW* 9: 39). Regarding his own work, Hughes poses an honest question: "Is life among the better classes any cleaner or any more worthy of a poet's consideration?" (40). Answering this question in the ironically titled "Our Wonderful Society: Washington" (1927), Hughes notes that he found only intraracial prejudice and snobbery among many of the black elite in Washington, DC (9: 41). For the black artist, the racial mountain remained a major concern.

As the Harlem Renaissance continued on into the turbulent 1930s, Hughes retained his interest in issues affecting black Americans while also expanding his earlier conceptions of a truly racial art. While he did not abandon his commitment to drawing literary material from within African American culture, his understanding of a distinct black art broadened out to include an equal commitment to representing in his writings the oppression of people of color throughout the world. Drawing from personal experiences gained from extensive travel in the United States and abroad, Hughes wrote powerfully in the 1930s of imperialism in Haiti, Korea, Japan, and China; the Scottsboro trials and racial violence in the American South; Victorian attitudes and segregationist practices at historically black colleges; life in the Soviet Union after the revolution; the West Coast longshoremen's strike; and the Spanish Civil War, among other topics.

Although the 1930s in many ways appear to have set Hughes on a path as a writer far removed from the impassioned challenge he posed to black artists in "The Negro Artist and the Racial Mountain" to embrace a racial art and aesthetic originating in black America, the decade also led him back to those ideas regarding the duty of black artists as the financial strains of the decade compelled him to rethink a subject he knew very well—artistic patronage. Hughes's experiences with patronage during the 1920s certainly contributed to his criticism of such philanthropy in the next decade. Charlotte Mason, a wealthy white woman, had financially supported Hughes during the writing of his first novel, allowing him to concentrate on his work rather than worry about his next paycheck. As Hughes's work became more politically and socially conscious, however, Mason ceased to support it. This hypocrisy that seemed inherent to the system of patronage remained a concern of Hughes long after the 1920s. In "To Negro Writers" (1935), Hughes urges African American writers to expose

> the lovely grinning face of philanthropy—which gives a million dollars to a Jim Crow school, but not one job to a graduate of that school; which builds a Negro hospital with second-rate equipment, then commands black patients and student-doctors to go there whether they will or no; or which, out of the kindness of its heart, erects yet another separate, segregated, shut-off, Jim Crow Y.M.C.A. (139)

Hughes calls upon writers to use the transformative power of words to effect social change: eliminate stereotypes, "wipe out . . . all the old inequalities of the past," and expose the false leaders within organized religion and the black community who do nothing to combat injustice (139). Different from the black aesthetic that he championed in "The Negro Artist and the Racial Mountain," the racial art that Hughes articulated as the Harlem Renaissance drew to a close remained true nevertheless to his youthful vision of the 1920s, and indeed to the vision of his intellectual forebears such as Wheatley, Harper, Chesnutt, Cooper, Matthews, and Du Bois: that African American writers had a distinctive message for the world and were bound by a certain duty to convey it with power, pride, and conviction.

Works Cited

Berry, Faith. *Langston Hughes: Before and Beyond Harlem*. Westport: Hill, 1983.

Chesnutt, Charles W. *The Journals of Charles W. Chesnutt*. Ed. Richard H. Brodhead. Durham: Duke UP, 1993.

Cooper, Anna Julia. *A Voice from the South*. 1892. New York: Oxford UP, 1988.

Du Bois, W. E. B. "The Negro in Literature and Art." *Annals of the American Academy of Political and Social Science* 49 (1913): 233-37.

_____. *The Souls of Black Folk: Essays and Sketches*. Chicago: McClurg, 1903.

Hale, Grace Elizabeth. *Making Whiteness: The Culture of Segregation in the South, 1890-1940*. New York: Pantheon, 1998.

Harper, Frances Ellen Watkins. *A Brighter Coming Day: A Frances Ellen Watkins Harper Reader*. Ed. Frances Smith Foster. New York: Feminist, 1990.

Herskovits, Melville J. *The Myth of the Negro Past*. New York: Harper, 1941.

Hughes, Langston. "American Art or Negro Art?" *Nation* 18 August 1926: 151.

_____. *The Collected Works of Langston Hughes*. Ed. Arnold Rampersad et al. 16 vols. Columbia: U of Missouri P, 2001-03.

_____. "The Negro Artist and the Racial Mountain." *Nation* 23 June 1926: 692-94.

_____. "To Negro Writers." *American Writers' Congress*. Ed. Henry Hart. New York: International, 1935. 139-41.

Matthews, Victoria Earle. "The Value of Race Literature: An Address Delivered at the First Congress of Colored Women of the United States." 1895. *With Pen and Voice: A Critical Anthology of Nineteenth-Century African-American Women*. Ed. Shirley Wilson Logan. Carbondale: Southern Illinois UP, 1995.

Rampersad, Arnold. *The Life of Langston Hughes*. Vol. 1. New York: Oxford UP, 1986.

Reising, Russell. *Loose Ends: Closure and Crisis in the American Social Text*. Durham: Duke UP, 1996.

Schuyler, George S. "The Negro-Art Hokum." *Nation* 16 June 1926: 662-663.

Thurman, Wallace. *The Blacker the Berry: A Novel of Negro Life*. New York: Macaulay, 1929.

Wheatley, Phillis. *The Collected Works of Phillis Wheatley*. Ed. John C. Shields. New York: Oxford UP, 1988.

The Creative Voice in the Autobiographies of Langston Hughes

Joseph McLaren

Langston Hughes's two autobiographies, *The Big Sea: An Autobiography* (1940) and *I Wonder as I Wander: An Autobiographical Journey* (1956), go beyond the details of his travels and personal associations by offering a creative voice of internationalism. In *The Big Sea*, Hughes recounts his early years and family relationships, his journeys to Africa and Europe, and his initial years in New York during the 1920s and the Harlem Renaissance. As noted in the *New York Times Book Review*, the work is "sensitive and poised, candid and reticent, realistic and unembittered" (Woods 5). What distinguishes Hughes's voice in this first volume is the re-creation of the era through the perspectives of race, identity, labor, and culture. In June 1920, Hughes journeyed to Africa, a rare experience for an African American creative writer of that era. His later travels in Europe resulted in recollections of the black expatriate experience of jazz artists and other African Americans such as the legendary Ada "Bricktop" Smith. Similarly, Hughes's second autobiography, *I Wonder as I Wander*, is about the creative writer and the international journey to such locations as Cuba, Haiti, Paris, the Soviet Union, and the Far East. Hughes's internationalism, his global vision, underlies his creative articulations in the two autobiographies. In this regard, he was clearly a visionary who understood the local and the global and their connections to African American life.

The Big Sea: Beyond Childhood and the Harlem Renaissance

Divided into three parts, *The Big Sea* opens with Hughes reimagining his moment of departure from New York City. In his newfound role as a novice seaman, Hughes tosses into the ocean books from his Columbia University experience. This moment represents his desire to understand the world, but not from the perspective of books. It is ironic that perhaps the last volume to go overboard is one by H. L. Mencken, an important figure in the publishing and newspaper world of the 1920s. Hughes's creative approach is that of the observer, cognizant of details and personality traits.

Although the ship on which he sails is identified by Hughes as the S.S. *Malone*, it was, according to Hughes biographer Arnold Rampersad, the *West Hesseltine*, and the reasons for the name discrepancy are uncertain (1: 71). The importance of Africa for Hughes is expressed with exuberance and perhaps the romantic fervor of an African American whose images of Africa are, like those expressed in Countee Cullen's poem "Heritage," a product of reading books. Hughes's celebrated poem "The Negro Speaks of Rivers," considered by Onwuchekwa Jemie to be "the most profound of these poems of heritage and strength" (Jemie 103), is also echoed in *The Big Sea*: "the people dark and beautiful, the palm trees tall, the sun bright, and the rivers deep." Most important, the opening chapter addresses Hughes's recognition of racial difference based on color when he recalls that the "Africans looked at me and would not believe I was a Negro" (11).

Hughes's realization of color becomes a point for reconstructing his early life in Kansas. He is especially concerned with ancestry and lineage, with tracing the background of the paternal and especially maternal side of his ancestry. His brown color is the result of racial mixture, with "white" blood on both sides and "Indian blood" deriving from his maternal grandmother. One of Hughes's most recognized ancestors was abolitionist Charles Langston, Hughes's grandfather, whose brother John Mercer Langston had been a Virginia congressman. Hughes, born in Joplin, Missouri, on February 1, 1902, was deeply affected by the separation of his parents, Carrie and James (12–13). His rendering of his early childhood in *The Big Sea* is marked by movement and his problematic relationship with his father. One of the major movements was to Lawrence, Kansas, where he resided with his grandmother, whose invigorating stories were about "people who wanted to make the Negroes free" (17). Hughes's childhood experiences also involved exposure to the black church. The section titled "Salvation" shows his sense of creative irony in reconstructing the day when he was supposed to have been "saved" and his inability to "*see*" Jesus (19).

The educational experiences of Hughes during his young adult years are also a part of his recollections, and in one particular instance, he links the throwing overboard of his books with the "vine-covered library" in Topeka, Kansas. The young Hughes "believed in books more than in people," an emotion that he identifies as "wrong" (26). His later educational background at Central High in Cleveland would form the foundations of his poetic leanings, when "poems came to [him] now spontaneously" (34).

Hughes devotes two sections, "Abrupt Encounter" and "Father," to his relationship with his father, who resided in Mexico. The time spent south of the border in the summer of 1919 is described as "the most miserable [he had] ever known" (39). Hughes was troubled by the realization that his father "hated Negroes" (40) and also had "a contempt" for "Mexican laborers" (Rampersad 1: 32). In 1920, on Hughes's second trip to visit his father, the train journey was a catalyst for his most celebrated poem, "The Negro Speaks of Rivers," formulated as the train crossed the Mississippi.

Mexico was clearly a transitional stage for Hughes's educational pursuits, which led him to Columbia University, where he discovered his dislike for the institution and the course material. Although a Columbia education had been his father's desire, Hughes emphasizes other New York experiences, such as attending Bert Williams's funeral and numerous performances of the 1921 all-black musical *Shuffle Along*. Hughes admittedly "adored Florence Mills," one of the leading African American stage celebrities of the era (*Big* 85).

Hughes's decision to forgo higher education suggests the uniqueness of his creativity. His approach to survival was manual labor, a prelude to his more extended experience as a seaman. His attraction to "the smell of the sea" began earlier in Vera Cruz. At this juncture in the autobiography, Hughes recounts his association with *Crisis* magazine members such as managing editor Jessie Fauset and his lunch outing at the Civic Club. Hughes projects himself not as a literary figure but as someone disconnected from the literary establishment and reluctant to meet such figures as Alain Locke (94). Most important, Hughes's connection to the world of books is symbolically severed when his box of volumes comes to represent a range of emotional and psychological feelings: "like everything I had known in the past, like the attics and basements in Cleveland, like the lonely nights in Toluca, like the dormitory at Columbia, like the furnished room in Harlem" (97).

The first section of part 2, "Africa," chronicles Hughes's reactions to viewing West Africa in 1923, when European colonization remained well entrenched. As observed by Michael Chaney, "Africa became a galvanizing but also much disputed center of intellectual and political interest" (51). This is summarized creatively in Hughes's statement: "We took away riches out of the earth, loaded with human hands." Hughes also acknowledges Marcus Garvey, whose name "was known the length and breadth of the West Coast of Africa" (*Big* 102). Over the course of four chapters, Hughes makes numerous observations about such places as Dakar, Senegal; Luanda, Angola; the Ivory Coast; the Gold Coast; and Lagos, Nigeria. One of his poems inspired by his voyage and included in *The Big Sea*, "African Fog," evokes "singing black boatmen" and "the thick white fog at Sekondi." To be sure, Hughes witnessed a good number of contradictions and realities of West Africa, including the sexual exploitation of "African girls" and the plight of a mixed-race boy named Edward (104–07). Certain descriptions are indicative of the way in which "the imaginative writings of Hughes resist colonialism" (Miller 70).

Hughes's involvement in the laboring life of a seaman brought him to Europe on another voyage. This journey would prove a turning point and the beginning of Hughes's entry into the world of African American expatriates in Paris. Here again there is the creation of the romantic mood of exhilaration as Hughes recounts his experiences in this unfamiliar city: "I was torn between walking up the Champs Elysées or down along the Seine, past the Tuileries" (*Big* 145). Hughes's job as a doorman for a small club in Montmartre for five francs per night serves as another example of the humble laboring life of the poet. However, it was his exposure to the world of the Grand Duc, a notable nightclub, that increased his awareness of the expatriate scene as he encountered African American singer Florence Embry and saw the wealthy white patrons of the club, including Lady Nancy Cunard and "various of the McCormicks" (159). Musicians, such as pianist Palmer Jones, Embry's husband, were also part of Hughes's European education. The list of jazz musicians in Paris at that time also included trumpeter Cricket Smith, violinist Louis Jones, clarinetist Frank Withers, and drummer Buddy Gilmore, but perhaps the most notable African American expatriate was Ada "Bricktop" Smith, who created an atmosphere at the Grand Duc "almost like a Harlem night club" (162, 179). Hughes's chronicle of the developments at the Grand Duc following the arrival of Bricktop is a unique social history.

After his seagoing adventures, Hughes discovered the realities of black bourgeois society and its "conventional-mindedness" in Washington DC. In keeping with his interest in urban black folk, he found Seventh Street to be in 1924 the location of the blues, "watermelon, barbecue, and fish sandwiches" (208, 209). He locates a singular, ironic moment, recounting his alleged discovery by poet Vachel Lindsay while working as a busboy at the Wardman Park Hotel, during which time Hughes was also assisting Carter G. Woodson in the final proofing and organizing stages of the book *Thirty Thousand Free Negro Heads of Families*. In general, Hughes shows a particular aversion to black middle-class pretentions and the idea "that a colored poet should be a credit to his race" (212). As noted African American novelist Richard Wright observes, "Hughes was not ashamed of those of his race who had to scuffle for their bread" (600). Despite his reluctance to be recognized, Hughes shows how his poetic reputation began to develop through his winning of an *Opportunity* magazine poetry prize and subsequent introduction to James Weldon Johnson, Zora Neale Hurston, and Eric Walrond. Hughes also notes the importance of patrons such as Casper Holstein, "a wealthy West Indian numbers banker," who would not have been recognized in "polite Washington society" (214–15).

Following this period, Hughes became associated with individuals who would define the Harlem Renaissance. His representation of what he calls the "Black Renaissance" rather than the "New Negro" or "Harlem" Renaissance is framed whimsically in part 3, "When the Negro Was in Vogue," suggesting that the public interest in black artistic production was temporary or faddish. His creative reconstruction of the time is that of a cultural interpreter who sees the landscape of the early 1920s as a network of events, including the premiere of such stage works as *Shuffle Along* in 1921 and Eugene O'Neill's *The Emperor Jones* in 1937. *Shuffle Along* is described by Hughes as "a honey of a show," featuring the musical collaboration of Eubie Blake and Noble Sissle. Josephine Baker, who would later gain international attention in Paris, was "merely in the chorus." Uptown, the Harlem scene attracted whites, who "began to come to Harlem in droves," a phenomenon that, from Hughes's perspective, affected performance styles as dancing at the Savoy began to include "absurd things for the entertainment of the whites" (223, 224, 226). Race mixing in Harlem was viewed as somewhat artificial and snobbish, for even the gatherings of A'Lelia Walker, a black millionaire, had attendees who were white social elites. In addition to social class, "color consciousness" was an important element of the Harlem Renaissance (Tarver and Barnes 17).

Hughes saw the formation of the "Harlem literati" while living in an apartment on 137th Street in 1926. The autobiography's extended discussion of Wallace Thurman, who also lived at the same location and was managing editor of the *Messenger*, shows another side of the Harlem Renaissance. The formation of the magazine *Fire!!*, created by younger writers of the era including Hughes, Thurman, Aaron Douglas, Gwendolyn Bennett, and Bruce Nugent, was a sign of publishing interests. *Fire!!* exposed the generational differences of the Harlem Renaissance; as Hughes notes, writers from the older generation such as W. E. B. Du Bois refused to "have anything to do with" it (*Big* 235–37). Hughes recalls other seminal authors, especially Rudolph Fisher and Jean Toomer, and shows the relationship between the "Downtown" literary establishment and Harlem writers.

The Big Sea clarifies other divisions among black intellectuals and critics by alluding to such writers as George S. Schuyler and the controversy over white patron Carl Van Vechten's 1926 novel *Nigger Heaven*. Hughes defends Van Vechten and argues that black critics had "written so stupidly" about the novel (270), although as Emily Bernard notes in her introduction to a volume of Hughes and Van Vechten's correspondence, "many consider [the novel] the least of [Van Vechten's] contributions to the Harlem Renaissance" (xviii). Meanwhile, Hughes's poetic career was firmly on its way to greater recognition by 1926, a pivotal year in which his poem "Mulatto," about America's race-mixing dilemma, was published by the *Saturday Review of Literature*. His success can also be measured by his publication of two collections of poetry during the 1920s, *The Weary Blues* (1926) and *Fine Clothes to the Jew* (1927).

Although Hughes is undoubtedly associated with the Harlem Renaissance, he was also a student at Lincoln University during the height of the era. In addition to Hughes, Lincoln attracted African students who would become national leaders in Africa's move toward independence, including Nnamdi Azikiwe of Nigeria and Kwame Nkrumah of Ghana. Yet, Hughes became aware of a "color line" at Lincoln, an "unwritten one" that implied that "no Negro could teach on that faculty" (279).

Along with recollections of a Southern journey and interpretations of Jim Crow, part 3 of *The Big Sea* includes a telling section titled "Patron and Friend," in which Hughes discusses the impact of patron Charlotte Osgood Mason on his career. The next section introduces his perspective on the Caribbean, especially Cuba, where he journeyed in search of a "Negro composer" and "met everybody, Negro, white and mulatto, of any interest in Havana," but more telling is his realization afterward of the dilemmas of Mason's patronage. "She possessed the power to control people's lives" and wanted Hughes "to be primitive and know and feel the intuitions of the primitive" (324, 325). Mason also funded the work of Zora Neale Hurston, with whom Hughes collaborated on the folk comedy *Mule Bone*. As a result of their falling out, the play was not staged during the period, although *Mule Bone* did reach the New York stage in 1991.

Although Hughes suggests that the Harlem Renaissance ended with the close of the 1920s, the era can be extended into the 1930s. His decision to earn a living by his pen is signified by his observation that "poetry became bread; prose, shelter and raiment." For Hughes, creativity through literary craft was like fishing in "a big sea full of many fish" (335).

I Wonder as I Wander: International Sources of Creativity

Hughes's second autobiography, *I Wonder as I Wander* (1956), continues his creative explorations through the retracing of his international journeys. At the close of *The Big Sea*, which "failed to sell" on its publication (Rampersad 2: 5), Hughes indicates his need for the "sun," a useful transition to the first of the eight sections of *I Wonder as I Wander*. "In Search of the Sun" begins this far-ranging second volume, which covers Hughes's travels in Cuba, Haiti, the southern United States and California, the Soviet Union, Japan, China, and Spain. Hughes reaffirms his goal as a writer, calling his life "the story of a Negro who wanted to make his living from poems and stories" (3). The journey through the South on the way to the "sun" involved a stop at Bethune-Cookman College in Daytona Beach, Florida, where black advocate Mary McLeod Bethune was president. Her suggestion that Hughes tour the South and read his poems would manifest itself later in his sojourn, and Bethune, a cultural celebrity known in the South, would accompany Hughes on his "poetry to the people" tour to such places as Cheraw, South Carolina, the birthplace of jazz trumpeter Dizzy Gillespie (40–41). Luther Jackson, reviewing the autobiography for the *Crisis*, considered the Caribbean and southern tour sections to be "best" parts of the book (119).

Hughes's Cuban experience is documented with the creative style of a novelist-observer. On this trip to Cuba, his third, he was able to capture cultural elements especially relating to music. Accompanied by Zell Ingram, Hughes identifies the "Negro musicians at Marianao" as retaining African rhythms "out of all the centuries of slavery and all the miles and miles from Guinea" (*Wonder* 7). His view is similar to that of a cultural anthropologist, but with a soulful touch, as in his description of rumbas and *sones* as "essentially hip-shaking music—of Afro-Cuban folk derivation" (8). Hughes's observations of race are also pointed, as when he describes the "triple color line" in Cuba based on variations of skin color, a clear allusion to Du Bois's notion of the "color line" (10). Haiti, too, affected Hughes "from both a creative and an intellectual point of view" (Mullen 33). There, he made connections with Haitian writer Jacques Roumain, a cabinet member who recognized the importance of folk culture.

Hughes's observations about Haiti, such as his description of Port au Prince as a "city of squalid huts, unattractive sheds and shops near the water front, but charming villas on the slopes that rise behind the port," are indicative of the vivid details used by creative writers (*Wonder* 15). Haiti as well exhibited class distinctions, which Hughes links to musical associations and divisions between the "barefoot Haitians who dance to the drums" and the shoe-wearing Haitians "who dance indoors to an orchestra" (22).

In contrast, Hughes's confrontation with race was direct during his southern poetry tour, during which he confronted Jim Crow barriers in North Carolina, where he saw blatant signs demarcating "COLORED" (45). Despite these obstacles, "poetry took [him] into the hearts and homes of colored people all over the South" (48). The experience of reading poetry there helped Hughes to fashion a creative method of presentation, which started with his earliest verses and moved toward his jazz poems while including his more political and socially relevant writing, such as his poems about the Scottsboro Boys. The Scottsboro case, which involved nine black men falsely accused of raping two white women on a freight train in Alabama in 1931, is captured in such lines as "Justice is a blind goddess. / To this we blacks are wise" (lines 1–2, *Wonder* 58). As novelist Paule Marshall observes, Hughes was among a "generation" that had "done their part" in the "fight to free" the Scottsboro Boys (21). Hughes's wide-ranging poetry readings were held in Alabama, Mississippi, Texas, and California, where in San Francisco he was hosted by Noël Sullivan and met journalist Lincoln Steffens. But Hughes also found the Jim Crow barrier in Oregon, where at a hotel reception desk he was told, "We don't take Negroes" (66).

The wandering motif of the second autobiography is enhanced by Hughes in the transition to chapter 3, where he notes his move from Russian Hill in San Francisco "to Russia itself" (67). He was part of a group of twenty-two African Americans, "youthful intellectuals," traveling to Moscow in 1932 as part of a Soviet film project (69). Their home in Moscow, the Grand Hotel, is given descriptive treatment as Hughes notes its "enormous rooms with huge pre-tzarist beds" (73), but given Hughes's interest in music, it is logical that he found the Metropol Hotel, where a jazz band performed, more attractive.

In particular, Hughes's observations suggest the relevance of race issues in the Soviet Union and the international exposure given to the Scottsboro case. For this reason, he posits that the friendliness of the Muscovites may have been due to their recognition of the group as black. Phrases such as "the Negro comrade" are indicative of the social interactions Hughes experienced on Moscow streets (74). Culturally, the theatrical world of Moscow, including the Opera, the Moscow Art Theatre, the Vakhtangov, the Meyerhold, and the Kamerny, was of particular interest. However, the experience was marred by difficulties with the film script, written for Meschrabpom Films and titled *Black and White*, which Hughes and the others considered "mistakenly conceived" (77). The failure of the film venture was covered widely in the international press. The report in the *New York Herald Tribune*, quoted in *I Wonder as I Wander*, suggests that the film was canceled for fear that it would "prejudice American opinion against the Soviet Union" (96).

Despite the dilemmas of the film production, Moscow under Stalin was for Hughes a place where he could observe the black presence, especially in the personage of Emma Harris, the widely known "Mammy of Moscow," who was present at the "enormous Scottsboro benefits" (82, 84). By 1932 Hughes was also aware that African American performing artists Paul Robeson and Marian Anderson as well as Harlem Renaissance writer Claude McKay had also visited the city.

Hughes's journey to the Soviet Union sparked his imagination and race consciousness. Within the country, he traveled to cities such as Kiev and Odessa, where the group stayed at a "de luxe Soviet resort" that reminded Hughes of the racial discrimination he faced in the United States; he would never be permitted to stay in such a hotel at home (93). As a train traveler, Hughes was introduced to Turkmenistan via the Moscow–Tashkent express, where along with a number of others, including trade union representatives, he journeyed "beyond the Urals." Noteworthy events along the way included the fortieth anniversary celebration for Russian author Maxim Gorky. Another of Hughes's creative observations echoes a humorous truism, "that there is at least *one* [black person] everywhere," and in this case it was Bernard Powers, a Howard University graduate in engineering (103–04).

Among Hughes's possessions as a traveler were his typewriter, Victrola, and records. Calling a chapter of the autobiography "Ashkhabad Adventure," he chronicles a series of encounters and shapes them around the conviviality of music; jazz becomes a mode of international communication that "can break down almost any language barriers." In other words, the trumpet of Louis Armstrong "creates spontaneous friendships" (114).

In the re-creation of individuals, Hughes shapes the autobiography with additional novelesque characterizations. In addition to the head of the Turkoman Writers Union, a poet named Kikilov, Hughes also encounters writer Arthur Koestler, who would later criticize the

Communist Party in *The God That Failed* (1949). Hughes's interactions with Koestler are covered over a series of chapters. In "Koestler Washes His Hands," the title of which alludes to Koestler's interest in cleanliness, they journey to a remote village called Permetyab, where the houses are constructed with "sunbaked bricks of thistle and mud" (129). Another link to experiences back home is the description of Nichan, an Uzbek who "was in his way as amiable and as thoughtful a host as had been Mrs. Bethune in Florida, Amy Spingarn at Troutbeck, or Noël Sullivan in San Francisco" (156). Hughes is reminded of the racial discrimination of the United States when he learns about the racial classifications in Uzbekistan that would have once relegated "a brown young Uzbek" to the "back of the streetcars in Tashkent" (172). In general, Hughes links "international communism" with "the struggle for black equality in the United States" (Scott 99).

In "South to Samarkand," Hughes recognizes that art can have beneficial results even if it is used for propaganda and that "even propaganda in talented hands took on dramatic dimensions" (173). Hughes notes that Samarkand reminds him of the hundreds of miles of cotton fields in Mississippi, Georgia, and Alabama, but the crops are transported by camels rather than mules. Images of the cotton fields "bursting white in the sun" as "the white bolls lift their precious heads" show a blending of poetic creativity and prose style (174). But the living situation for workers in the cotton collective he visits in Central Asia is difficult; the journey to get there is "physically worse than any Jim Crow train trip [he] ever made in the United States" (177).

After returning to Moscow, Hughes began to work as a correspondent for the newspaper *Izvestia*. During this time he met noteworthy playwright Sergei Tretiakov and novelist Boris Pasternak, encounters that helped further his sense of an international literary community (197). While living at the New Moscow Hotel, Hughes was able to acquire additional theatrical knowledge by attending performances at Stanislavsky's Moscow Art Theater and at other theaters that "housed productions untouched by Soviet ideology" such as Chekhov's *The*

Cherry Orchard and Gogol's *The Inspector General*. Hughes's observations of theatrical productions were crucial to the creation of his own dramatic works, such as his "Negro history play" *Don't You Want To Be Free?*, staged in Harlem in 1938 and influenced by Meyerhold's "constructivist" staging. Hughes notes that he was most "fascinated" by Oklopkov's Krasni Presnia, which was "the most advanced in production styles of any playhouse" he had seen (199–200). In addition to creative inspiration, Hughes documents cases of "dire disillusionment with the Soviets" in "Illusion and Disillusion" (209).

In "Color Around the Globe," Hughes's descriptive style captures recollections of the Far East. In Kyoto, he saw the ritual services offered by the geisha, who, Hughes reminds us, were not prostitutes (238). Hughes's notoriety in Tokyo may have been the result of the translation of some of his blues poems into Japanese and the appearance of his image on the cover of a Japanese literary magazine (242). Significantly, Hughes notes the presence of jazz in Tokyo and the popularity of W. C. Handy's "The St. Louis Blues," which had been translated into Japanese and was "whirling on Tokyo jukeboxes." Jazz had taken off as well through live performances involving groups that included Filipino musicians, who "played good jazz" (242). The Kabuki theatre, with its multihour performances, is also described in detail.

Hughes arrived in Shanghai, China, in July of 1933, when, as noted by biographer Faith Berry, Japan had been "pushing hard its invasion of China" (193). Hughes calls it "Incredible Shanghai," a "multi-racial city" that rivaled Chicago for its underworld (*Wonder* 246). But what seems to have most interested Hughes about Shanghai was the replication of racial issues, as "none of the leading hotels in the International Settlement accepted Asiatic or Negro guests" (248). Significant for Hughes, however, was the presence of jazz, which he documents in "Jazz in China." The location for "the best American jazz band" was Canidrome Gardens, where Teddy Weatherford played with his all-black band. In addition to Weatherford, such artists as Nora Holt, Midge Williams, Valaida Snow, Bob Hill, Jack Carter, and Buck Clayton could be heard. Hughes also met the political elite of China, such as Madame Sun Yat-sen, "wife of the founder of the Chinese Republic and sister-in-law of [Sun Yat-sen's successor] Chiang Kai-Shek" (251, 255).

On his return to the United States, Hughes passed under the Golden Gate Bridge, and although his travels had been enlightening he was, nevertheless, "glad to be in [his] own land" and in San Francisco (281). In "Writing for a Living," Hughes returns to his life as a creative writer with the aid of Noël Sullivan, whose patronage of a sort places Hughes among illustrious company at Hyde Park, where he witnesses such "fascinating guests" as Duke Ellington, Roland Hayes, Marian Anderson, and William Saroyan (282). Later, Hughes encountered film personages, including James Cagney, and social activist writer John Steinbeck, author of *The Grapes of Wrath* (1939). During this phase of the Great Depression, Hughes furthered his writing, especially his short fiction, while at the same time remaining politically committed. He focused on writing short stories that "had their roots in actual situations" he knew of or had experienced firsthand. His intensely productive "ten or twelve hours a day" creative process was also motivated by the need for family stability, particularly the support of his mother (285).

I Wonder as I Wander becomes personal once again in an exploration of Hughes's relationship with his father—a problematic one, as they "never liked each other" (288). Though Hughes was not mentioned in his father's will, and though he claims to have been "unperturbed," there may have been some residual disappointment. Nevertheless, Hughes encountered notable individuals in Mexico, including Henri Cartier-Bresson, a French photographer; Diego Rivera, a Mexican painter; and Miguel Covarrubias, who had designed the jacket art for *The Weary Blues* in 1926 (294).

The autobiography also discusses Hughes's 1935 play, *Mulatto*, and its Broadway production. His surprise at finding that *Mulatto* was in production is expressed as re-created dialogue. Arriving in New York, Hughes is asked whether he is there for the "rehearsals" of his play; he responds, "What play?" *Mulatto*, the longest-running play by an

African American to reach Broadway during its era, was produced by Martin Jones and dealt with the highly charged issue of mixed-race identity in the South.

One of the most significant parts of *I Wonder as I Wander* is Hughes's account of his experience as a journalist covering the Spanish Civil War for the *Baltimore Afro-American* in 1937. As described by Michael Thurston, the conflict became "a microcosmic conflict between the international Left and the Right, or between democracy and autocracy" (203). "World Without End," subtitled "Bombs in Barcelona," documents his initial observations and his association with Cuban poet Nicolás Guillén (321), who recognized Hughes's "ability to capture a certain image of blacks in the Diaspora" (Sawyer 140). In the rich description of the bombings, Hughes suggests the power of the moment: "A *terrific* explosion somewhere nearby had literally lifted me out of my bed." He became accustomed to "the sound of machine gun fire" but could not forget the "baleful, high, eerie, wailing sirens of warning" (*Wonder* 325–26). Of the many issues to investigate, Hughes was concerned with "color prejudice" that might affect the "dark troops" from North Africa brought to Spain by fascist leader Francisco Franco. He was interested in the situation of the Moors as well as the treatment of black Americans who "came on furlough from the Brigades" (327). Hughes's focus on the Moors is significant because he acknowledges that black people were "not strange to Spain" and that "there was not the slightest trace of color prejudice" (351). In addition, he mentions that racial integration had occurred in the International Brigades before it had happened in the United States military (381).

Traveling to cities such as Valencia, Hughes made connections at the Alianza del Intelectuales, a club for artists and writers in Madrid (334). As in other situations, his jazz records were useful. During a heavy bombardment, jazz music, particularly Jimmie Lunceford's "Organ Grinder's Swing," helped to pass the night (341).

His reflections on Madrid indicate the autobiography's title as he "wonder[s]" "how much longer could they resist like this" (345).

In Madrid, he met a number of celebrated writers including Ernest Hemingway, who stayed at the Hotel Florida; *New York Times* journalist Herbert Matthews, who resided at the "safest hotel," the Victoria; and Cuban poet Alejo Carpentier (342, 344). In addition to Hemingway, Hughes met white American writers such as Dorothy Parker, Leland Stowe, Malcolm Cowley, and Lillian Hellman (362). Hughes found Hemingway to be "a big likable fellow whom the men in the Brigades adored" (363). Hemingway and Herbert Matthews, along with other journalists, gave "a little farewell party" for Hughes when he left Spain (391–92).

His thoughts in Paris, where he traveled after Spain, suggest the possibilities of global destruction. In wondering if "the world [would] really end," he voices the concern of the 1930s as Mussolini and Hitler prepared to "turn their planes on the rest of" the world after the devastation in Ethiopia and Spain (405). This prophetic moment is a fitting close to an autobiography in which the theme of wondering recurs. In both autobiographies, Hughes narrates many of the sources for his literary voice.

Works Cited

Berry, Faith. *Langston Hughes: Before and Beyond Harlem*. Westport: Hill, 1983.
Chaney, Michael A. "International Contexts of the Negro Renaissance." *The Cambridge Companion to the Harlem Renaissance*. Ed. George Hutchinson. New York: Cambridge UP, 2007. 41–54.
Hughes, Langston. *The Big Sea: An Autobiography*. New York: Hill, 1940.
_____. *I Wonder as I Wander: An Autobiographical Journey*. 1956. New York: Octagon, 1974.
Hughes, Langston, and Carl Van Vechten. *Remember Me to Harlem: The Letters of Langston Hughes and Carl Van Vechten, 1925–1964*. Ed. Emily Bernard. New York: Knopf, 2001.
Jackson, Luther. "Globe-Trotting Bard." Rev. of *I Wonder as I Wander*, by Langston Hughes. *Crisis* 64 (1957): 119–20.
Jemie, Onwuchekwa. *Langston Hughes: An Introduction to the Poetry*. New York: Columbia UP, 1976.
Marshall, Paule. *Triangular Road: A Memoir*. New York: Basic, 2009.
Miller, R. Baxter. *The Art and Imagination of Langston Hughes*. Lexington: UP of Kentucky, 1989.

Mullen, Edward J., ed. *Langston Hughes in the Hispanic World and Haiti*. Hamden: Archon, 1977.

Rampersad, Arnold. *The Life of Langston Hughes*. 2 vols. New York: Oxford UP, 1986–88.

Sawyer, Mark Q. "Du Bois's Double Consciousness versus Latin American Exceptionalism: Joe Arroyo, Salsa, and Négritude." *Transnational Blackness: Navigating the Global Color Line*. Ed. Manning Marable and Vanessa Agard-Jones. New York: Palgrave, 2008. 135–47.

Scott, Jonathan. *Socialist Joy in the Writing of Langston Hughes*. Columbia: U of Missouri P, 2006.

Tarver, Australia, and Paula C. Barnes, eds. *New Voices on the Harlem Renaissance: Essays on Race, Gender, and Literary Discourse*. Madison: Fairleigh Dickinson UP, 2006.

Thurston, Michael. "Montage of a Dream Destroyed: Langston Hughes in Spain." *Montage of a Dream: The Art and Life of Langston Hughes*. Ed. John Edgar Tidwell and Cheryl R. Ragar. Columbia: U of Missouri P, 2007. 195–208.

Woods, Catherine. "A Negro Intellectual Tells His Life Story." Rev. of *The Big Sea*, by Langston Hughes. *New York Times Book Review* 25 Aug. 1941: 5.

Wright, Richard. "Forerunner and Ambassador." Rev. of *The Big Sea*, by Langston Hughes. *New Republic: A Journal of Opinion* 103 (1940): 600–01.

I'm Lonely: I'll Build Me a Family: Functional Family Relationships in the Life and Art of Langston Hughes

Carmaletta M. Williams

Langston Hughes rarely revealed his personal feelings or the deepest details of his being. His closest friends and acquaintances admitted that he spoke freely but revealed little of his emotional and intimate life. Harlem Renaissance writer Wallace Thurman discusses Hughes's reticence in talking about personal matters by describing Hughes as "the most close-mouthed and cagey individual" he had ever met. He suggests that this secrecy was deliberate because "when it came to personal matters [Hughes] fended off every attempt to probe his inner self and did this with such an unconscious and naïve air that the prober soon came to one of two conclusions: Either [Hughes] had no depth whatsoever, or else he was too deep for plumbing by ordinary mortals" (qtd. in Rampersad 119). Novelist and philosopher Arthur Koestler reinforces Thurman's claim with his own: "one felt an impenetrable, elusive remoteness which warded off all undue familiarity" (qtd. in Rampersad 260). Examinations of Hughes's work make clear that he was by no means shallow. His writings reveal complex and complicated situations told simply and in accessible language. We do recognize, however, that although Hughes did not talk about the details of his intimate or sexual life as he had a right to privacy, his writings openly reveal his personal feelings, especially in regard to his friends, his family both natural and fictive, and his relationships with them.

Dr. John Q. Adams, in his "Socio-cultural Interaction Vocabulary," defines "fictive kinship" as the kinship-like relationship between persons not related by blood or marriage in a society but who have some reciprocal social or economic relationship.[1] Family systems theory expands this definition to one of "functional" relationships. Persons in functional relationships, in addition to having a fictive relationship, also claim each other in words, emotional closeness, or deed as "family." They function in their chosen familial roles. For example, a female raising children to whom she did not give birth is the functional mother. The same holds for a male raising children who are not his biological children; he is functioning as their father.

Hughes, like all persons in the twentieth and twenty-first centuries, lived in the midst of what Thomas Merton in his *Conjectures of a Guilty Bystander* identifies as

> the greatest revolution in history—a huge spontaneous upheaval of the entire human race; not the revolution planned and carried out by any particular party, race or nation, but *a deep elemental boiling over of all the inner contradictions that have ever been in man, a revelation of the chaotic forces inside everybody. This is not something we have chosen, nor is it something we are free to avoid.* (72, emphasis added)

As hard as he tried, Hughes could not avoid the "boiling over" of those inner contradictions, but he successfully reveals those chaotic forces driving his life and, through his art, wages a successful personal revolution.

Hughes's deepest desire was for a close family, and he held tight to the seed of that dream. His early life, largely constructed and framed by his mother's life choices, was filled with contradictions and held none of the "dream" he imagined as a child. Year after year of disappointment in trying to get that dream seed to germinate and grow into a close family forced Hughes to face the impossibility of acquiring an emotionally close "natural" family and accept the reality that the only way he was to have healthy familial relationships was to step outside the boundaries of his nuclear family and build lasting functional ones.

Psychiatrist Roberta M. Gilbert argues that relationships, if not love, are what make the world revolve. After basic human needs of food, water, and shelter, the prime determinant of the quality of one's life is the quality of the relationships in which one is involved. Those extraordinary relationships that everyone seeks do not occur by accident or appear as products of fate but evolve over time and require reciprocity of the parties involved. Relationships are delicate and fragile and demand constant consideration, much effort, and a great deal of objectivity. Due vigilance is required because emotions are always in flux. In addition, one person cannot be the sole determinant of the success of a relationship. Both or all parties involved must work at creating a balance in the relationship. A frequently overlooked factor in relationships is that it is impossible to change others. One can only change oneself.

Family systems theory argues that there are two opposing basic life forces: the preservation of self in relationships and the need for togetherness. Ideally, these two forces can come together, and one can retain autonomy and individuality while being part of a close, emotionally healthy relationship. In many relationships, however, there is no real balance. One person gains, while the other loses. The tension in these relationships causes anger, disappointment, hurt, and physical and emotional distance. If only one person attempts to change the relationship, nothing changes. That person either loses individuality, sacrificing himself or herself for the sake of the relationship, or must find a more balanced relationship. In the case of Langston Hughes, he could not change his mother, father, or stepsiblings. So, in order to preserve himself, he developed functional relationships outside of his nuclear family. A functional family built of people who want to be family, and not just those whom nature has decreed a family, is just as real and valid. Hughes created long-lasting functional relationships throughout his entire life.

In his work, Hughes is very much aware of the tensions in his family relationships, as he has constantly fought against them. He addresses the glaring distinctions and contradictions between his inner emotional life and outer public life through his writings as he exposes the relationships he has with his natural family. He alerts the readers of his intent to build functional family relationships in truth and in art in his autobiography *The Big Sea*, in which he confesses that while writing his first novel, *Not without Laughter*, he wanted to write about a typical midwestern family, but as his family was not "typical" at all, he had to create a family that was. Part of Hughes's complexity is evident in his candidness, especially when he couples that statement with his revelation that he was "trying to write a truthful and honest book." Regennia N. Williams and Carmaletta M. Williams, in their essay "Mother to Son: The Letters from Carrie Hughes Clark to Langston Hughes, 1928–1938," submit that contrary to Hughes's declaration that he created the fictional family in *Not without Laughter*, he uses his own family as the model for the characters in the novel. He is very honest in his portrayal of his mother, Carrie, showing three facets of her character in the three sisters in the novel, Tempy, Harriette, and Annjee. Hughes clearly reveals his personal feelings, especially toward Carrie, in that novel and in many of his other works.

What Hughes tells us about his family members, within and without the cloak of fiction, is that he had very complex emotional relationships with each of them. He spent his formative years being raised in extreme poverty by his maternal grandmother in Lawrence, Kansas, where he felt lonely, isolated, and abandoned by his parents.[2] He learned to hate his absent father and resent his vagabond mother. The love he initially felt for his stepbrother over time grew into disappointment and disgust. In the absence of an emotionally satisfying relationship with his own family and rather than compartmentalize this lacuna as a lost segment of his being, Hughes created functional families to fill the void in his life and in his art.

In his early life, Hughes tells us in *The Big Sea*, he was "very lonesome growing up all by [him]self, the only child, with no father and no mother around" (24). Indeed, he had no father present for years at a time and his mother only for short sporadic periods, but he did have his maternal grandmother, Mary Sampson Patterson Leary Langston. He also had James and Mary Reed, who had no biological connection to him but were his functional aunt and uncle. Grandmothers often must function as mothers, and Mary Langston demonstrated no resentment in having to assume that role. In addition to supplying his basic human needs of food, water, and shelter, a primary parental responsibility she willingly accepted and generously engaged in was the transmission of family history. Langston writes of the importance of storytelling in the development of their relationship in his poem "Aunt Sue's Stories":

> Aunt Sue has a head full of stories.
> Aunt Sue has a whole heart full of stories.
> Summer nights on the front porch
> Aunt Sue cuddles a brown-faced child to her bosom
> And tells him stories.
>
> Black slaves
> Working in the hot sun,
> And black slaves
> Walking in the dewy night,
> And black slaves
> Singing sorrow songs on the banks of a mighty river
> Mingle themselves softly
> In the flow of old Aunt Sue's voice,
> Mingle themselves softly
> In the dark shadows that cross and recross
> Aunt Sue's stories.
>
> And the dark-faced child, listening
> Knows that Aunt Sue's stories are real stories.
> He knows that Aunt Sue never got her stories
> Out of any book at all,
> But that they came
> Right out of her own life.
>
> The dark-faced child is quiet
> Of a summer night
> Listening to Aunt Sue's stories.

Langston was never a slave—in fact, she and both of her husbands were abolitionists—but that fact does not lessen the validity or parental necessity of her stories. Hughes admits that through her stories, he learned a great deal about his family history, but more importantly, he learned that

> always life moved, and moved heroically toward an end. Nobody ever cried in my grandmother's stories. They worked or schemed or fought, but no crying. When my grandmother died, I didn't cry either. Something about my grandmother's stories (without her ever having said so) taught me the uselessness of crying about anything. (*Big* 17)

Hughes and his grandmother did not cry when they ate dandelion greens for dinner for days on end, nor did they cry when they had to leave their home in order to save it. Unable to make the mortgage payments, Langston rented rooms and sometimes the entire house to University of Kansas students.[3] The rent money was enough to pay the mortgage but not enough to lift them out of the abject poverty they experienced, so the two moved in with the Reeds as family, not as boarders. Auntie and Uncle Reed opened their doors to Hughes and his grandmother and treated them like blood kin, seeing to their needs. The Reeds served as additional parents for Hughes, and the four individuals together functioned as family. Uncle Reed allowed Hughes to help herd the cows and work with the chickens. He also spent much time talking with him.

When Langston died, Carrie and her new husband, Homer Clark, and stepson, Gwyn, visited Hughes in Lawrence, but they left town quickly after the funeral. The Reeds continued to care for Hughes, with Auntie Reed maintaining the duties of her familial role including overseeing Hughes's religious training.[4] Hughes notes that his functional relatives, Uncle and Auntie Reed, had differing views on religion:

> Auntie Reed was a Christian and made me go to church and Sunday School every Sunday. But Uncle Reed was a sinner and never went to church as long as he lived nor cared anything about it. . . . But both of them were very good and kind— the one who went to church and the one who didn't. And no doubt from them I learned to like both Christians and sinners equally well. . . . For me there have never been any better people in the world. I loved them very much. (18)

Hughes speaks freely about love when describing his relationships with family, natural or functional. He especially admits to deeply loving his mother, Carrie. Regardless of his grandmother's lessons on the futility of crying, he confesses that the only times he did cry were out of his loneliness and longing for a close relationship with his mother. Carrie, on the other hand, seems to have been oblivious to her son's need for familial closeness. Her continual abandonment and emotional blackmail created an internal conflict that caused Hughes to grow to resent her, but he never stopped loving her. He came to recognize that his separations from Carrie were largely due to her "travel[ing] around the country looking for [his] step-father or for a better job, always moving from one house to another where the rent was cheaper or there was at least a bathroom or a backyard to hang out clothes." His resentment toward her is evident as he describes "growing up living with [his] grandmother, with aunts who were really no relation, with [his] mother in rented rooms, or alone trying to get through high school—always some kind of crisis in [their] lives" (36). Even as a child he felt deeply that mothers were not supposed to treat their children the way Carrie treated him; hence, he retaliated the only way he could, sabotaging her public performances.

As an adult, he could only balance his feelings of love and resentment for her by putting physical space between them, living alone for much of his adult life and traveling at every opportunity. He still had no control over their relationship because Carrie used emotional blackmail to retain her power. In her letters to Hughes, Carrie writes in what becomes her traditional fashion, connecting her love for her son with his providing for her needs. She also places the blame for the emotional distance between them on him:

> Dear, why don't you love me, why aren't we more loving and chummy, why don't you ever confide in me. I know I have no sense to help you in your work but I'd enjoy your confiding. Now Langston, I have no one else to talk to. You will agree with me and help if you can. (Williams and Williams 110)

Unable to counter Carrie's emotional assaults, Hughes instead built a mother-son relationship with Charlotte Osgood Mason. The elderly, rich, white widow who was patron to Hughes for two years, in exchange for power over his art, operated rather successfully for that time as Hughes's functional mother. Their relationship was balanced, as she took care of his financial and emotional needs and he provided the adoring, talented protégé she needed. Mason eased much of the financial strain he constantly carried with an allowance, freeing him to write without worrying about food or a place to live. In addition to money, limousine rides, and tickets to Broadway performances, which they often attended together, Mason provided emotional support and encouragement for his writing, lifted his spirits, and listened to him. Hughes, as he had in talking about his relationship with the Reeds, uses "love" in his description of their relationship: "I was fascinated by her, and I loved her. No one else had ever been so thoughtful of me, or so interested in the things I wanted to do, or so kind and generous toward me" (*Big* 315). While Carrie refused to feed him when he would not go out and get a job to support her, Mason even saw to the needs of his "real" family. For example, when Carrie wrote to Hughes asking for money to help her stepson, Gwyn, whom they called Kit, Mason arranged for Kit to attend a northeastern boarding school. Hughes's relief when Mason provided for Kit's education is described in terms of how it helped not him, but his mother. He also acknowledges the blended family relationship and refers to Kit as his brother rather than his stepbrother: "at least the burden of my kid brother's care had been lifted from my mother" (318). Kit's time away, however, was short lived. Because of her own emotional needs, Carrie sabotaged Kit's schooling, which forced him to return home to her and forced Carrie to continue demanding financial support from Hughes.

In the end, it seems as though both the mother he was born to and the one he created were emotionally fickle, neither caring how her actions affected Hughes. Mason abruptly ended her patronage, which left Hughes financially and emotionally despondent. Mason refused even to listen to him or answer his letter pleading for reconciliation, or at least for an understanding of the rift. Unable to break down the wall between him and his functional mother, Hughes fell ill. He was treated, at times undergoing surgery, for illnesses he knew he did not have. It was almost as if having part of his body excised, in this case his tonsils, would rid him of the pain he was feeling for the loss of his functional mother. In *The Big Sea*, Hughes recognizes that his psychosomatic illnesses were caused by his recurring loneliness for a mother. He speaks of his deep need for someone to care about him and for him, acknowledging that he "enjoyed paying for attention" (331), a justifiable step for one who was paid so little attention by the "mothers" in his life. In a largely ironic action, Hughes went home to Carrie to recover from the loss of Mason.

Neither Carrie nor Kit had developed the essential elements of a functioning family: equal interest in the needs of others, support and encouragement of personal goals, emotional bonding, resistance to inappropriate fusing of individuals so that each person could grow independent of one another, personal respect, and, if possible, love. Instead, Kit had followed Carrie's model too well and grown dependent on Hughes for the financial support he should have assumed, especially as a man. The young Kit had "kicked out his shoes" too often for Hughes to keep pace financially. As a teenager, Kit grew too fast, forcing a constant need for clothes; furthermore, he did not do well in school and was responsible for impregnating his cousin. Kit's pattern of being interested only in partying, drinking, and womanizing remained firmly entrenched as he entered adulthood.[5] He continued to ask Hughes for financial assistance, a need grown largely from his alcohol addiction. Families often face such problems and deal with them successfully. In this case, however, Kit did little to develop a reciprocal emotional support system, as needed in well-functioning relationships between siblings. Instead, Hughes became the overfunctioning sibling, giving advice, doing things for Kit that Kit should have been doing for himself, worrying about and feeling responsible for Kit, and experiencing periodic, sudden "burnouts."[6] Hughes did all the giving, and Kit did all the taking. Despite this, Hughes had no intention of financing Kit's drinking and womanizing after his death. His first will left his estate to Carrie. After her death, the second will provided for the education of Kit's children by his first wife.[7] Hughes's final will left his estate to Lincoln University in Pennsylvania.[8]

Hughes entered into another stepsibling relationship when his father married his housekeeper, Frau Schultz. Schultz, who had many children, took only her ten-year-old daughter Lotte with her to Mexico. Hughes writes that he and the child got along well, but as Lotte spoke German and Hughes did not, and because of their difference in age, their relationship was superficial. He admits that he still felt lonesome in Mexico even with his father, stepmother, and stepsister there with him.

Hughes seems never to have had any substantial father-son relationship in function or in fact. The relationship between Hughes and his father was problematic from the beginning. There is no evidence that James Nathaniel Hughes was in Joplin, Missouri, on February 1, 1902, when his son James Langston Hughes was born. Indeed, he probably was in Cuba at the time. It is very possible that the first time the father and son saw each other was when Carrie and James attempted to reconcile. Carrie, her mother, and Hughes traveled to Mexico to meet his father, but an earthquake shook their familial foundation apart. Hughes had only vague memories of his father carrying him the night of the earthquake in Mexico City and none before then. Carrie refused to stay in Mexico, fearing another quake. The reconciliation failed, and instead of "wearing diamonds," as James later asserted she would have had she come back to him, Carrie worked a series of menial jobs. At their next meeting, Hughes and his father initially walked past one another, each not recognizing the other. Hughes describes that meeting in unemotional terms:

> I saw the little bronze man with a moustache coming rapidly up the street toward me. We looked closely at each other as we passed. Then we turned and looked back.
> The man said: "Are you Langston?"
> I said: "Yes, are you my father?" (37)

Their relationship was strained from the beginning, but it ruptured when Hughes recognized that his father hated black people and probably hated himself for being black. Hughes likely believed that his father must hate him, his black child. Hughes never speaks of loving his father, and in all his writing, James Hughes is the only person Hughes admits to hating. His father's insistence that Hughes move out of the United States and get a classical European education, or at least get an American education in a field that would support him well financially, and his mother's insistence that he stay and support her are represented by the parents and grandmother he writes about in "Piggy-Back."

> My daddy rides me piggy-back.
> My mama rides me, too.
> But grandma says her poor old back
> Has had enough to do.

Hughes admits to liking his stepfather, Homer Clark, "a great deal," but over time Clark established a familiar pattern of abandoning, rejoining, and again leaving the family. His constant movement and eventual complete disappearance from the lives of Carrie, Kit, and Hughes did not allow the building of a functional father-son relationship. Instead, it had a twofold effect: it forced Hughes to assume more responsibility for his mother and stepbrother, and it made his father look better in Hughes's view, for "he at least stayed put" (*Big* 36)

Hughes never stopped attempting to build a functional family. In fact, he built several functional family relationships. He came very close to having a "real" family in the stable relationship he built with his mother's friend from Kansas, Ethel "Toy" Harper, and her husband, Emerson. The Harpers and Hughes bought a townhouse in Harlem, which the three shared. They held family celebrations, hosted friends, supported each other's work, and respected each other as artists, as individuals, and as family. The Harpers functioned as Hughes's "uncle" and "aunt," and he referred to them as such. In his wills, Hughes left his interest in the townhouse to Toy upon his death. When she died, he changed his will to specify that while the property would be bequeathed to Lincoln University, his "uncle" Emerson could occupy the townhouse, rent-free, as long as he lived.

The Hughes-Harper relationship lasted a lifetime, as family relationships should. But there was another important person with whom Hughes developed a close, emotionally healthy familial relationship: Arna Bontemps. Hughes describes Bontemps, at the time of their first meeting, as a "poet and coming novelist, quiet and scholarly, looking like a young edition of Dr. DuBois"—the "mysterious member of the Harlem literati" (248). Hughes admired Bontemps's scholarship and intellect, while Bontemps had a lifelong admiration for Hughes's skill as an artist. Together they built a relationship often desired by those raised without siblings: a brotherhood.

In many ways, it would seem unnatural if the two men had not developed a brotherly relationship. Born the same year, the men looked alike and were characterized by what Charles H. Nichols, in his introduction to a volume of their correspondence, describes as the firmness of their commitment to African and Afro-American culture through the world, the creation of a vital and productive art among Negroes, the effort to fulfill the splendid promise of an often-despised minority. This sense of mission obsessed them both and drew them into a lasting bond of mutual interests and deep affection. (Hughes and Bontemps 1)

The sheer heft of their letters, thousands over a forty-year span, is testament to their closeness. Their friendship, however, did not come without a price. Bontemps was deeply impressed with Hughes. He recited his poetry, admired his ease with speaking publicly, and shared his pride in being African American. Bontemps's relationship with Hughes was problematic in that it ran counter to the rules and image set by his employer, the Seventh-Day Adventist Oakwood School. The school's administration threatened to fire Bontemps for "subverting Oakwood School with racial ideas" (v). In order to keep his job he would have had to burn all his books and abandon the source of his roots—the Deep South—and his commitment to the black masses, the folk Hughes often called "the people lowest down." In addition, he would have had to sever his relationship with Hughes. This would have been damaging for Bontemps, for their brotherhood had helped him overcome the restrictions of his upbringing and find his truth in his art. Bontemps left Oakwood School and retained his personal integrity. After working a variety of jobs, he accepted the position of librarian at Fisk University, a position he held for the remainder of his professional career.

In addition to their personal commitment to the race, the men shared somewhat parallel family situations. Neither had a father who was proud of the folk tradition of the African American masses. Both fathers were ambitious, educated men who saw racial uplift as abandoning those vestiges of black life in language, music, literature, art, and economics that marked African Americans with what they viewed as a shameful past. Bontemps's father was a brick mason and lay minister in the Seventh-Day Adventist Church. Bontemps was born in Louisiana, but his father shipped him off to a northern white boarding school with instructions not to go "up there acting colored" (i). Hughes's father built up an intense hatred for racial restrictions in the United States, which had denied him the opportunity to take the state bar exam after finishing law school by correspondence course. James Hughes reviled his son's passion to live among Negroes, not understanding why he would want to "live like a nigger among niggers."

Both men were raised without mothers and spent a good deal of their formative years under the care of their grandmothers or isolated from their families. The vast differences in the two men's socioeconomic and religious statuses account for the quality of isolation each felt. Bontemps's mother died when he was young, and even though his father was present, his grandmother was his primary caretaker. Hughes's mother abandoned him to her mother in Kansas. Bontemps's father sent him to a white boarding school, essentially banishing him to the north. He graduated from San Fernando Academy, a private Adventist high school, and Pacific Union College. After his family moved to California, they became staunch members of the Seventh-Day Adventist Church, which Nichols describes as "fundamentalist Christians—with their Hebraic theology and other worldly outlook" (2). Hughes had given up on religion, especially Jesus, since the day in Lawrence, Kansas, when he faked a conversion to please Auntie Reed. He "didn't believe there was a Jesus any more, since he didn't come to help." As a teenager he lived alone in Cleveland, trying to put himself through high school with the allowance his father sent. He shared part of that money with his mother, which forced him to eat the only things he knew how to cook and could afford: hot dogs and rice. After Hughes's graduation from Central High School, his father wanted him to leave the United States altogether to get a classical education in Europe. He finally agreed to fund Hughes's education at Columbia University in New York, but only if he would study engineering. Hughes tried, but his soul called out for him to be a writer, so he left Columbia and later attended and graduated from Lincoln University in Pennsylvania.

Both fathers remarried, giving their sons stepmothers. Bontemps built a fairly close relationship with his, and his father and stepmother remained married for the rest of their lives. Hughes and his stepmother, Frau Schultz, did not have as long a relationship, as she and his father divorced. But Hughes and Schultz did share the joy of surreptitiously spending his father's money on meats, cheeses, and other foods his father objected to buying because he thought them too expensive.

Both men pressed past the pressures of their fathers and their families and found each other in Harlem, New York, in 1924. Their paths continued to cross at the homes of friends and other artists through the next few years. Bontemps, who worked in the New York City Post Office at that time, was deeply impressed with Hughes's creativity and the ease with which he infused his poetry with the sounds of the folk through jazz and blues rhythms. To embrace poetry, fiction, blues, and jazz ran counter to Bontemps's Seventh-Day Adventist upbringing, and he struggled to reconcile the burgeoning internal conflict. The teachings and beliefs of his family, who focused only on the Second Coming and saw all things outside of the Word as sin, were at war with his need for *Sankofa*—a return to his roots. So, Bontemps embraced his Louisiana past, used his errant Uncle Buddy as a model, and allowed his creativity to work freely.

Hughes had no such background to overcome. Once he refused his father's money in exchange for abandoning his blackness, he was free to explore his art his way. An advantage he had over Bontemps was his mother. An incredible model for being socially active in the black world, Carrie was deeply rooted in her African American heritage and proud of being Negro. She loved to interact with other black folk, especially at parties. She and her husband Homer spent so much of their time and money on weekends socializing with their friends that Hughes found them financially frivolous.

[My father] was interested only in making money. My mother and stepfather were interested in making money, too . . . But they were interested in making money to *spend*. And for fun. They were always buying victrolas and radios and watches and rings, and going to shows and drinking beer and playing cards, and trying to have a good time after working hours. But my father was interested in making money to *keep*. (*Big* 39)

Hughes captures his mother's free spirit in his life and in his work. However, this was not a welcoming time for the shifts in black aesthetics, politics, or personal ideology. In the words of Harlem Renaissance writer Wallace Thurman, quoted in *The Big Sea*, the young artists of this time worked hard to affirm "the SELF in an environment that would reduce them to zero" (5). In his seminal essay "The Negro Artist and the Racial Mountain," Hughes writes of the freedom he, Bontemps, and the other Harlem Renaissance artists embraced: "We younger Negro artists who write now intend to express our individual dark skinned selves without fear or shame. . . . We built our temples for tomorrow, strong as we know how, and stand on top of the mountain free within ourselves" (692).

They did express themselves freely, but more important than embracing the same literary and sociopolitical ideology was the development of a functional brotherhood between Hughes and Bontemps. The two men follow the model for family support discussed by Harold W. Neighbors, which allows that when faced with serious stress and crises, whether financial or emotional, men are more likely to call on family members than nonfamily, particularly brothers. Being able to obtain help during difficult times is essential for the emotional and physical health of the person. When faced with his personal stressors and crises, of which there were many, Hughes turned to Bontemps, not Kit, for assistance. Bontemps also served as Hughes confidant and vice versa. Hughes thanks Bontemps for his support on many occasions in their letters, especially for writing him because "a good long newsy letter from [Bontemps] . . . with so many burdens on [his] head . . . indeed helped to bear [him] up" (Hughes and Bontemps 279).

The two men further supported each other in their career choices. Hughes was determined to earn a living with his writing, but Bontemps, faced with the reality of caring for a wife and six children, stayed at Fisk until he retired. They informed each other of possible paid presentations and looked over each other's contracts with publishers. Hughes considered himself a "documentary poet" reporting the lives of black Americans, and he considered Bontemps an intellectual. Bontemps considered Hughes "a genius and a scholar—honestly" (35).

The two men even resembled each other in the color of their complexions, hair texture, and manner. Hughes constantly teased Bontemps about being the heavier person, measuring the difference in ounces, and joked that they could substitute for each other "whenever there's a lecture date one or the other of [them did not] want to fill" (39). Bontemps was fond of telling the story of visiting Countee Cullen's stepfather, who immediately took him to be Hughes. They were even mistaken for each other over the telephone.

They openly shared their families. Hughes never married or had any children, but Bontemps married his former Harlem Academy student Alberta Johnson. Hughes recalls that she was "a shy and charming girl, holding a golden baby on her lap. A year or two later there was another golden baby. And every time I went away to Haiti or Mexico or Europe and came back, there would be a new golden baby, each prettier than the last" (*Big* 248). The Bontempses had six "golden babies," and Hughes developed relationships with those children that lasted his entire life. He chose Poppy as his favorite and sent her loving messages and special gifts, yearned to see Constance with her new teeth, and continually sent messages urging Alberta and Arna to kiss Camille for him and to give the children in high school some money. He also asked them to spare the rod. Hughes remained close to Paul, Bontemps's eldest son, through his childhood, military service, college, and life in New York; he and his wife would often visit Hughes. Hughes referred to the townhouse he shared with Toy and Emerson as the Harpers' and told Bontemps the guest room was always available to him, especially since Bontemps was "Mrs. Harper's favorite guest" (Hughes and Bontemps 248).

An inherent aspect of family building is being recognized as such. Hughes's and Bontemps's friends and the public recognized their closeness. To honor them, people named their children after them as individuals and as a pair. Their friend Dorothy Johnson had a student in her school named Langston Arna. Zora Neale Hurston biographer Robert Hemenway named his son Arna. Hughes had a "name-sake cousin," and his "New York god son," his favorite godchild, was named Langston Hughes Mickens after him.

Hughes and Bontemps were best friends, indeed, but their relationship ran deeper than just friendship. They built a family together. They freely and openly shared their families, their lives, and their art. They supported and encouraged each other. They built individual self-differentiated personalities; yet, they created and maintained a state of togetherness. Their relationship was equitable, reciprocal, and loving. They were brothers.

In addition to building lifelong functional family relationships with individuals, Hughes also transferred his emotional needs outside of his family and developed relationships with the larger black community. Hughes biographer Arnold Rampersad identifies Hughes as being "psychologically mortgaged" to the masses of blacks who "for certain intimate reasons [Hughes] craved the affection and regard of . . . to an extent shared by perhaps no other important black writer" (*Big* xv). In fact, he queries how Hughes "came to discover that he should and could install the black race in the place in his heart vacated by his absconding parents." Hughes's best friend and functional brother, Bontemps, provides an answer when he notes that "few people have enjoyed being Negro as much as Langston Hughes" (qtd. in Harper 9). Writer Richard Wright explains that "unlike the sons and daughters of Negro 'society' Hughes was not ashamed of those of his race who had to scuffle for their bread" (qtd. in Harper 9). Hughes scholar Donna Akiba Sullivan Harper attributes this attachment to the likely fact that

Hughes "loved, respected, and identified with ordinary African Americans" (9).

Such ordinary Americans helped Langston Hughes fill the empty spaces in his life with respect, laughter, and love. He did not have a close nuclear family, so he built functional families for himself. Through reading his magnificent art, which has lived longer than he or any of his factual, fictive, or functional relatives, we are able to absorb and understand the value of family in this artist's life.

> When a man starts out with nothing,
> When a man starts out with his hands
> Empty, but clean,
> When a man starts out to build a world,
> He starts first with himself
> And the faith that is in his heart—
> The strength there,
> The will to build. ("Freedom's Plow" 1–8)

Notes

1. Dr. John Q. Adams is a professor in the Department of Educational and Interdisciplinary Studies at Western Illinois University, Macomb, Illinois.
2. This is not an unusual phenomenon. According to a report released by the Pew Research Center, the number of children living with one or more grandparent rose from 2.5 million in 2000 to 2.9 million, or 10 percent of all children in the United States, in 2008.
3. Hughes writes that when Langston died "the house went right straight to the mortgage man, quickly" (*Big* 13).
4. Langston had refused to attend church because churches were segregated.
5. Money that Hughes had left to pay Carrie's rent while he was in Russia was possibly used instead to pay for an abortion for a girl impregnated by Kit. Letters between Carrie and the girl's mother, who lived in Kansas City, Missouri, appear to confirm that Carrie paid a portion of the cost and that the girl's mother was to pay the balance. Letters from the girl to Kit months later, in which she complains about how hard it was to be pregnant, make clear that the abortion was not performed.

6. See Roberta M. Gilbert's *Extraordinary Relationships: A New Way of Thinking about Human Interactions* for a deeper discussion of over- and underfunctioning roles in family relationships.
7. Kit's second wife also had children, but they are not mentioned in the will (Hughes and Bontemps 126, 136, 140).
8. Hughes's wills are available in the James Weldon Johnson Collection at the Bieneke Rare Book and Manuscript Library at Yale University.

Works Cited

Adams, J. Q. *Socio-cultural Interaction Vocabulary*. Macomb: Western Illinois U, n.d.

Gilbert, Roberta M. *Extraordinary Relationships: A New Way of Thinking About Human Interactions*. Minneapolis: Chronimed, 1991.

Harper, Donna Akiba Sullivan. *Not So Simple: The "Simple" Stories by Langston Hughes*. Columbia: U of Missouri P, 1995.

Hughes, Langston. *The Big Sea*. New York: Hill, 1940.

———. *The Collected Poems of Langston Hughes*. Ed. Arnold Rampersad and David Roessel. New York: Random, 1994.

———. "The Negro Artist and the Racial Mountain." *Nation* 23 June 1926: 692–94.

Hughes, Langston, and Arna Bontemps. *Arna Bontemps-Langston Hughes Letters 1925–1967*. Ed. Charles H. Nichols. New York: Paragon, 1990.

Merton, Thomas. *Conjectures of a Guilty Bystander*. New York: Doubleday, 1968.

Neighbors, Harold W. "Husbands, Wives, Family and Friends: Sources of Stress, Sources of Support." *Family Life in Black America*. Eds. Robert Joseph Taylor, James S. Jackson, and Linda M. Chatters. Thousand Oaks: Sage, 1997. 279–94.

Rampersad, Arnold. *The Life of Langston Hughes*. 2 vols. New York: Oxford UP, 1986–88.

Williams, Carmaletta M., and Regennia N. Williams. "Mother to Son: The Letters from Carrie Hughes Clark to Langston Hughes, 1928–1938." *Montage of a Dream: The Art and Life of Langston Hughes*. Ed. John Edgar Tidwell and Cheryl Ragar. Columbia: U of Missouri P, 2007. 106–24.

Hughes and Lynching
W. Jason Miller

Lynching has haunted America for at least three centuries. As early as the eighteenth century, the term merely designated the punishment assigned to a horse thief who received "thirty-nine blows to the back" (Gussow 52). In Virginia, Judge Charles Lynch reportedly punished Tories during the American Revolution, and "lynch law" was "understood to be execution without due process of the law" (Apel 23). By 1922, the term "lynching" was defined in unsuccessful antilynching legislation as "five or more persons acting in concert for the purpose of depriving any person his life without authority of law" (Dray viii). While lynching can mean many different things, it often meant something even more brutal and sadistic during the lifetime of Langston Hughes. In the early parts of the twentieth century, lynchings sometimes lasted for five hours. They often included brutal beating, castration, and burning. Lynch mobs often used chains rather than rope because the chain links wouldn't burn over the long course of torture. As a result of heat, eyes exploded. Small children took fingers, teeth, and toes home as souvenirs.

Justice was blind to these events. The term "lynching," unlike hanging, means that these murders were committed without juries, testimony, or evidence. Throughout the twentieth century, the main targets were African Americans. Thousands of these victims were innocent. They were the sons, brothers, sisters, or mothers often killed when the accused could not be located. Those who committed these murders went unpunished even after they posed in broad daylight for photos with their victims. By 1909, sales from lynching postcards featuring such photos reached the staggering sum of fifty million dollars (Snyder 164–65). These were stamped and mailed to friends and relatives.

Hughes was all too familiar with lynching. He had seen photos, heard oral stories, and read about such events in the publication of the National Association for the Advancement of Colored People

(NAACP), the *Crisis*, as well as in the black press. Three distinct types of lynching were noteworthy during Hughes's life. First, the publications Hughes often read offered highly detailed and sometimes embellished accounts of *spectacle lynchings*. Crowds numbering in the tens of thousands sometimes witnessed such lynchings on courthouse lawns after traveling long distances by trains. A second form of lynching is commonly referred to as *mob lynching*. Although spectacle lynching was advertised, lynchings also occurred at the hands of angry mobs. Appearing to be more spontaneously organized, these groups sometimes stormed jail cells or victims' homes, with the lynching occurring later the same day. Beginning in 1882, Tuskegee Institute began keeping official records of both forms of lynching. In 1892 alone, 161 black lynching victims were confirmed and documented. Many more were never officially recorded. Third, beginning in the early 1930s, America also engaged in the practice of *legal lynching*. While at least "4,742 blacks met their deaths at the hands of lynch mobs . . . [a]s many if not more blacks were victims of legal lynchings (speedy trials and executions)" (Litwack 12). For African Americans, the threat of lynching in all three of these forms served as a potent and violent means of control.

Hughes's works are rife with references, responses, and critiques of lynching too numerous to mention in full. Briefly, lynching is at the heart of *Mulatto* (1935), the longest running play on Broadway by an African American until Lorraine Hansberry's *A Raisin in the Sun* (1959). The short story "Home" (1934) ends with a lynching. Moreover, Hughes's *Fight for Freedom: The Story of the NAACP* (1962) recounts the lynchings of Cordie Cheek, Mack Parker, Felton Turner, and Jesse Washington. In fact, Hughes refers to lynching so frequently in this work that he even uses alternative terms and phrases such as "torture-death" just to offer some variety (*CW* 10: 73). In Hughes's dramatic works *Esther* (1956) and *The Gospel Glow* (1962), he describes the hanging deaths of Haman and Christ in the language of lynching; the death of Christ is described with the line "they lynched Him on the cross" (*CW* 6: 399). Most important, by the time of his death in 1967, Langston Hughes had written nearly three dozen poems about lynching. Because poetry was so central to Hughes's artistic achievement, Hughes's antilynching poems stand as a testament to the ways in which he addressed this topic throughout his professional life.

The 1930s: "Christ in Alabama"

Hughes's most overt poetic response to lynching came as a result of the Scottsboro case. On March 25, 1931, nine young black men were arrested in Scottsboro, Alabama, and charged with raping two white women named Victoria Price and Ruby Bates. These men were referred to as the "Scottsboro Boys." Price's past criminal offenses, which included misdemeanor convictions for fornication and adultery that resulted in her serving time in jail, were regarded as inadmissible evidence in the trials. The original trials were a judicial farce. In the first hearing, eight of the men were sentenced to death. After no fewer than five appeals to other courts, including the US Supreme Court in November 1932, the men were not sent to the electric chair. All of the men spent at least six and a half years in prison for a crime they clearly did not commit. Two men spent more than seventeen years in jail.

Eventually a letter penned by Bates surfaced in which she states that "those policemen made me tell a lie. . . . [T]hose Negroes did not touch me. . . . [I] wish those Negroes are not Burnt on account of me" (Cunard 273). Nancy Cunard's report on the second trial of Heywood Patterson finds that Bates eventually testified in the second hearing that she had "not even known the meaning of the word 'rape'" (279). Despite this testimony from one of the supposed victims of this crime, Patterson was found guilty. Bates's appearance alongside five of the mothers of the Scottsboro Boys in Washington, DC, on May 14, 1934, was a failed attempt to earn a presidential appeal for the young men. Corruption surrounded the trials to the extent that the case was regarded as a legal lynching.

Hughes's controversial poem "Christ in Alabama" was published in *Contempo* with an accompanying illustration by Zell Ingram. On the night of November 19, 1931, Hughes gave a public reading in Gerrard Hall on the campus of the University of North Carolina at Chapel Hill. Hughes avoided being completely mobbed because the editors of the locally published *Contempo*, Anthony Buttitta and Milton Abernethy, waited to release the five thousand extra copies they had printed of the issue until the day Hughes appeared. However, the day was not without incident, as Hughes intentionally passed for Mexican at a local restaurant by speaking in Spanish. Friends accompanying him recall the server later tried to "catch [them] in a place or two and sock [them] in the jaw" when he discovered that Hughes was black (Rampersad 1: 225). Hughes was later told that this marked the first time a black man had ever eaten at a table in the dining room of one of Chapel Hill's restaurants (*CW* 14: 77). Hughes was originally scheduled to read on campus in the larger and more prominent Memorial Hall. When he was refused, a "campus demonstration for freedom of speech" ensued, and Hughes was then allowed to read at the smaller and far less prestigious Gerrard Hall (Buttitta 164).

Hughes was not the first to associate the crucifixion of Christ with lynching. Countee Cullen's poem "Christ Recrucified" (1922) had made this connection earlier. However, Hughes's tone, diction, imagery, and moral implications made his "Christ in Alabama" unforgettable:

> Christ is a nigger,
> Beaten and black
> *O, bare your back.*
>
> Mary is His mother
> *Mammy of the South,*
> *Silence your mouth.* (lines 1–6)

To parallel the behavior of a mob, lines in both roman and italic type offer "multiple subject positions that, like a Union Square protest rally, are crowded with potential speakers" (Thurston 34). In the context of lynching, the word "black" does not necessarily denote race. "Black" literally implies the charred remains of a lynch victim. His body is now black, not brown, because it has been burned. Hughes uses "black" in this way in his poem "Question" (1922), in which speaks of a "black torso" (7).

Hughes's powerful imagery comes in response to the fact that he regarded the Scottsboro case as a legal lynching. The fact that none of the men were literally lynched at the time of publication highlights the connections between Christ's appearance before Pontius Pilate and these men's appearance in similar courts that practiced their own form of mock-justice. Hence, Hughes ends the poem with volatile implications by pointing out the religious and moral hypocrisy of the South:

> God's His Father—
> *White Master Above,*
> *Grant us your love.*
>
> Most holy Bastard
> Of the bleeding mouth:
> *Nigger Christ*
> *On the cross of the South.* (7–13)

Hughes's biting irony suggests that citizens of the South are acting like Pontius Pilate. He states this more directly in an essay that accompanied the first publication of the poem:

> Daily, I watch the guards washing their hands. The world remembers for a long time a certain washing of hands. The world remembers for a long time a certain humble One born in a manger—straw, manure, and the feet of animals—standing before Power washing its hands. No proven crime. Farce of a trial. Lies. Laughter. Mob. (*Good* 60)

Now a full eight months past the initial arrests, Hughes compares American citizens to Pilate. This is particularly condemning given the South's long history of being located in the "Bible Belt" of the United States. The poem accuses the South of allowing innocent men to die the types of deaths that they decried the Romans for when they crucified Christ. It is interesting to note that Hughes posed for a photograph on Franklin Street during his visit to Chapel Hill in 1931. The steeple of a church is framed perfectly in the background, reminding viewers of the religious hypocrisy he saw at work in the nation (Miller 53).

The poem's accusations of ethical hypocrisy are even more potent. In the essay that accompanied his poem, Hughes writes: "But back to the dark millions—black and half-black, brown and yellow, with a gang of white fore-parents—like me" (*Good* 58). The powerful irony of this point is reinforced in the poem, undermining the essential myth of lynching and the Scottsboro case. Although these black men were falsely accused of raping white women, the poem reminds readers that many more white "masters" have brought children into the world through black women. Hughes reminds his readers of the ethical hypocrisy of fearing that blacks might rape white women while ignoring the harsh reality that white men have been raping black women for centuries. Given the metaphor of justice, Hughes's poem becomes the one place where these past offenses can receive accurate testimony, a fair trial, and a real hearing.

In the wake of publishing this poem, the fate of *Contempo* itself provides a measurable way to document the poem's controversial nature. The June 1931 issue of *Contempo*, which appeared before the "Christ in Alabama" issue, featured exactly ten advertisements in its pages. Two issues after the magazine's publication of Hughes's volatile poem, the January 1932 issue featured only one ad. Future issues of *Contempo* included the magazine's own ads, in which the magazine drew attention to its plight by printing that "little can be expected from local advertising" and "Local Advertising Completely cut." Although *Contempo* eventually weathered this loss of advertising dollars, the situation changed slowly, with only three ads appearing in the issue released July 5, 1932.

Like *Contempo*, Hughes paid a dear price for his beliefs. During his trip to Chapel Hill, the Carolina Inn refused to let Hughes and Zell Ingram have a room to sleep in during their stay, and they were forced to spend the night with a local black minister (Buttitta 164). Like Christ himself, Hughes had "no place to rest his head." In fact, securing money to pay Hughes for his visit was difficult. Many people cited two main reasons for their reluctance, objecting to his visit being "a *Contempo* affair" and asking whether the organizers were "bringing Mr. Hughes [to Chapel Hill] as a poet or as a communist" (Miller 55).

Although Hughes was scheduled to visit Guy Johnson's 8:30 a.m. sociology class the day after his reading to discuss the subject of the "Negro," Hughes left town prematurely. It is interesting to note that just as Christ had often "left town before his time had come," Hughes himself escaped unharmed. Nonetheless, one exchange in the *Charlotte Observer* blatantly states one man's desire to make an example of Hughes by covering him in a "coat of tar" (55). Hughes himself soon received several concerned letters from those closest to him after other readers saw the poem. Elmer Carter writes to Hughes, "I have been a little fearful about your safety. The fervor . . . might cause some of the more hot-headed cracker type to attempt to do you bodily harm" (Rampersad 1: 225). On February 10, 1932, four months after the Chapel Hill appearance, Hughes writes to Carl Van Vechten, "Friends in the North are writing me that I'll surely be lynched. And my mother has wired that I come back at once: prayers are being said at the altar for me in Cleveland!" (Hughes and Van Vechten 93).

Despite this, Hughes continued to write in defense of the Scottsboro Boys throughout the 1930s. The details surrounding the exact date of publication for another poem, "August 19th," illuminate Hughes's attempt to exert his influence on Clarence Norris's fate. Hughes's poem was published on June 28, 1938, in *The Daily Worker*. It is a direct response to the Alabama Supreme Court's ruling earlier in the month that upheld the penalty of the death sentence for Clarence Norris. Soon after publication, Norris's death sentence was commuted to life imprisonment, and he was eventually pardoned in 1976. Hughes also wrote "Ballad of Ozzie Powell," published in 1936. Powell's case set the standard by which all law is now practiced. After this 1932 case, all defendants were granted the right to legitimate legal counsel. If a defendant could not afford counsel, the government was required to provide it. The Powell case marked the first time in legal history that such counsel was ruled mandatory.

The 1940s: "Dream Deferred"

The 1940s saw Hughes publish more poems about lynching than any other decade. Hughes stood all the more determined because of the failure of antilynching legislation and the fervor with which Americans fought racism abroad during WWII while ignoring similar racism at home. His most obvious example is "The Bitter River," in which Hughes's speaker tires of being told to "wait, be patient" (38). Hughes wrote in direct response to the lynching of two fourteen-year-old boys named Charlie Lang and Ernest Green, who were lynched from the Shubuta Bridge in Mississippi. One of Hughes's most complex poems during this period, titled "Harlem" in *Montage of a Dream Deferred* and retitled "Dream Deferred" in *Selected Poems*, was written in 1948. Its elusiveness rests in its interlocking use of visual imagery, references to food, and allusions to the song "Strange Fruit." The poem, which asks a series of unanswered questions, was written during a period in which Hughes was limited by censorship of his work.

As early as 1940, several of his works had been censored. These included three radio plays he attempted to get CBS to broadcast: *The Organizer* and its theme of forming a sharecroppers' union were too controversial in 1940, comparing Americans who used lynch ropes to "little Hitlers" kept *Brothers* off the air in 1941, and *Pvt. Jim Crow* never made it to production.

During this time, Hughes was forced to function "within the bitter limits of censorship" (*CW* 6: 475). Furthermore, Hughes fell under FBI surveillance in 1944 and was denounced as a communist by the Senate in 1948. Not even Hughes's editors were immune to such issues of control and power; many of them at Henry Holt were fired for their roles in publishing Hughes's works in 1951 and 1952 as a result of pressure from Texas conservatives (Rampersad 1: 85).

In addition to repeatedly offering public denials that he had ever been a communist, Hughes also later asserted that censorship in America took on a racial dimension. He suggested that censorship "begins at the color line" and informed listeners that "many black writers live abroad . . . [b]ecause the body of little Emmett Till drowned in a Mississippi River and no one brought to justice, haunts them, too" (Rampersad 2: 270).

Censorship played a critical role in advancing Hughes's poetic complexity. "Dream Deferred" can be read as an exploration of how America has figuratively lynched the dreams of African Americans. The sequencing of poems was always important to Hughes. Given more liberty when he published overseas, Hughes placed this poem directly after another of his lyrics entitled "Not for Publication" in the French and English bilingual edition of *La poésie Negro-Americane*, a text he edited. The title of this preceding poem not only gestures toward the constraints Hughes faced but also specifically activates the imagery of lynching, as its last line places crucifixion in readers' minds. It is little wonder that Hughes would engage this topic so adroitly given that, in the original and larger poetic project of *Montage of a Dream Deferred*, "the concealment of anger becomes the dominant mode of the sequence" (Smethurst 160).

Hughes was actively engaged with the world of photography during this period. He worked with celebrated photographers such as Henri Cartier-Bresson, Roy DeCarava, Griffith J. Davis, and Marion Palfi. Surrounded by some of the art form's most innovative and celebrated practitioners, Hughes wanted to create a photo-text of Harlem. Hughes pitched the complete idea for the project he titled "Ups and Downs," "down to page layouts, and specific photo choices," to a photographer in 1950 (Blair 54). Though this idea fell through, Hughes's next collection of poems, *Montage of a Dream Deferred*, blurred the line between the visual and verbal realms. In fact, the collection was dedicated to Ralph and Fanny Ellison; Ralph regarded himself as both a noted writer and a professional photographer. The images in the poem give Hughes the means to show the reader what he dares not say.

It is the subtle invocation of repeated food imagery in "Dream Deferred" that offers insight into the poem's ability to reactivate the connection between food and the history of lynching. It is important to note that cultural connections between food and lynching were very common. It is no small matter that food, in the form of "strange fruit," became the preferred vehicle of the most powerful metaphoric statement ever made on lynching. This metaphor resulted in part from the language used in newspaper reports, which often featured headlines such as "Colored Man Roasted Alive," and the public burning of blacks was commonly referred to as a "Negro Barbeque" (Apel 23). Other common food imagery included referring to lynchings as "coon cooking, and main fare" (Allen 175).

Although Billie Holiday's musical rendition of Abel Meeropol's poem "Strange Fruit" was first popularized more than twelve years before "Dream Deferred," it was still very fresh in Hughes's mind when he wrote his opera *Esther* in 1956. Hughes cannot resist portraying the character Haman in the context of lynching culture. As a result, Hughes has Haman speak these lines as he revels in the idea of hanging Mordecai from the gallows:

> Let his eyes be eyes
> For the crows to pluck
> And his lips be lips
> For the wind to suck. (*CW* 6: 123)

Hughes plays off of lines 9 and 10 of Holiday's song by rhyming "pluck" with "suck" and by specifically citing the "crow" and "wind," which are mentioned in the same lines of the song. Evidently the connection between lynching and food was so ingrained in Hughes through his knowledge of Holiday's song that he clearly alluded to it decades after its release.

Hughes's 1962 history of the NAACP uses the metaphor of food as he recounts the coverage of a lynching he knew all too well. Within a full-paragraph summary of the lynching of Jesse Washington, Hughes writes, "Innumerable photographs were taken of the gruesome spectacle.... [The] findings concerning this human barbeque were published in a special 8-page supplement to *Crisis* entitled 'The Waco Horror'" (*CW* 10: 51). Hughes repeatedly connected food with lynching in very sophisticated ways.

It is uncanny how much of Hughes's imagery in "Dream Deferred" resembles the lynched body. Lynching appears to be a striking analogy for conveying how Harlem residents could feel after having their dreams deferred. Given Hughes's need to negotiate censorship, it would not be surprising if he used analogy to allude to the plight of those living in Harlem. Under the constraints of censorship, Hughes's analogy creates its forceful meaning ambiguously.

"Dream Deferred" offers its readers a series of images that circle from one bright image to another like photographic images being projected from a slide-show carousel:

> What happens to a dream deferred?
> Does it dry up
> like a raisin in the sun?
> Or fester like a sore—
> And then run?
> Does it stink like rotten meat?
> Or crust and sugar over—
> like a syrupy sweet?

> Maybe it just sags
> like a heavy load.
>
> *Or does it explode?*

It is not hard to compare the images in "Dream Deferred" to images of lynching victims. While Holiday sings of fruit that the sun would rot, Hughes's first image in the poem more specifically supplies readers with the image of what the sun does to a raisin. It is not difficult to liken this image to a black body wrinkling in the sun after being burned. "Strange Fruit" describes the eyes that bulge after a man has been lynched, and Hughes ends his poem by suggesting an explosion. In line eight of her song, Holiday sings of the scent of burnt flesh; Hughes wonders about the stink of rotten meat.

Because lynch victims were often tortured in a sadistic fashion for extended hours before their public executions, they would also develop open wounds. Hughes's second image in the poem is that of a sore that festers and runs. Such lesions could result from lashing with strips of thin tree branches, chains, or a whip. The smell of burnt flesh is unforgettable, and Hughes next wonders if unfulfilled dreams "stink like rotten meat" (6). Hughes's image furthers the connections between the body and a piece of meat. Historically, lynch victims were discussed and labeled as if they were the main course for some perverse feast. Hughes's idea that dreams can "crust and sugar over / like a syrupy sweet" (7–8) continues the association with what happens when the human body is exposed to heat. Dreams cannot dry up, stink, or crust over, but human bodies can. The victims who are hanged sag from trees, looking like something heavy to carry.

No official lynchings were recorded between 1952 and 1954. However, by inflicting "nonlethal assaults," American lynching culture had uncovered "more than one way to deny African Americans their rights as citizens," thus "there was less reason for whites in the North or South to resort to lynching as a means to dominate black people"

(Goldsby 289). Nonetheless, these assaults and denials of rights had many of the same effects on their victims as lynching. Hughes's poem captures the feeling of having to wait for full integration and equality. Metaphorically, it is as painful as having one's dreams lynched.

There are several ways to define Hughes's tactics. Some have noted that Hughes's poetry is often a masked performance in which the imagery, pain, and history are latent. Hence, this is a form of Hughes's "functions of masking" as he emphasizes "the politics of the page" (Summers-Brenner 272). Others have noted that some of Hughes's works resemble a "cryptic collage" with meanings so buried that they are in need of decoding (Higgins 5). Given Hughes's penchant for intentionally passing as Mexican, his use of either technique to slip such potent statements into mainstream publications during this era of censorship can be seen as a form of literary passing (Miller 12). In later poems, he addresses lynching by appearing to be only retelling history. In "Dream Deferred," he used lessons learned from photography and food imagery first popularized in the song "Strange Fruit."

The 1950s: Emmett Till, "The Negro," and "Mississippi"

Fourteen-year-old Emmett Till was a black youth from Chicago who was visiting his extended family who lived near Money, Mississippi, in the summer of 1955. After allegedly whistling at the white clerk working in the local store, Till was kidnapped and beaten. His body was found six days later. His face was bloated and horrifically disfigured when his body was recovered from the Tallahatchie River. He had been shot in the head, and a large wheel from a cotton gin had been secured around his neck with barbed wire. Later testimony has documented that Till was also castrated (Apel and Smith 62). Although two white men were acquitted of the murder, they later admitted in full detail that they had indeed committed the deed. The 2005 documentary *The Untold Story of Emmett Louis Till* asserts that as many as fourteen people may have been involved in the lynching.

Equally important to the African American community, the body was placed on display in an open casket during the funeral in Chicago, and extensive images of Till's face were published in *Jet* magazine. As many as 250,000 people may have viewed the body as it lay in the casket. The impact of Till's death was enormous. When Rosa Parks refused to give up her seat on a bus only three months later, "she related her decision to the shock of seeing the photographs of Emmett Till" (64). In fact, "many historians now argue that the modern civil rights movement was inspired by the protests that erupted across the country in the wake of Till's murder" (Goldsby 294).

The lynching of Emmett Till is reflected in two important poems published by Hughes in the 1950s. The sum of Hughes's achievement in these two poems is captured in one word: "still." This significance becomes most clear when viewed in the context of Hughes's public reading at the national poetry festival in Washington, DC in 1962. He began the reading symbolically by reading the poem "Still Here." Despite his own figurative lynching before the Senate Permanent Subcommittee on Investigations in 1953, during which the committee had tried to make him "stop laughin', stop lovin', stop livin'" (6), Hughes opened by stating defiantly that he was "still here!" (8).

Later during this reading, Hughes made his most significant reference to contemporary lynching in a poem titled "The Negro." Another central poem in Hughes's works, "The Negro" is set off from all others in his first full collection of poems, *The Weary Blues*. The poem appears alone as the introductory poem to the collection, serving as an overview of the themes that would continue to appear throughout his poetic career. In all earlier publications, this poem reads, "I've been a victim: / The Belgians cut off my hands in the Congo. / They lynch me now in Texas" (14–16). However, in the 1959 collection *Selected Poems* and during this public reading, Hughes significantly revises one line in the poem to account for the lynching of Emmett Till. In versions published after 1959, line 16 reads, "They lynch me still in Mississippi." The constraints of censorship relegate this statement against lynching to the space of a mere single-line revision in this very significant collection. However, the seemingly general nature of this line allowed Hughes's poem to escape censorship by appearing to only retell history.

This new revision simultaneously interrogates the United States on three counts. First, "still" elevates the intensity of American violence over what is mentioned earlier in the poem as coming to fruition in the past in Rome, Egypt, and the Congo. King Leopold's reign of terror spanned approximately twenty-five years (1885–1908); lynching is a present and even more violent reality. Second, the line slyly embeds Till's name. Censored, Hughes avoids overtly saying "They lynched Emmett Till in Mississippi." However, it is important to remember that the poet's realm is sound just as a painter's medium is color. Through this medium of sound, Hughes's revised line mirrors his implied statement as "lynch me still" subtly parallels "lynch Emmett Till." Hence, Hughes suggests Till's lynching to those who listen. Third, still haunted by his appearance before a Senate committee intent on identifying American communists, Hughes offers biting irony through his play on Till's name. It is as if Hughes is reminding the government that "Till" is the name of a victim whose murder, rather than alleged communist activity, they should be investigating.

Hughes also responds to Till's murder in an earlier poem, "Mississippi." As Christopher Metress has exhaustively traced, Hughes was the first African American to respond in writing to the lynching of Emmett Till. Metress notes that the first recorded appearance of the poem Hughes wrote in response to the lynching was dated September 16, 1955. It appeared as a sort of headnote to a newspaper article written by Hughes and directed to the primarily black readers of the *Chicago Defender*. Interestingly enough, in this same article, Hughes also addresses Congress's inability to investigate lynchings (Metress 140). Hughes greatly revised the poem so that Till's name is completely absent from its final version, which appeared in *The Panther and the Lash* (1967). Yet, Till is present in the subtle complexities of Hughes's verse.

Hughes consistently repeats the word "again" in the beginning of "Mississippi." This repetition survives even in the final 1967 version: "terror comes again / To Mississippi. / *Again?*" (6–8). Hughes engages in the practice of autocitation, intentionally alluding to ideas expressed in another of his published works. His repeated idea of this happening "again" becomes his own italicized question: "*Again?*" Readers who wonder when such an event happened before in Mississippi need look no further than Hughes's own poetry. "Again" references ideas from "The Bitter River." This use of "again" implies that only the names have changed since the day, almost thirteen years earlier, that two other fourteen-year-olds were lynched in Mississippi.

The second example of autocitation in the 1967 version of the poem comes in the second-to-last line. Hughes states that "tears and blood / Still mix like rain / In Mississippi" (18–20). Readers may wonder why Hughes would respond to the highly publicized lynching of Emmett Till by referencing the *state* in which it occurred rather than by directly mentioning Till by name. The answer becomes quite clear in light of the important time referent Hughes settles on in line 19 of the poem: "still." Hughes's poem collapses time rather than portraying specific events as "new," as a typical newspaper account might. For Hughes, individual experiences are often recontextualized to take on more expansive collective meanings. This collective meaning is the best means for discussing Hughes's choice: Hughes's use of the word "still" in "Mississippi" does not eliminate the memory of Till so much as it includes all other lynch victims who have died in Mississippi in the poem. This concept in fueled by Hughes's metaphor of "mixing" in the poem, an amplification of an idea mentioned in "The Bitter River." The idea of mixing is forever captured in the word "still." The last four letters are the last name of Emmett Till, and the opening *s* can be read as a quiet sibilant representing all the other nameless victims of lynching who hail from Mississippi. The letter *s*, so redundant in the state name "Mississippi," is an appropriate figurative representation of those who have died quietly throughout the state.

Such a reading explains a great deal. Black writers such as Gwendolyn Brooks, James Baldwin, Toni Morrison, and others responded specifically to the lynching of Till. Unlike these other writers, Hughes's response takes shape within the context of his own lifelong campaign against lynching and amid the reality that Till was only one of the many lynching victims who died in Mississippi. Hughes did not write about Till's lynching as an isolated incident; he transforms it into a greater, collective meaning that includes Green, Lang, and other victims. Hughes decenters Till and uses his death as a means to memorialize the others who were lynched without funerals, press coverage, and responses printed on the front pages of newspapers. Because the poem first appeared in a newspaper, it also seems likely that Hughes is critiquing the accuracy of most print coverage. Hughes regarded the lynching of Till as more than an isolated incident, and he used this incident as an opportunity to draw attention to the rest of Mississippi's nameless lynch victims.

Hughes's use of the word "still" culminates with the 1959 line revision and 1962 reading of the poem "The Negro." In this revision, Hughes broadens the reader's perspective of American lynching culture rather than isolating specific victims. Although many readers and listeners were unaware, Hughes was "still" writing about lynching, just as he had done throughout his entire poetic career.

Works Cited

Allen, James. *Without Sanctuary: Lynching Photography in America*. Santa Fe: Twin Palms, 2000.

Apel, Dora. *Imagery of Lynching: Black Men, White Women, and the Mob*. New Brunswick: Rutgers UP, 2004.

Apel, Dora, and Shawn Michelle Smith. *Lynching Photographs*. Berkley: U of California P, 2007.

Blair, Sara. *Harlem Crossroads: Black Writers and the Photograph in the Twentieth Century*. Princeton: Princeton UP, 2007.

Buttitta, Tony. *The Lost Summer: A Personal Memoir of F. Scott Fitzgerald*. New York: St. Martin's, 1987.

Cunard, Nancy Clara. "Scottsboro and Other Scottsboros." *Witnessing Lynching: American Writers Respond.* Ed. Anne P. Rice. New Brunswick: Rutgers UP, 2003. 272–81.

Dray, Philip. *At the Hands of Persons Unknown: The Lynching of Black America.* New York: Random, 2002.

Goldsby, Jacqueline. *A Spectacular Secret: Lynching in American Life and Literature.* Chicago: U of Chicago P, 2006.

Gussow, Adam. *Seems Like Murder Here: Southern Violence and the Blues Tradition.* Chicago: U of Chicago P, 2002.

Higgins, Scarlett. "How Long Must We Wait?: Langston Hughes's Cryptic Collage." *The Langston Hughes Review* 23.1 (Fall 2009): 5–18.

Hughes, Langston. *The Collected Works of Langston Hughes.* Ed. Arnold Rampersad et al. 16 vols. Columbia: U of Missouri P, 2001–03.

———. *Good Morning Revolution: Uncollected Writings of Social Protest.* Ed. Faith Berry. Secaucus: Carol, 1992.

Hughes, Langston, and Arna Bontemps. *Arna Bontemps-Langston Hughes Letters (1925–1967).* Ed. Charles H. Nichols. New York: Dodd, 1980.

Hughes, Langston, and Carl Van Vechten. *Remember Me to Harlem: The Letters of Langston Hughes and Carl Van Vechten 1925–1964.* Ed. Emily Bernard. New York: Knopf, 2001.

Litwack, Leon F. Introduction. *Without Sanctuary: Lynching Photography in America.* Santa Fe: Twin Palms, 2000.

Metress, Christopher. "Langston Hughes's 'Mississippi-1955': A Note on Revisions and an Appeal for Reconsideration." *African American Review* 37.1 (2003): 139–48.

Miller, W. Jason. *Langston Hughes and American Lynching Culture.* Gainesville: UP of Florida, 2011.

Rampersad, Arnold. *The Life of Langston Hughes.* 2 vols. New York: Oxford UP, 2002.

Sanders, Leslie Catherine. Introduction. *Gospel Plays, Operas, and Later Dramatic Works.* Ed. Sanders and Nancy Johnston. Columbia: U of Missouri P, 2001. 1–11. Vol. 6 of *The Collected Works of Langston Hughes.* Arnold Rampersad et al., gen. eds. 16 vols. 2001–03.

Smethurst, James. "The Adventures of a Social Poet: Langston Hughes from the Popular Front to Black Power." *A Historical Guide to Langston Hughes.* Ed. Steven C. Tracy. Oxford: Oxford UP, 2004. 141–68

Snyder, Robert E. "Without Sanctuary: An American Holocaust?" *Southern Quarterly* 39.3 (2001): 162–69.

Summers-Brenner, Eluned. "Unreal City and Dream Deferred." *Geomodernisms.* Ed. Laura Doyle and Laura Winkel. Bloomington: Indiana UP, 2005. 262–80.

Thurston, Michael. "Black Christ, Red Flag: Langston Hughes on Scottsboro." *College Literature* 22.3 (1995): 30–52.

The Blues I'm Not Playing?:
Langston Hughes in the 1930s

David Roessel

The February 1939 issue of *Opportunity* published a poem by Langston Hughes entitled "Six-Bit Blues." This was followed in August by "Red Clay Blues," written with Richard Wright, in the *New Masses*, and then "Hey-Hey Blues" in the *New Yorker* in November. Such information might seem rather unremarkable, given Hughes's reputation as a "blues" poet. Yet February 1939 was the first time that Hughes had used the word "blues" in a poem title since the appearance of his 1927 volume, *Fine Clothes to the Jew*. Throughout the 1920s, the blues was a major theme and motif not only in *Fine Clothes to the Jew* but also in *Not without Laughter* (1930), the novel that Hughes worked on in the late 1920s. A form of the blues is also used in "Sylvester's Dying Bed," which appeared in *Poetry* in October 1931. But from 1931 until 1939, the blues was largely absent from Hughes's verse in title and form, the major exception being "The Ballad of Roosevelt" in *The New Republic* in 1934, which seems more like a doggerel imitation of the blues.

> The pot was empty,
> The cupboard was bare.
> I said, Papa,
> What's the matter here?
> I'm waitin' on Roosevelt, son,
> Roosevelt, Roosevelt,
> Waitin' on Roosevelt, son. (lines 1–7)

This period during which Hughes turned away from the blues in his poetry coincides with the Great Depression and a rise in leftist politics in America. Hughes was not the only author who had some difficulty negotiating the 1930s poetically. The critic Malcolm Cowley, surveying the writing of the turbulent decade in 1941, states that the "1930s were a vigorous age for criticism, an experimental age for dramas, a really brilliant age for the realistic novel," indeed, "most branches of literature were flourishing; almost the only exceptions were poetry and strictly imaginative writing" (193). But the larger situation on the literary front helps to explain why Hughes concentrated on new and different forms of poetic composition in the 1930s, even when the blues had been so fruitful for him in the previous decade.

In 1939, when the blues returned to Hughes's verse, it was as if a dam had burst. After "Hey-Hey Blues," there followed "Love Again Blues" and "Out of Work" (both in *Poetry*, April 1940), "Seven Moments of Love: An Un-Sonnet Sequence in Blues" (*Esquire*, May 1940), and "Evenin' Air Blues" (*Common Ground*, spring 1941). Jazz and spiritual elements, which were also prominent in Hughes's poems in the 1920s, are similarly hard to find between 1931 and 1939; after "Rent Party Shout: For a Lady Dancer" (*Amsterdam News*, August 20, 1930) and *The Dream Keeper* (1932), a volume for young people composed entirely of previously published poems, those musical themes would disappear until the end of the decade. The African American folk poet seems to have put his folk elements in a drawer for most of the 1930s.

This observation about the poetry does not extend to his drama and fiction. In the mid-1930s Hughes wrote African American folk comedies for the Gilpin Players of Karamu House in Cleveland that contain all the folk and musical elements lacking in his poetry of the period. Among them were *Little Ham* (1935), which ends with the playing of the "St. Louis Blues," and *When the Jack Hollers* (1936), written with Arna Bontemps. In 1934 he published a volume of short stories dealing with race in America, *The Ways of White Folks*, in which African American music and folk culture play a role, especially in the story "The Blues I'm Playing." Some of his efforts in drama and fiction were attempts to make his work more commercial, but the folk comedies, as biographer Arnold Rampersad notes, were "perhaps also part of his renewal of racial bonding" (Rampersad 1: 323). The fact that this attempt at bonding was in the form of drama underscores the observation that in his poetry, Hughes was quite clearly not playing the blues in the 1930s.

Perhaps the most successful play artistically, and one of the most successful commercially, that Hughes produced in the 1930s was *Don't You Want to Be Free?: A Poetry Play, from Slavery through the Blues to Now*. The play was written for the Harlem Suitcase Theater and sponsored by the International Workers Order, which was also the publisher of Hughes's volume of radical verse, *A New Song* (1938). This was an innovative piece that used the African American musical and folk traditions to convey a radical message. The ending of this play resembles numerous other proletarian dramas, including another one of Hughes's plays, *Scottsboro Limited*.

> Who wants to come and join hands with me?
> Who wants to make one great unity?
> Who wants to say no more black and white?
> Then let's get together, folks,
> And fight, fight, fight! (*CW* 5: 569)

The use of the poetry earlier in the play to present character and situation gives it breadth most of Hughes's proletarian skits lack. Alain Locke, in his annual survey of African American writing in *Opportunity*, takes special note of these "dramatized 'Blues episodes'" in the play and sees them as a sign of a cultural revival of the 1920s ("The Negro" 10). But while Hughes was playing the blues in this piece, he was not writing it. Almost all of the poetry in the show was previously published in *The Weary Blues* (1926) and *Fine Clothes to the Jew*. If there was a moment that convinced Hughes that in order to be a poet, whether radical or not, he had to return to the themes and styles of his early work, it might have been the success of *Don't You Want to Be Free?* in 1938.

Two possible explanations stand out for Hughes's move away from the rhythms that predominate in *Fine Clothes to the Jew*, such as in "Homesick Blues":

> De railroad bridge's
> A sad song in the de air.
> De railroad bridge's
> A sad song in de air.
> Ever time de trains pass
> I wants to go somewhere. (1–6)

One is that the savage reception the volume received from the black press for its subject matter and vernacular language so singed Hughes that it would take some time before he would risk writing in that vein again. Hughes records some of this response in his autobiography *The Big Sea* (1940), such as the comment of Benjamin Brawley: "It would have been just as well, perhaps better, if the book had never been published. No other ever issued reflects more fully the abandon and the vulgarity of its age" (266). A few pages later, Hughes responds to the uproar:

> I felt that the masses of our people had as much in their lives to put into books as did those more fortunate ones who had been born with some means and the ability to work up to a master's degree at a Northern college. Anyway, I didn't know the upper class Negroes well enough to write much about them. (267–68)

Hughes says of the assault on *Fine Clothes to the Jew* that he understood that African American intellectuals were sensitive about how the black race was portrayed in literature and that he was sympathetic to their concerns. But he did not see why every black author had to write in the same vein, and he thought he should be free to portray the common people that he knew. He finishes by asserting:

> So I didn't pay any attention to the critics who railed against the subject matter of my poems, nor did I write them protesting letters, nor in any way attempt to defend my book. Curiously enough, a short ten years later, many of those very poems in *Fine Clothes to the Jew* were being used in Negro schools and colleges. (268)

This was hardly a defiant stand, for not only did Hughes make little attempt to defend his book, he also began to avoid in verse the style, subject matter, and diction that had caused the controversy. When Hughes embarked on an extensive tour of poetry readings in 1931, his audiences preferred material that was "uplifting, sentimental and formally conservative" (Smethurst 95)—it was clear to him that he would not be allowed to read blues poems in African American churches and schools, and he accepted that fact.[1] The interlude of music was consistently "classical pieces or spirituals; most likely, no one ever ventured to sing the blues, as Langston would have preferred" (Rampersad 1: 223). Despite Hughes's assertion that some of the poems from *Fine Clothes* were now part of the curriculum, that did not seem to be the case for the blues poems. When Hughes published the volume *Shakespeare in Harlem* (1942), which he describes in the preface as "Afro-Americana in the blues mood," "the reaction of most black reviewers to *Shakespeare in Harlem* was very much like their reaction to *Fine Clothes*; they saw neither virtue nor virtuosity in blues poems" (Rampersad 2: 40). If Hughes had waited to return to the blues until African American reviewers were ready to accept these efforts, he had not waited long enough.

The other explanation is bound up in Hughes's turn to the Left and his attempt to be a poet for a different kind of masses in the 1930s. It is not only the déclassé blues that disappears from Hughes's verse, but also those African American elements, such as the spirituals, that the "Talented Tenth" and black intellectuals embraced. In its place were poems such as "Revolution," which begins:

> Great mob that knows no fear—
> Come here!
> And raise your hand
> Against this man
> Of iron and steel and gold
> Who's bought and sold
> You— (1–7)

Such poems were no more likely to please the black establishment, and no more likely to be read in a black church or school, than those that appeared in *Fine Clothes to the Jew*.

Critics have observed, for how could they not, that Hughes was not playing with the blues in the 1930s as he had in the 1920s or would in the 1940s. Indeed, Alain Locke notes in his 1933 survey of African American literature that "as the folk-school tradition deepens, Hughes, formerly its chief exponent, turns more and more in the direction of social protest and propaganda" ("Black Truth" 17); he goes on to say that *The Dream Keeper*, a volume of previously published verse that came out in 1932, showed "a delightful echo of the old Hughes, who sings of his people as 'walkers with the Dawn'" instead of the "indignant proletarian reformer" he had become (17). The consensus, at least among Hughes scholars and nonleftist scholars, is that, as Rampersad puts it, Hughes lost his "essential identity" for a period in the 1930s: "Only Hughes could have written 'The Negro Speaks of Rivers' but—given the right mixture of radical rage and literary adroitness on the part of a writer—'Good Morning Revolution' could have been written by almost anyone" ("Critics on the Left" 40). This is a strong judgment, but taking into account Hughes's whole career, not an unfair one—and one that Hughes himself had helped to create.

In his essay "The Negro Artist and the Racial Mountain," Hughes chastises "one of the most promising Negro poets" for saying "'I want to be a poet—not a Negro poet.'" Hughes interprets this statement by the promising poet, clearly Countee Cullen, to mean that he wants to be white—a leap in logic that Cullen could well protest. In that piece, Hughes declares that he admires "the serious black artist . . . who would produce a racial art" and says that he is ashamed of the "colored artist who runs from the painting of colored faces to the painting of sunsets after the manner of academicians." He writes, "Let the blare of Negro jazz bands and the bellowing voice of Bessie Smith singing Blues penetrate the closed ears of colored intellectuals until they listen and understand" (*CW* 9: 31, 35–36). Hughes was a young man at the time of this essay, but the self-construction he produced has affected his image ever since; readers of this piece have listened to the blues in his work as a sign of authenticity. So when, in the 1930s, Hughes seemed to want to be a red poet, or at least a black poet who ran after the class struggle in the manner of the theoreticians, some critics both then and now have felt that he moved away from his mission and genius as an artist. It is, of course, unfair to judge Hughes's whole career by a manifesto he wrote at the age of twenty-five, but part of the staying power of "The Negro Artist and the Racial Mountain" is that Hughes appeared to follow its precepts in every decade but the 1930s. One could add that it is only fair to hold him accountable to the same standards he applied to Cullen.

Still, Hughes was certainly not the only poet, African American or white, to have to renegotiate his aesthetics in the world of the Great Depression. Locke, in his survey of African American literature for 1935, draws a connection between the 1930s and the writing produced before the era of the Harlem Renaissance:

> Our art is again turning prosaic, partisan, propagandistic but this time it is not on behalf of striving, strident racialism, but rather a protestant and belligerent universalism of social analysis and protest. Yesterday it was Beauty at all costs and local color with a vengeance; today it is Truth by all means and social justice at any price. ("Deep River" 7)

If the blues was, as Hughes writes in "Songs Called the Blues" in 1941, "folk-songs born of heart-ache" for when one is "troubled in mind and don't know what to do and nobody cares," then its individualism might well be out of key with an era that wanted poetry to advocate group action and mass protest (*CW* 9: 212–13).

There have been a few attempts to reexamine Hughes's verse from the 1930s; two of the most cogent are by Richard Barksdale and James Smethurst. Barksdale notes that in this decade, "one area in which Hughes developed as a poet was in the quality and power of some of his occasional poems published during this time in *Crisis* and *Opportunity*" (42), pointing to pieces such as "The Town of Scottsboro."

> Scottsboro's just a little place:
> No shame is writ across its face—
> Its court, too weak to stand against a mob,
> Its people's heart, too small to hold a sob.

Barksdale is clearly correct; there had been almost no occasional verse in either *The Weary Blues* or *Fine Clothes to the Jew*, and the occasional poem, such as "Birmingham Sunday" in *The Panther and the Lash* (1967), would remain an important piece of Hughes's repertoire and a vehicle for him to speak out about contemporary events until his death. Barksdale is again correct when he states that Hughes "broadened his poetical range of subject matter, moving beyond the treatment of Harlem's folk types to black folk throughout the African diaspora" as well as "his poetical scope to include leftist issues and causes" (41), but his assertion that Hughes "expanded his literary interests to meet new and different political and social contingencies" (42) seems a bit of an overstatement. Expansion suggests that Hughes added to his literary interests, and if that were true then the blues would not have been abandoned in title and style. It would be more appropriate to say that Hughes changed his literary interests to meet new and different political and social contingencies, and that somehow the blues did not fit those.

Smethurst notes that the "largest part of Hughes's poetic production during the 1930s was his 'revolutionary poetry,' often seen as his weakest or strongest according to the political bent of the critic" (101). But even he acknowledges that those with a political bent to judge those poems the strongest are few; for the majority of critics, both black and white, "no portion of Hughes's literary career has been more commonly dismissed than the 1930s" (93). What is refreshing about Smethurst, as with Barksdale, is that he examines the revolutionary poems as poetry and asks how they fit into Hughes's art. The point is not that Hughes's poetry of the 1930s is radical and therefore bad—some of the poems, among them "Let America Be America Again," Letter to the Academy," and "Advertisement for the Waldorf Astoria," have great merit. The point made here is the one Hughes makes at the start of "Note on Commercial Theatre": "You've taken my blues and gone," and as a result the poems "don't sound like me" (1, 6). Hughes published that poem in 1940. If he had published it in 1938, he would have had no one to blame but himself for the disappearance of his blues.

Smethurst writes:

> What is formally most interesting in the 1930s is that the wide variety of voices, styles and themes employed by Hughes in the late 1920s and early 1930s and addressed to equally disparate audiences become largely unified by the end of the decade in a manner that is crucial to the development of his later work. (94)

Like other critics, he observes that during the 1930s, Hughes stopped writing the types of poems featured in *Fine Clothes to the Jew*: "poems formally rooted in the secular and sacred musical forms of the blues and gospel music, as well as in black rhetoric and representing as speaking subjects such 'low-life' characters as prostitutes, gamblers, murderers, drunks, and suicides" (94). So once again, there is an argument for expansion when there is change and, it could be argued, contraction. Hughes's verse certainly changed in the 1930s, and one can see that change as a sign of poetic growth. Smethurst, like many critics of Hughes, finds that Hughes achieves a new power when he returns to and integrates those abandoned elements back into his poetry in the 1940s and in *Montage of a Dream Deferred* (1951).

Did the Left, and specifically the communists, influence Hughes's verse so much that it is not a coincidence that the years of his most intense engagement were the years without blues poems? In "Moscow and Me," an essay published in *International Literature* in 1933, Hughes announces that communist Muscovite "editors welcome frank stories of American Negro life" as well as material about race relations that commercial publishers in American would not touch (*CW* 9: 61). Hughes seems to implicitly say in this piece that in the Soviet Union, he did not have to please either the white middle-class or the black bourgeoisie; he could stand as a black artist on the mountaintop and create poems such as "Red Silk Stockings" just as he pleased. Hughes clearly felt a freedom in the Soviet Union—there was no color line and he was paid well for his writing (Rampersad 1: 252). But in Russia in early 1933, when Hughes discovered the stories of D. H. Lawrence and was inspired to compose the first of the stories that would appear in *The Ways of White Folks*, "almost certainly he did not try to find out what Lydia Filatova and other Muscovite critics thought of these pieces" (269). Hughes was already aware that the Russian editors welcomed "frank stories of American Negro life" as long as they were frank in the proper way, and that did not include the blues or jazz.

As Rampersad observes about *I Wonder as I Wander*, Hughes's second autobiography, which begins in 1931, Hughes "could tell of no conflict as wrenching as that with his mother, no hatred as intense and yet as germinal as what he had felt for his father, no clash as apocalyptic as his break with 'Godmother'" (2: 259).[2] For both Wright and Ellison, the conflict with the Communist Party would be the apocalyptic break. Rampersad seems to be unique in his suggestion that the collapse of Hughes's relationship with his white patron, Charlotte Osgood Mason, in 1930 drove Hughes "to the left for many years, and in other ways affect[ed] the entire course of the rest of his life" (1: 200). Hughes's own account of his break with Mason in *The Big Sea* begins with the composition of the poem "Advertisement for the Waldorf Astoria," about the opening of the deluxe hotel, which would not employ blacks, in a city with tens of thousands unemployed: "'It's not you,' said my benefactor . . . 'it's a powerful poem! But it's not you.' I knew she did not like it. I began that winter to feel increasingly bad, increasingly worried and apprehensive" (323).

There are problems with Hughes's account, as the Waldorf Astoria had not yet opened, nor was Hughes's poem written, until after the final break with Mason. So, it is interesting that Hughes employs the poem in his autobiography to suggest both aesthetic and political conflicts with Mason. His letters to Mason confirm his distress with her wish that he write according to a certain schedule and plan. In a letter dated June 6, 1930, Hughes writes, "In all my life I have never been free. I have never been able to do anything with freedom, except in my writing. . . . I must never write when I do not want to write. That is my last freedom and I must keep it for myself" (LHP; Rampersad 1: 184).

If pressure from Mason about what to write caused Hughes great discomfort, one would expect that, at some point, he would experience some unease if the Communist Party exerted pressure on his artistic freedom. In *I Wonder as I Wander*, Hughes addresses this only briefly:

Arthur Koestler asked me one day why in Moscow I did not join the Communist Party. I told him that what I had heard concerning the Party indicated that it was based on strict discipline and the acceptance of directives that I, as a writer, did not wish to accept. I did not believe political directives could be successfully applied to creative writing. They might well apply to the preparation of tracts and pamphlets, yes, but not to poetry or fiction, which to be valid, I felt, had to express as truthfully as possible the individual emotions and reactions of the writer, rather than mass directives issued to achieve practical and often temporary political objectives. Koestler agreed with me that it was very difficult to write both politically and individually at the same time, especially when the political lines were applied from above by bureaucrats who had no appreciation of creative impulses. But he said, at certain historical periods, collective social aims might be worthy of transcending individual desires. (121–22)

There is a certain amount of disingenuousness in this response—Hughes professes to know only what he has heard about party discipline and directives. In two passages that follow, however, he indicates that he knew at least something about those directives and why he could not accept them. He goes on to say:

> Once, I gave as my reason for not joining the Party the fact that jazz was officially taboo in Russia, being played only at the déclassé Metropol hotel, and very badly there.
>
> "But jazz is decadent bourgeois music," I was told, for that is what the Soviet press had hammered into Russian heads.
>
> "It's my music," I said, and I wouldn't give up jazz for world revolution. (122)

This is an interesting passage, because although Hughes claims he would not give up jazz even for a world revolution, he was, based on his verse, willing to leave jazz and blues styles and themes out of his poetry for nearly a decade.

As if to underscore that being both an African American and a red poet was problematic, Hughes recounts one more conversation in Moscow:

> While I was in Moscow my third book of poems, *The Dream Keeper*, was published in the United States. When copies reached me, I gave one to Ivy Litvinoff, the cultivated English woman who was most gracious to members of our movie group, and whose husband later became the Soviet Ambassador to Washington. Mrs. Litvinoff said that she liked my poems, all save those in the religious group. When I informed her that they were

based on the old folk forms of the spirituals, she said that such poems had no place in the class struggle and were not worthy of a Party member. When I told her I was not a Party member, she asked why, and I gave her the same reasons I gave Koestler. (122–23)

I Wonder as I Wander was published in 1956, after a decade or more in which authors, both black and white, who had joined the party offered explanations for why it had been a great error, so there has been some suspicion that the views offered within were more for public consumption and did not represent Hughes's true convictions. But it is interesting to note that in drafts of *I Wonder as I Wander*, Hughes is a bit more forthright about his issues with the party and comes across as more literarily sophisticated. The first of these excised passages reads:

And in writing the most complex to me and difficult taboos existed. Modernism was discouraged as being, I gathered, beyond the interest or understanding of the people—which I thought absurd. Long arguments with Madame Lunacharsky and others could not bring me to understand why, for instance, it was wrong to write poems in the manner of the Negro spirituals of the South, or why poems in which no mention of the class struggle occurred were considered frivolous and of no consequence, thus better left undone. (LHP)

It would, of course, be wrong to take this passage as a more authentic reaction to communist taboos on writing than the one Hughes actually published, but it is curious how much more direct it is. What is noteworthy is that Hughes says that he was told it was wrong to write poems in the manner of the spirituals, or jazz, or the blues, and for a long time in the 1930s he did not write them. There does, then, seem to have been some tension between what Hughes felt he was supposed to write and what he at times wanted to write. That Hughes really did want to play his part with the Left is signified by the fact that, for as long as he could, he did try to write poems in the accepted revolutionary and proletarian manner.

In the draft of *I Wonder as I Wander*, he is also more forthright about not joining the Communist Party:

> And in spite of the urging of the ardent comrades whom I know, I never joined the Communist Party, nor did I ever think seriously of joining. In the first place, I did not want to accept its discipline—which is its first tenant and strength. . . . I did not agree with the party on a number of scores, my main disagreement being its inability to accept without the most illogical and screamingly vituperative rebuttals even the mildest criticism of its tactics and politics. In the second place I could not feel comfortable concerning its attitude to poetry and writing. The orthodox Communists—many of them—are very much like certain staunch hide-bound Christians I knew in my youth. "Are you with us, Son?" they would ask. If you weren't, there was not use to go any further. Hell had you! (LHP)

What is remarkable is that while Hughes seemed to want to distance himself from his radical past, he did not include this passage, which echoes many of the ideas anticommunist intellectuals wanted to hear in 1956, in the published book. But again, this passage was written in hindsight, and the poetic evidence suggests that Hughes was aesthetically more supportive of the communists than not for most of the 1930s. It is also noteworthy that in both the published and unpublished versions of his reasons for not joining the Communist Party, he makes no objection on political grounds.

Was Hughes encouraged to think that a good proletarian wrote in a certain style? It certainly seems so, based on his comments in his autobiography, the critique by Lydia Filatova of his work in *International Literature*, and his correspondence with party members. In her survey of Hughes's works, Filatova takes note of his recent revolutionary poetry and how different it is from *The Weary Blues* and *Fine Clothes to the Jew*, writing that "his new poetical *credo* is the total negation of his former creative position" ("American Writer" 104). As Rampersad observes, of the five poems from *Fine Clothes to the Jew* mentioned in the article by Filatova, "not one is in the blues form; in fact, in reviewing a book defined by the blues, the word 'blues' is never mentioned."[3] Rampersad goes on to say that "Hughes evidently accepted, at this point in his career, Filatova's analysis of his work" ("Critics on the Left" 38).

After Hughes left Russia and returned to the United States, he exchanged letters with Walt Carmon, the editor of *International Literature*. Hughes had stayed in the Moscow apartment of Walt and Rose Carmon for a month after his return from a trip to Soviet Asia. After Hughes mailed Carmon copies of two stories, "Cora Unashamed" and "Slave on the Block," that marked both an artistic and commercial breakthrough, Carmon responded on September 4, 1933. He writes: "I got the sheets of the *Mercury* with your story and a copy of *Scribner's* came in the same mail. Congratulations on the breaks and all but don't stop at those kinds of stories. You're a rev. writer now and they slow your pace up, swell as they are. I'm serious" (LHP). Carmon goes on to ask Hughes about the status of a projected volume of proletarian verse. In a letter written November 2, 1933, Carmon writes: "You lowlifer. I come back from the wild of Siberia expecting loads of stuff from one Hughes, rev. writer, and I get a song for the Music Union. Now I ask you! But being a gentleman, I cursed only the normal amount and turned over the song as directed" (LHP). Indeed, Carmon pushed Hughes toward more revolutionary or proletarian work in every letter. The hints were scarcely subtle.

But if Hughes felt some pressure to publish in a certain vein from leftist friends and critics, it had nowhere near the kind of force that he had felt from Mason. He seems to have willingly adopted the "revolutionary" style in the 1930s, even though many critics since have thought it was an artistic detour from his "essential identity." When he moved away from the proletarian style and back to the blues, he did so with apparently little angst. This may just be because he was older and wiser than he had been during his relationship with Mason, and more wary about commitment. It may also be because his abandonment of the blues for revolutionary verse was voluntary—he wrote what he thought the times needed, or he thought the blues too individual a vehicle in an era that called for social protest.

The poem "Poet to Patron," published in 1939, reads:

> What right has anyone to say
> That I
> Must throw out pieces of my heart
> For pay?
>
> For bread that helps to make
> My heart beat true,
> I must sell myself
> To you?
>
> A factory shift's better,
> A week's meagre pay,
> Than a perfumed note asking:
> *What poems today?*

The mention of a perfumed note clearly evokes Hughes's problems with Mason, suggesting that perhaps the poem was written on the tenth anniversary of the start of the problems in their relationship, and Hughes marked the date, still, with this effort. It is intriguing that the poem appeared during the period in which Hughes resumed including the blues in his poetry. Did it take Hughes ten years to recover from what was clearly an emotionally shattering experience? Was he now ready to confront again the African American critics who had rejected his use of the blues and jazz in the 1920s? Did this poem to Mason also serve as a message to those such as Filatova and Carmon, asserting that he would no longer be Langston Hughes, "revolutionary writer"? Or, is it just coincidence that he wrote "Poet to Patron" when he resumed playing the blues in poetry? Once Hughes returned to the blues form in 1939, he never again abandoned it for such a number of years. In his later career, he would find that he was able to express social and political contingencies with rhythms he first played in the 1920s.

> Good morning, daddy!
> Ain't you heard
> The boogie-woogie rumble
> Of a dream deferred? ("Dream Boogie" 1–4)

We have all now heard that rumble in a way that we will never forget.

Notes

1. For a description of the contents of a typical reading on the tour, see Rampersad 1: 223–24.
2. Louise Thompson Patterson indicates to Arnold Rampersad that her experience with Mason was "as decisive as any in urging her into an association for life with communism," so it is not a stretch that it could also have that effect on Hughes. She also notes that Hughes "got sick. . . . When I got over it, I got mad" (1: 200).
3. Curiously, Mike Gold, in his introduction to *A New Song*, a volume of Hughes's radical poetry published by the International Workers Order, writes that folk literature was the "best Negro literature" as it was "close to the joys and sorrows of the people" (Wald 89). However, there was not much folk tradition in the poems that followed his introduction.

Works Cited

Barksdale, Richard. *Langston Hughes: The Poet and His Critics*. Chicago: ALA, 1977.
Cowley, Malcolm. *Think Back on Us: A Contemporary Chronicle of the 1930s*. Ed. Henry Dan Piper. Carbondale: Southern Illinois UP, 1967.
Filatova, Lidia. "Langston Hughes: American Writer." *International Literature* 1 (1933): 99–107.
Hughes, Langston. *The Big Sea*. 1940. New York: Hill, 1993.
_____. *The Collected Poems*. Ed. Arnold Rampersad and David Roessel. New York: Knopf, 1994.

———. *The Collected Works of Langston Hughes.* Ed. Arnold Rampersad et al. 16 vols. Columbia: U of Missouri P, 2001–03.
———. *Good Morning Revolution: Uncollected Writing of Social Protest.* Ed. Faith Berry. Secaucus: Carol, 1992.
———. *I Wonder as I Wander.* 1956. New York: Hill, 1993.
———. Langston Hughes Papers. James Weldon Johnson Collection. Beinecke Rare Book and Manuscript Lib., Yale U, New Haven.
Locke, Alain. "Black Truth and Black Beauty." *Opportunity* (1933): 14–18.
———. "Deep River: Deeper Sea" *Opportunity* (1936): 6+.
———. "The Negro: 'New' or Newer." *Opportunity* (1940): 6–10.
Rampersad, Arnold. "Langston Hughes and His Critics on the Left." *The Langston Hughes Review* 5.2 (1986): 34–40.
———. *The Life of Langston Hughes.* 2 vols. New York: Oxford UP, 1986–88.
Smethurst, James Edward. *The New Red Negro: The Literary Left and African American Poetry, 1930–1946.* New York: Oxford UP, 1999.
Wald, Alan. *Exiles from a Future Time: The Forging of the Mid-Twentieth Century Left.* Chapel Hill: U of North Carolina P, 2002.

Hughes's Stories and the Test of Faith
Sharon L. Jones

Although Langston Hughes has been widely celebrated and recognized as a poet, he was an accomplished autobiographer, playwright, and fiction writer. His numerous short stories reveal his ability to compose sophisticated, thoughtful, and innovative tales focusing on the diversity of human beings. In stories such as "On the Road," "Big Meeting," and "Blessed Assurance," he demonstrates the importance of African American textual and structural irony throughout the middle third of the twentieth century. Consequently, he provides readers with a greater and more sophisticated understanding of how religious irony is inherent in the lives of African Americans. In addition, he resists treating his subject matter in a simplistic and condescending manner. Rather, he shows a dynamic, multidimensional, and nuanced representation of African American spirituality from a variety of perspectives.

"On the Road," "Big Meeting," and "Blessed Assurance" illustrate that Hughes used short fiction as a means of exploring theological ideas. Hughes focuses on characters whose acceptance or rejection of the Christian concepts of faith and hope illustrate his willingness to write about important moral issues. His artistic courage in representing such matters reveals his remarkable ability to address this topic in enlightening ways. Hence, these stories reveal the position of his work within the African American literary tradition in relation to the significance of religion. His fiction serves therefore as a reminder of the ways in which his writing showcases the centrality of Christianity to the evolution of the African American presence in the United States.

Hughes provides readers with a greater comprehension of how he adopted and appropriated the short story form to convey powerful revelations in a sociohistorical context. He uses conflicts about faith as a central idea in his fiction to symbolize the ways religion can reinforce or challenge the status quo. Ultimately, his stories suggest that the individual's response to questions of faith dictates whether such belief expands or restricts the opportunities for economic advancement and personal well-being. All of the major characters in the three stories must decide whether to embrace faith. Ultimately, the choices result in consequences for believers and for others around them. In turn, Hughes challenges the readers to interrogate their own beliefs about faith as it relates to other aspects of their identities.

The Christian concept identifies faith as an important quality of the individual or community's relationship with God. According to the concept, people must have faith that God is the father of all people and that Jesus, his son, died for the sins of all. Individuals can find redemption and salvation if they ask for forgiveness for their sins. Later, they can hope for everlasting life in heaven as a reward for their faith and allegiance to God and Christ. In "On the Road," "Big Meeting," and "Blessed Assurance," the protagonists' faith is frequently tested as characters must determine whether the Christian concept is relevant and meaningful to their own lives and those of others around them.

In "On the Road," Sargeant, the protagonist, finds his hope tested during the Great Depression when he is rejected by a white pastor and attacked by law enforcement officials for attempting to enter a white church. The pastor and his flock represent religion, and he discovers that as a black male of low economic status, he is an outcast. His encounter with an imaginary Christ presents him with a situation in which he must decide whether to accept or reject his faith. In "Big Meeting," the narrator finds his perspective on religion transformed when he attends a religious service to observe the participants. While he views what he sees and hears as something initially amusing, he undergoes a gradual conversion in recognizing the importance of hope for African Americans. The comments of the black pastor during the sermon make a powerful connection between the suffering of Jesus and the figurative Black Christ of African American literary and cultural tradition. The figure signifies empathy with individuals who are socially and economically marginalized and for a figure who was crucified unjustly (Douglas 21). In the context of black liberation theology, the crucifixion bears similarities to the lynchings of African Americans in the nineteenth and twentieth centuries.

Black liberation theology emphasizes the connection between the everyday lives of black people in America and biblical story. James H. Cone, author of *A Black Theology of Liberation*, articulates the impetus behind the expression of Christianity for African Americans: "Black theology is a theology of liberation because it is a theology which arises from identification with the oppressed blacks of America, seeking to interpret the gospel of Jesus in the light of the black condition. It believes that the liberation of the black community *is* God's liberation" (4–5). The pastor in "Big Meeting" preaches a powerful sermon that embodies the theological perspective by showing the applicability of biblical teachings to the people at the religious service; at the same time, the pastor empowers the black narrator by showing that hope in God and Jesus Christ can be uplifting. The service tests both the narrator's faith and the devotion of the white onlookers. Ultimately, the black narrator chooses to understand and accept the power of an activist liberation to challenge oppressive forces, but the white onlookers reinforce the ideas of racial prejudice. Obviously, the distinction between the two theologies is that one—the African American—really works for positive change in the social world. This is the structural irony of black belief.

The representation of the Black Christ in Hughes's "Big Meeting" recurs within a longstanding tradition of African American cultural expression. During the colonial period, many enslaved blacks adopted Christianity due to the influence of British and European slaveholders who claimed to be Christian. But African Americans appropriated aspects of Christianity, including biblical figures such as Moses and Christ, based on their own experiences. As Kelly Brown Douglas points out in *The Black Christ*, "Jesus' significance for the slaves was based upon an interpretation of Christianity that stressed the centrality of Jesus' ministry and relationship to the oppressed during his own time" (21). This relation and connection with Jesus prompted slaves to compose and sing songs that portrayed themselves as analogous to Christ during the 1700s and 1800s as well as during the Harlem Renaissance of the 1920s. In the poem "The Black Christ" by Countee Cullen, a contemporary of Hughes, the speaker laments the lynching of his black brother in the South. After the lynched victim dies, he is resurrected. Cullen's "Simon the Cyrenian" represents a black male who agrees to carry Christ's cross. According to *My Soul's High Song*, edited by Gerald Early, "Cullen explained that seeing Simon the Cyrenian as a black is a tradition among African-Americans" (87). When the pastor in "Big Meeting" emphasizes the race of the Christ figure, the persona completes the *analogue* or implied comparison. As a crucial link in the chain, the story shows that black literary tradition emerges from black oral tradition and complements it well.

Hughes's short fiction does not present the acceptance or rejection of faith as an easy journey for anyone. "On the Road," "Big Meeting," and "Blessed Assurance" illustrate that spiritual conviction remains a complex one that can be best understood in terms of political contexts. Through examining the structural irony of faith in the stories, readers gain an appreciation for how Hughes wrestles with these ideas to develop historical and moral irony.

The story "On the Road" skillfully blends the complementary dimensions of history and morality. According to *A Langston Hughes Encyclopedia*, the tale first appeared in the January 1935 issue of *Esquire* magazine as "Two on the Road"; it was later published in Hughes's second volume of short stories, *Laughing to Keep from Crying* (1952; Ostrom 287). Critical commentary on the work typically focuses on the resolution, the tone, the treatment of religion, and the status of the protagonist. Hans Ostrom writes, "The plot is spare and parablelike, concerning an African American man, Sargeant, who is trying merely to survive during the Great Depression in the United States" (287). The same literary historian acknowledges in *Langston Hughes: A Study of the Short Fiction* that "in fact, Sargeant's innocent goodwill becomes a powerful indictment of institutionalized religion, and jail is not depicted as the end of the road for him" (53). In the introduction to *The Short Stories*, volume 15 of *The Collected Works of Langston Hughes*, Hughes biographer Arnold Rampersad adds, "The main character, Sargeant, is a black hobo who seeks refuge from the bitter cold of a northern city in winter by pounding on the door of a white church" (6). In her article "Liberating Christ: Sargeant's Metamorphosis in Langston Hughes's 'On the Road,'" Carolyn P. Walker concludes, "In his short story 'On the Road,' Langston Hughes has created a powerful indictment of racial discrimination" (745). Milton Meltzer, in *Langston Hughes: A Biography*, observes that the protagonist and Jesus share a similar status (188). Ostrom, Miller, Walker, and Meltzer all agree that the story explores a new racial theology.

The plot is rather rudimentary. Sargeant desires kindness, sympathy, and shelter from a pastor at a white church but confronts oppression as a result of his efforts. Hughes portrays the pastor and his flock as unwelcoming to impoverished black people. Meanwhile, the setting of a snowy night encapsulates the frozen communications in race relations. Initially, the protagonist, who suffers from being wet and cold, does not feel the snow. Rather, he concentrates on his hunger, waiting so wearily for sleep. If snow suggests whiteness, as night does blackness, then it is a most cold moment for contemporary America. As Hughes writes, "The Reverend Mr. Dorset, however, saw the snow when he switched on his porch light, opened the front door of his parsonage, and found standing there before him a big black man with snow on his face, a human piece of night with snow on his face—obviously unemployed" (*Short Stories* 272). To achieve racial equality in the midst of the Great Depression and the prevailing bigotry of the time would mean to illuminate the protagonist's plight. It would mean to recognize the way that an acculturating whiteness glosses over the authentic blackness of African American socioeconomics.[1] As Carolyn P. Walker points out, "The man of God asks no questions. He shuts the door in Sargeant's face" (746). Indeed, the economic downturn of the 1930s affected the lives of individuals in the United States. Indeed, many people struggled to obtain sufficient food and lodging. The economic devastation created startling statistics: "National income dropped by nearly 50 percent, from $81 billion in 1929 to $40 billion in 1932; unemployment rose to an estimated 25 percent of the labor force; and nearly 20 million Americans turned to public and private relief agencies to prevent starvation and destitution" (Trotter 434–35). Hence, the faith that appears in the story as a dream alters in no direct way the material realities of the 1930s. Faith therefore informs the story so much more than such hope transforms the real world. Though such faith is quite wonderfully literary, it may not indeed be quite so real.

Due to the situation and the economic hardships of the Depression, the protagonist experiences racial discrimination. When seeking refuge at havens for homeless people in the past, he learned there was no furniture for sleeping, the meal time had often ended, and there was no room for any additional people. In biblical terms, there was no room at the proverbial inn. His situation reinforces the types of injustices that African Americans faced during the period. When whites notice what the protagonist attempts to do, they react by shouting at him. Despite his realization that blacks are not allowed admission to the church, he desperately needs somewhere to stay. Law enforcement officials arrive to deter him, but he resists them, holding the pillars of the church while they assault him. He imagines the edifice collapsing onto the snow, including the cross with Jesus on it, and then experiences a situation in which it falls onto Reverend Dorset, who is in a moral-free Fall of his own. Sargeant imagines that Christ is nearby after the imagined crumpling of the church. As Ostrom observes in *A Langston Hughes Encyclopedia*, it appears that Jesus speaks to the protagonist (287).

The structural irony has become insufferable for him, so Christ, freed now from the hypocrisy of the Christian order, leaves the town for Kansas City. As the subtle manifestation of Jesus (the Black Christ) on earth, the protagonist visits a haven of the destitute. The church and Reverend Dorset have rejected him, but, eventually finding acceptance among the disinherited, he imagines himself attempting to board a train. Awakening from the imagined state, he realizes that a law officer is rapping his pained knuckles. Then he knows that he is a captive in jail, probably because of his attempted entrance into the white church. At the story's end, he remains defiant, musing about Christ while questioning if Christ had actually ventured to Kansas City at all. Meanwhile, the crumbling edifice represents by contrast the potential liberation of marginalized people. Dorset and the white church miss out on a chance to transform society, and they will certainly have to do much more in that regard before Christ would ever be willing to return to them. As R. Baxter Miller points out,

> the ancient story underlies the contemporary hardships of the modern African American wanderer—the homeless person today on our urban streets—who has so unsuccessfully sought sanctuary in the American Christian church, the walls crumbling like those of an ancient temple, "covering the cops and the people with bricks and stones and debris." (*Literary Criticism* 93)

Such symbolism recurs throughout Hughes's stories.

As Ostrom notes in *A Langston Hughes Encyclopedia*, "Big Meeting" appeared in a 1935 issue of *Scribner's*; it was also published in *Laughing to Keep from Crying* (1952). Ostrom observes that "the narrative captures the ambience of an African American evangelical gathering or 'tent meeting'" (34). In addition, in *Langston Hughes: A Study of the Short Fiction*, Ostrom remarks that Hughes understood the importance of religious activity for black people (28). Similarly, Mary Beth Culp, in the essay "Religion in the Poetry of Langston Hughes," analyzes the significance of the spiritual subject to Hughes (240).

"Big Meeting" focuses on a man who attends an outdoor religious service with another. As the former serves as the narrator of the tale, the reader acquires a view of various activities. To the white voyeur Mr. Parkes, the revival is so entertaining that he must assure a white female companion that she will appreciate the music. Meanwhile, a black singer who completes her song during the revival reveals many of her day's troubles. Instead of showing empathy for her, her white counterpart finds the former's story to be humorous, as does her white male companion. Neither of the two understands the spiritual compulsion behind the singer's song. When the pastor finally preaches the sermon, he focuses on the crucifixion of Jesus; he presents Christ as someone marginalized by his socioeconomic world. Jesus has agency, the ability to make things happen in life, but the listeners may as well have no agency at all, for they lack the will to transform the oppressive America in which they live. Yet, the sermon reminds them that they, too, can be agents of transformation. Indeed, the sermon form serves as a means for the pastor's identification with Jesus since both of them are marginalized in society, the pastor by race and Jesus by empathy. Faith is therefore a quality that at least theoretically enables human sympathy across race and class.

The pastor emphasizes that a black male, even darker than he, actually carried the cross on which Jesus was crucified. The narrator, despite his earlier view of the presumed entertainment, his sarcastic projection of a white perspective, becomes engrossed in his own ironic tale. The pastor next compares the crucifixion to a lynching. What was initially a form of the white voyeur's entertainment changes into a moral judgment of her whiteness. Indeed, the impact of the service shifts for both black and white onlookers in the scene. The narrator says, "I didn't realize I was crying until I tasted my tears in my mouth" (*Short Stories* 287). The concluding sentence proves very important, for the speaker may be crying due either to the departure of the whites or the crucifixion of Jesus. The narrator's experience becomes a conversion in which he is presented with a metaphor of suffering and comes to recognize the grandeur of the metaphor.

Hughes's story "Blessed Assurance" resembles "On the Road" and "Big Meeting" in its emphasis on faith. The piece appears in *Something in Common and Other Stories* (1963; Ostrom, *Encyclopedia* 45). The story tells of a relationship between two generations of men in a family as a means of commenting on political and cultural linkages. In *Langston Hughes: A Study of the Short Fiction*, Ostrom observes the complicated treatment of identity in the story: "To some extent, [Hughes] seems to want to ask rhetorically whether homosexuals are welcome in church and to show that John's son, for example, is in some sense blessed by God" (49). Ostrom also suggests that the representation of homosexuality may be stereotypical. Rampersad, in the introduction to *The Short Stories*, writes, "In 'Blessed Assurance,' Hughes treats the intertwined themes of homosexuality and religion in a story written from the point of view of a young black man's father, who is obviously upset about his suspicion that his son might be gay" (7). Rampersad suggests that Hughes's position on the subject remains ambiguous. Anne Borden, in the essay "Heroic 'Hussies' and 'Brilliant Queers': Genderracial Resistance in the Works of Langston Hughes," stresses the depiction of sexual inclination and the possibility of public transformation: "Thus, 'Blessed Assurance' works to move homosexuality out of the realm of the dangerous and deviant in our minds, and creates dialogue on its possible uses in promoting positive social change" (339). In "Langston Hughes, 1902–1967: A Brief Biography," published in *A Historical Guide to Langston Hughes*, R. Baxter Miller observes, "Despite the audience's discomfort with a boy singer, especially the troubled father's, the uniqueness of the boy's voice compels the female audience to suspend the rules of sexuality" (59).

    The story focuses on Delmar, a young black male known more popularly as Delly. As well as displaying a wonderful singing voice in the church choir, he demonstrates academic excellence and intelligence. His father, John, feels great anxiety due to his unproven belief that his son is gay. Hughes depicts much of the father's concern over the son's sexuality as the fear that the son's orientation will eventually foster more discrimination against him. Hughes's story tests faith in the context of a parental bond. The father's faith in God has declined due to his feeling that the son, Delmar, may not be heterosexual; the fact that the son (Christ, the unrecognized *Son*) does not exhibit more normative behavior makes the father question the son's sexual orientation and therefore God. Once a part of the Great Chain of Being or Belief is challenged, the whole hierarchy suddenly threatens to collapse. As E. M. W. Tillyard points out in *The Elizabethan World Picture*, "This metaphor [of the Great Chain of Being] served to express the unimaginable plenitude of God's creation, its unfaltering order, and its ultimate unity." He adds, "The chain stretched from the foot of God's throne to the meanest of inanimate objects. Every speck of creation was a link in the chain, and every link except those at the two extremities was simultaneously bigger and smaller than another: there could be no gap" (25–26). When the father in "Blessed Assurance" finds his faith in God tested, have his ideas about the Great Chain of Being changed? While the son seems comfortable in his somewhat fluid sexual orientation, the father rejects the perceived femininity of the son's church performance: a high-pitched musical rendition inspired by the biblical story of Ruth and composed by Dr. Jaxon. Perhaps the son believes that God would appreciate him for himself, but the father rejects the "queerly" talented son, the singer God has given him. While the son's faith enables him to cope with the alleged difference, the father's negative response manifests an unhappiness and contempt for the son (*Son*). The Christian idea of hope enables the son to achieve a freedom, but the father's religious attitude confines the range of his approval.

In reflecting on earlier work for a moment, Hughes's representation of generational conflict reflects his interest in the dynamic; his short story "Father and Son" echoes the tension that develops between generations of a family when people have different desires. Bert Lewis, who has a black mother named Cora and a white father named Colonel Thomas Norwood, experiences anger at his plight in Georgia during the early 1900s. Bert attempts to assert his manhood in an environment that seeks to emasculate black men. When Bert gets into a fight at a post office and his white father finds out about it, Norwood decides that he must control and dominate his son and even threatens to kill him. When Norwood himself later dies, Bert and his brother Willie are both lynched in connection with the father's death. As R. Baxter Miller asserts in *A Literary Criticism of Five Generations of African American Writing*, "the long story, reappearing twenty-eight years after its first publication, unifies consequently the pattern of [Hughes's] life's work in short fiction" (88). In recalling the explosive tension between father and son, in other words, the white father and the mulatto (so imperfectly God the Father and Christ the Son), Hughes reexplores in *Something in Common* an idea he had left unfinished in *The Ways of White Folks* (1934). While the themes of racial history near the beginning of his career and of sexual orientation so near the end may not be the same, the disturbing rupture between races and generations is still so. In refusing to accept the very different sons, both fathers violate the higher principles of God's law.

To return to "Blessed Assurance," John, a black male, disagrees with his son's behavior. He thinks the boy does not reflect his own ideas of manhood. Nevertheless, Delmar resists the idea of changing or altering his identity. The father's ability to send the son to a university implies that the family probably has a comfortable middle-class income. Meanwhile, Dr. Jaxon, the music minister of the church, desires for Delly to perform a woman's role rather than a man's in a song about the relationship between the biblical figure Naomi and her daughter-in-law Ruth. John's hostile reaction to the event and his ultimate anger reveal his profound worry over sexual orientation. John speculates that his son's name, Delmar, might have influenced the son's identity. He wonders if his son's sexuality derives from his own wife's family ancestry and then wonders, too, if there perhaps is a history of homosexuality in his own family. He believes he should have named his son John Jr., irrationally implying that the son would have therefore assumed the father's attributes and been heterosexual as well. Delly does not fit the socially prescribed role for young males. While he does not resist domestic chores, he enjoys playing with dolls as well. He rejects football, the sport his father played. He wears glasses, making his appearance seem effeminate to the narrating father, who perceives the youngster's style of dress, shorts, as different than that of other males, who wear jeans. John worries that his son takes too much care laundering clothes, fears that his son holds a cigarette in a feminine manner, and so on. Ridden with great anxiety over his son's transgression of gendered boundaries, John is an unreliable narrator who brings cultural and political forces to a climax.

In the book of Ruth in the King James Version of the Bible, Ruth is the daughter-in-law of a woman named Naomi. Naomi's husband and both of her sons die, leaving behind two widows named Ruth and Orpah. When Naomi decides to relocate to Bethlehem, Ruth shows loyalty to her mother-in-law by accompanying her. After they arrive, Ruth continues to show her allegiance to Naomi, and her treatment of her mother-in-law impresses Boaz, a relative of Naomi's deceased husband. Boaz eventually marries Ruth, and they have a child. Ruth's commitment to Naomi illustrates the close-knit bond that can unite individuals of the same gender.

Yet, such a bond is clearly feared among men. In a reversal of gender roles, Delmar sings the traditional female lead. So overcome by passion, Dr. Jaxon becomes emotionally spent by the youngster's voice and faints. Amid the tragicomic effects, Reverend Greene insists that the religious service must continue. As Delmar's sister Arletta perceives the impact of her brother's voice on women, she implies that the music minister's reaction may be even more excitable. To no avail, John yells for his son to stop singing. When Reverend Greene calls for people to donate money at the conclusion, the lyrics finish in the title hymn, "Blessed Assurance." Nearly thirty years after "Father and Son," Langston Hughes recognized that sexual orientation could be nearly as divisive as race.

In all three stories, "On the Road," "Big Meeting," and "Blessed Assurance," Hughes interrogates the concept of faith. He tests whether an idealistic faith can survive the Great Depression of the 1930s. By the end of his life, he still wanted to know whether the figurative divide between father and son was any different in 1963 than it had been in

1934. For nearly three decades, he had internalized and experimented with the metaphor of the Black Christ to test his faith. The result was a profound and moral contradiction. Rather than being only a theory, Christianity was actually to be *lived*. The emerging paradox became a distinguishing quality of his most quiet belief.

Notes

1. In fact, it is the precise imagery of Richard Wright's *Native Son* (1940).

Works Cited

Borden, Anne. "Heroic 'Hussies' and 'Brilliant Queers': Genderracial Resistance in the Works of Langston Hughes." *African American Review* 28.3 (1994): 333–45. *JSTOR*. Web. 9 May 2011.

Cone, James H. *A Black Theology of Liberation*. Maryknoll: Orbis, 1986.

Cullen, Countee. *The Black Christ and Other Poems*. New York: Harper, 1929.

_____. "Simon the Cyrenian Speaks." Early 87.

Culp, Mary Beth. "Religion in the Poetry of Langston Hughes." *Phylon* 48.3 (1987): 240–45. *JSTOR*. Web. 9 May 2011.

Douglas, Kelly Brown. *The Black Christ*. Maryknoll: Orbis, 1994.

Early, Gerald, ed. *My Soul's High Song*. New York: Doubleday, 1991.

The Holy Bible. Iowa Falls: World Bible, n.d.

Hughes, Langston. *The Short Stories*. Ed. R. Baxter Miller. Columbia: U of Missouri P, 2002. Vol. 15 of *The Collected Works of Langston Hughes*. Ed. Arnold Rampersad et al. 16 vols. 2001–03.

Meltzer, Milton. *Langston Hughes: A Biography*. New York: Crowell, 1968.

Miller, R. Baxter. "Langston Hughes, 1902–1967: A Brief Biography." *A Historical Guide to Langston Hughes*. Ed. Stephen C. Tracy. Oxford: Oxford UP, 2004. 23–62.

_____. *A Literary Criticism of Five Generations of African American Writing: The Artistry of Memory*. Lewiston: Mellen, 2008.

Ostrom, Hans. *A Langston Hughes Encyclopedia*. Westport: Greenwood, 2002.

_____. *Langston Hughes: A Study of the Short Fiction*. New York: Twayne, 1993.

Tillyard, E. M. W. *The Elizabethan World Picture*. New York: Vintage, 1959.

Trotter, Joe William. *The African American Experience*. Boston: Houghton, 2001.

Walker, Carolyn P. "Liberating Christ: Sargeant's Metamorphosis in Langston Hughes's 'On the Road.'" *Black American Literature Forum* 25.4 (1991): 745–52. *JSTOR*. Web. 9 May 2011.

Madam Alberta K. Johnson and the Women of the "Simple" Tales

Donna Akiba Sullivan Harper

As the 1940s began, Langston Hughes was already a well-established and celebrated writer who had made his mark with numerous volumes of poetry, a successful Broadway play (*Mulatto*, 1937), a novel (*Not without Laughter*, 1930), and short stories (*The Ways of White Folks*, 1934). What he had not yet done was create enduring characters who would become so real that readers would claim to know people just like the characters and even send gifts to them. Perhaps World War II and the urban race riots provided the catalyst for Hughes to show the world that ordinary African Americans needed to be understood and appreciated. Two enduring characters who emerged from Hughes's writing in the 1940s were Madam Alberta K. Johnson, in his poetry, and Jesse B. Semple, better known as "Simple," in his short fiction. This essay observes characteristics of several prominent women in the Simple stories and of poetic protagonist Madam Alberta K. Johnson. Taken collectively, these female characters affirm Hughes's insistence that black women should be considered in their full range of personalities, aspirations, attitudes, and situations.

Many contemporary scholars and casual readers of Langston Hughes recognize the similarities between the character Jesse B. Semple of Hughes's short fiction series and Madam Alberta K. Johnson, the narrator of a set of poems from the 1949 volume *One-Way Ticket*. However, as established scholars Sandra Y. Govan and Helen R. Houston remind readers, in some ways Madam preceded Simple, and in many ways she is neglected (96).

Correspondence with friend and collaborator Arna Bontemps indicates that Hughes drafted the poems featuring Madam as a series, *Madam to You*, while he was in residence at Yaddo, a writer's colony in New York. He had diverted his attention from his second autobiographical volume, *I Wonder as I Wander*, and was sending three of his Madam poems to *Poetry* magazine (Hughes and Bontemps, 139). Arnold Rampersad, award-winning biographer of Hughes and one of the executors of the Hughes estate, suggests that the role of Margie Polite in setting off the Harlem Riots of 1943 may have "put the creative mischief in him" that led to the creation of the suite of poems. Rampersad also points out that by naming the poetic protagonist Alberta Johnson, Hughes may have intended "to tease Arna Bontemps' wife, whose maiden name had been Alberta Johnson, although she was nothing at all like his creation" (78). In any case, as Rampersad notes, the quarterly journal *Common Ground* published the first four Madam poems in the summer 1943 issue (79). These four poems, "Madam's Past History," "Madam and Her Madam," "Madam and the Army," and "Madam and the Movies," introduced Madam Alberta K. Johnson to the world. Since Rampersad notes that the first two Madam poems had already been written in 1942, and given the time between submission and publication, one can certainly recognize that Madam had already asserted her full name and her own history before Jesse B. Semple even had his name. First mentioned in Langston Hughes's "Here to Yonder" column in the *Chicago Defender* on February 13, 1943, he was only called Hughes's "Simple Minded Friend." Not until November 3, 1945, did the character announce, "My name is Jess" (Harper, *Not So Simple* 87). Thus, while some analysts consider Madam to be "a poetic spin-off" from Simple (Barksdale, "Comic Relief" 109), she was actually the original creation.

Hughes demonstrated a lifelong tendency to express deeply felt views and attitudes of female characters. Through Madam Alberta K. Johnson, readers became acquainted with a woman who is feisty, sassy, and undaunted by anyone, including the agent for her landlord, the census taker, the telephone company, or even death. She demonstrates the same kinds of heroic attitudes that Hughes had advocated in his 1941 essay in the *Crisis*, "The Need for Heroes." Hughes writes, "We have a need for books and plays that will encourage and inspire our youth, set for them examples and patterns of conduct, move and stir them to be forthright, strong, clear-thinking, and unafraid" (*CW* 10: 225). Since his essay clearly reveals that he considers inspiration and patterns of conduct to include the everyday operations of life, Madam and Simple both qualify as the kinds of heroes he wanted to see in literature. This essay in the *Crisis* explicitly heralds those "whose English is by no means perfect." In fact, Hughes cautions young people not to be misled by movies or radio sketches into believing "that lack of proper English is always attended by servility, grotesqueness, and stupidity" (228). Hughes insists, "We know we are not weak, ignorant, frustrated, or cowed" (229). In this essay, Hughes retains a remarkable balance in gender references, signaling his intention to appreciate and to engender heroic actions in both men and women. Thus, it is evident that Hughes consciously and intentionally sought to create in his writing courageous everyday African Americans "whose words and thoughts gather up what is in our own hearts and say it clearly and plainly for all to hear" (228).

The audience reaction to the fictional Simple was far more immediate than that to the poetic Alberta K. Johnson, and the medium was certainly responsible. Although Hughes had not yet published a book-length collection of his Simple stories in 1949, when twelve of the Madam poems were published in *One-Way Ticket*, his fan mail had already made him aware that readers of the *Chicago Defender* identified with Simple. By publishing in one of the most popular and most well-read black newspapers of that era, Hughes reached a large audience, almost entirely black, that was very interested in and sympathetic to the situations in which Simple found himself. Poetry, even from beloved and popular poets such as Hughes, did not attract as large an audience among ordinary African American readers. Readers of poetry sometimes expected more complex and more erudite subjects than Madam Alberta K. Johnson. Thus, the Simple stories garnered a larger immediate audience.

Both the Madam poems and the Simple stories reflect Hughes's maturity as a writer capturing Harlem in his works. In his earliest representations of Harlem in *The Weary Blues*, daytime is scarcely represented. There is "no getting up and going to work" in those early poetic images, only the nightlife and music scene. In *Montage of a Dream Deferred*, published in 1951, Hughes reflects a full and complex portrait of Harlem. Arthur Paul Davis, the late Howard University professor and astute analyst of African American literature, demonstrates how Hughes's representation of Harlem matured by the late 1940s ("The Harlem" 277). As Davis states, both Madam Alberta K. Johnson and Jesse B. Semple reveal "Hughes's humorous yet profound understanding of the Negro urban character" ("Cool Poet" 35). Indeed, in his detailed study *Langston Hughes: The Poet and His Critics*, noted scholar and inaugural president of the Langston Hughes Society Richard K. Barksdale finds that when *One-Way Ticket* first appeared, *only* Davis perceived the link between Madam Alberta K. Johnson and Jesse B. Semple (86).

Even Hughes's treatment of his own manuscript shows a distinction and growth. According to Emily Bernard, who has scrutinized the correspondence between Hughes and his patron and friend Carl Van Vechten, Hughes broke his old pattern of sending Van Vechten his manuscripts. Bernard writes that with *One-Way Ticket*, for the first time, Hughes did *not* send his manuscript to Van Vechten. Instead, he sent it first to Bontemps (Hughes and Van Vechten 249). Hughes was comfortable with his work and with his representations of Harlem, and he no longer needed the approval of Van Vechten. Instead, he seemed more interested in having Bontemps verify the racial authenticity of the material.

Barksdale considers Alberta K. Johnson to be "Hughes' greatest comic creation in poetry" ("Comic Relief" 109). His assessment of Madam clearly matches Hughes's intentional creation of everyday heroes: "Self-reliant and aggressively independent, [Madam] represents the resolute Black matriarch who, despite ghetto pressures of ever increasing magnitude, revives and survives" (110).

While Barksdale finds that all of the "Madam to You" poems reveal "a light comic touch," he deems two of the Madam poems, "Madam and the Number Writer" and "Madam and the Phone Bill," to "reveal considerable mastery of the comic technique" (110). In *Langston Hughes: The Poet and His Critics*, Barksdale insists, "Hughes was more than a poetic dramatist; he had a comic vision that enabled him to cover the pain and suffering of black urban existence with protective layers of wit, humor, and sympathetic understanding" (86). What Barksdale describes as a "cover" can also be considered a balance. In either case, the strength and heroism of surviving pain and suffering without resorting to despair, murder, or madness exemplifies the qualities Hughes demands in his 1941 essay.

While Barksdale focuses upon the comic aspects of the poems, Anne Borden explores the ways the Madam poems present what she calls "genderracial resistance in Black women's lives." Emphasizing the exchange in "Madam and Her Madam," Borden notes that Madam Alberta K. Johnson must call her employer "Madam," but the employer calls her by her first name, even insisting, "You know, Alberta, / I love you so!" (lines 19–20).

> The fact that Madam is overworked and exploited by her employer, yet her employer claims to "love" her, points to the historic relationship between white and Black women of racist *and* sexist oppression. Though both Madam and her employer share a subordinate, female status, the oppressions heaped upon Madam are in no way lessened by the fact that her oppressor is a woman. In fact, by calling her out of her [preferred] name, Madam's female employer is attempting to *negate* Madam's status as a "real" woman. (Borden 335)

Madam Alberta K. Johnson, of course, does not succumb to the intentional or incidental demeaning of her worth and dignity. She responds to her employer with a full measure of her own dignity.

> I said, Madam,
> That may be true—
> But I'll be dogged
> If I love you! (21–24)

In other encounters, we find Madam equally assertive about her own worth and her own autonomy. She insists that the census taker should write her name exactly as she intends it to be written. "You leave my name / Just that way!" she demands in "Madam and the Census Man" (19–20). She also dismisses the billing agent for the phone company: "You say I gave my O.K.? / Well, that O.K. you may keep— / But I *sure* ain't gonna pay!" ("Madam and the Phone Bill" 38–40). While these encounters do not involve that extra level of gender identity, the reader clearly sees that Madam has no fear of authority figures.

The late poet, novelist, essayist, and social scientist Calvin C. Hernton describes categories of women in the works of Hughes. He identifies Madam Alberta K. Johnson as a kind of "Blues Jazz Woman." He considers her ownership of businesses, a beauty parlor and a barbecue stand, as evidence of her having "plant[ed] her feet in the men's world" (109). In his explication of Madam's outspoken interactions with persons of power, Hernton declares that Madam "is a womanish woman." Moreover, in his analysis of her confident independence, Hernton finds Madam to be "an existential woman" (111).

> She will accept nothing less than equality with men, and hardly any man can stand equality with a woman. Madam is an urbanized, modernized version of Blues Jazz Women who are alone and like it. They are women who are refined and have adapted themselves to coping effectively with the realities of their lives. Though her circumstances are less than ideal, she will "get along." Madam is *Madam* to the world. (112)

Dellita Martin, scholar of world languages and past president of the Langston Hughes Society, explores the dramatic monologue technique in the Madam poems. She asserts that the technique is at least suggested by the silent implied listener to whom Madam reveals her circumstances. Martin argues, "Langston Hughes is one of very few male writers to achieve complex female characterizations" (99).

R. Baxter Miller, distinguished scholar and past president of the Langston Hughes Society, discusses the Madam poems within a broader analysis of the archetypes of woman in Hughes's works. Miller asserts, "To the archetype of woman, Hughes could graft his own ethnic vision; indeed, he could build upon it his most captivating themes: heroic endurance, human mortality, marital desertion, and enduring art" ("'No Crystal'" 109). Miller finds that "the 'Madam Poems' restore a comic sense to the archetype, but they eliminate the mythic level" (113). Miller notes that "the thematic range of the [*Madam to You*] collection includes the following: nationalism, self-reliance, and self-doubt. Here humor and worldly vision supplant myth" (113).

Most critics only evaluate the twelve poems that were published in *One-Way Ticket*. However, based upon *The Collected Poems of Langston Hughes*, there were actually eighteen Madam poems. "Madam and the Army," "Madam and the Crime Wave," "Madam and the Insurance Man," "Madam and the Movies," "Madam and the Newsboy," and "Madam's Christmas" were not included in the published volumes Hughes compiled—and rightly so. Their topics and narrative techniques fall short of those in the poems Hughes reprinted in *One-Way Ticket* and *Selected Poems*.

Composer Elie Siegmeister, characterized as a composer who "wrote music for the common folk" (Oja 158), wrote a song cycle for voice and piano called *Madam to You*. He and Hughes evidently shared their creative ideas while both were at Yaddo. Identified as part of Siegmeister's "large and important output of solo songs and of works for musical theater," *Madam to You* (1964) was only one of Siegmeister's songs set to poetry by Langston Hughes (175). In his liner notes for *Madam to You*, the composer calls Madam "the typical black woman of the Harlem tenements, spunky, bright, in love with life, and standing up (long before women's lib) to all 'put-downs'" (qtd. in Oja 176). Thus, although Govan and Houston bemoan Madam's absence from most anthologies, she is clearly recognized and celebrated in much scholarship and in some musical compositions.

How does Madam Alberta K. Johnson compare to the women of the Simple tales? Langston Hughes launched his episodic narratives in February of 1943, and he continued to bring Simple's voice to the public until 1965. While Simple can easily be considered hostile or insensitive to women, or misogynistic—particularly in the stories most commonly read because of their inclusion in *The Best of Simple*—other stories present a more balanced and often respectful view of women. A few stories even feature women, and several women reappear throughout the twenty-two year history of the Simple stories.

Donna Akiba Sullivan Harper was one of the earliest critics to urge readers to see how Simple distinguishes between the various kinds of women in his life. In "Langston Hughes as Cultural Conservator" (1988), she offers a summary of the women in the Simple stories.

> Simple deeply appreciates the genuine, abiding, sensitive love he has received from some women, and he responds to those women by striving to accomplish his personal best. By contrast, Simple recognizes deceit, exploitation, and disrespect exhibited towards him by other women. He responds to these other women with callousness, hostility, and insult. . . . Simple categorizes women, but he does not stereotype them. He distinguishes individuals within the categories. Moreover, he recognizes and praises the benefits of support and encouragement from loving women. (15)

So, which women does he insult? Which women does he appreciate?

The most prominent woman is Simple's primary love interest, Joyce Lane Semple. She epitomizes the sensitive and loving woman—and she is never a doormat! Her love for Simple does not exempt him from the requirement to behave in the manner she deems appropriate. Aspiring for acceptance in the highest echelons of society, Joyce insists upon respectable behavior from Simple when they are dating. She insists upon his divorce from his first wife—even if she has to pay for one-third the cost of it. In "Blue Evening," when she observes another woman holding a party in his room to which she was not invited, Joyce walks away in a dignified manner that shatters Simple. As his wife, Joyce Lane Semple insists that the budget must be balanced. Simple points out the gendered difference in her handling of the family finances:

> [A] woman balances different from a man. You [Boyd] are not married so, whenever you want to, you can shift your balance around—and pull a hype on yourself. But my wife wants our budget to come out even each and every week. A woman's voice is sweet to hear when it is full of love, but not when the budget don't balance. Joyce can figure backwards, count pennies down to the last Indian head, and don't mess with dollar bills! Every time I break a dollar, I think about what will happen at home. (*CW* 8: 255)

Ultimately, Joyce motivates Simple to move out of Harlem. Considering how dearly he loves Harlem, her success in effecting that move testifies to her persuasive powers.

Like most topics and characters in the Simple stories, Joyce is revealed to readers primarily through Simple's biased views. We seldom hear her voice except as parroted or interpreted by Simple, who does not share all of her views and social aspirations. Although *The Best of Simple* depicts her as a social climber comfortable with shallow markings of high society, episodes placed into book-length collections such as *The Return of Simple* and volume 8 of *The Collected Works of Langston Hughes*, both edited by Harper and published after Hughes's death, reveal that Joyce also was politically aware and had an African-centered identity.

The female character in the Simple stories who is most like Simple's "bar buddy" and foil, Boyd, and least like most of Hughes's other recurring female characters is Simple's cousin Lynn Clarisse. She only appears in a few episodes, first collected in *Simple's Uncle Sam*, but she makes a lingering impression on Boyd and represents the well-educated, politically active women who helped to make the civil rights movement a success. Introduced in the episode named for her, Lynn Clarisse reads extensively and boasts a degree from Fisk University, the first historically black college to form a chapter of Phi Beta Kappa. Hughes alludes to his good friend Bontemps when Lynn Clarisse announces that Fisk "has one of the best libraries in the country, and a librarian who helps students choose good books" (*CW* 8: 210). Bontemps was for many years the chief librarian at Fisk.

The "Lynn Clarisse" episode is one of the few Simple stories from which Simple himself is essentially missing. Instead, Boyd and Lynn Clarisse discuss literature, theater, and the Freedom Rides—all of which have been meaningful to this young woman visiting the North for the first time. In "Soul Food," Boyd also refers to her as being "pretty" (228). Boyd finds her a "mystery," however. He is intrigued by a woman who navigates existentialism and Southern violence with equal grace.

> "There are no limits to where the mind or body goes," said Lynn Clarisse. "My body has been on Freedom Rides. See that scar where an Alabama cop tried to break my neck with his billy club. He just broke my shoulder, but it left a scar on my neck where his club burst the skin open. It might sound pretentious to say it, but while my body was in Alabama that night, my mind was on Sartre and Genet." (209)

Lynn Clarisse is not evident in many Simple stories, but she represents a very important aspect of the variety of women Langston Hughes included in his short fiction.

The female character most similar to Madam Alberta K. Johnson is Jesse B. Semple's landlady, also known as "Madam." In nearly every episode in which Simple mentions her, he insults and resents her. The qualities of business ownership and refusal to be trampled are as evident in the landlady as they had been in the Madam poems. The huge distinction between these two Madam characters is that Madam Alberta K. Johnson dramatically narrates her own story, while the landlady's messages are usually filtered through the biased delivery of Simple himself.

When represented only through the eyes of Simple, the landlady's house rules appear capricious, and she seems hostile to Simple. However, in one episode, "Nothing but Roomers," she narrates her own story in detail. Madam Butler reveals that she has hardened herself because of disappointments in love and sabotage in business. Indeed, when Madam Butler says she would tell any woman "a roof over your head is better than a husband in your bed," for a moment the standard male-to-male dialogue typical of the Simple stories is disrupted convincingly. For some reason, Hughes did not choose to collect "Nothing but Roomers" in *The Best of Simple*. Thus, only by reading *Simple Takes a Wife*, volume 7 of the *Collected Works*, or *The Return of Simple* can readers actually hear from Madam Butler. Unless they read "Nothing but Roomers," readers will not fully appreciate how similar these two no-nonsense Madams are.

Another familiar female in the Simple stories is Zarita, the friendly frequenter of the bar where Simple drinks his beer. Simple has mixed reactions to Zarita, depending upon whether she has interfered with his relationship with Joyce. Zarita is what Hernton considers "the third and ultimate progression of Blues Jazz Women in Hughes's work," which he calls "the Wild Woman"—although she is not the "Warrior Woman" Hernton quickly connects to this type of woman. However, like Harriett Williams, the youngest daughter in *Not without Laughter* (1930), Zarita will "sing, dance, and make merry around the house," but she "will not have a 'respectable' job" (112).

Zarita's one moment to directly share her feelings about her love life comes in the play *Simply Heavenly* (1957). Compelled by theatrical requirements to divide lines and remove the typical fictional scene of two men conversing in a bar, Hughes gives Zarita a few moments of her own in act 2, scene 1. After promising the nearly married Simple that she will stay out of his life, Zarita is left in the bar with the other characters when Simple and Boyd leave—much earlier than Simple habitually used to leave the bar.

> ARCIE. It ain't but a quarter to twelve. What's happening to Simple?
> ZARITA. He's getting domesticated. You know, Arcie, I wish someone would feel about me the way Simple feels about Joyce, and she about him, even if they do have their ups and downs. I guess a little trouble now and then just helps to draw people together. But you got to have somebody to come together with. (*CW* 6: 219)

The vulnerability Zarita reveals resembles similar short-lived statements from Madam Alberta K. Johnson in "Madam and Her Might-Have-Been" and Madam Butler the landlady in "Nothing but Roomers." Hughes therefore preserves at least a small glimmer of the romantic in these women, despite their self-sufficient outer shells.

Other women in the Simple stories exemplify a broad range of attitudes and behaviors that range from exploitative to innovative. Cousin Minnie, Simple's cousin from Virginia, manifests traits that Simple had shown, such as a fondness for alcoholic beverages and pleasure in the opposite sex. Much like Harriett Williams and Zarita, Minnie is one of the "Wild Women" of the Blues/Jazz variety that Hernton outlines. However, whereas Madam Butler and Madam Alberta K. Johnson provide for themselves, Minnie proudly works schemes rather than jobs: "I pay the rent on my place—with *his* money, naturally, if I can get it. I close the door to my place when the dough don't come no more. I change the lock when I can no longer stand his face—and his contribution to the pot is a disgrace. I rule!" ("Miss Boss"; *CW* 8: 244). Moreover, Simple admits, "That chick carries her licker well and protects her ladyhood, too. Minnie knows she is a lone woman in this big city—except for me, her Cousin Jess" ("Ladyhood" 203).

Minnie may have no male to "protect" her, but she clearly knows how to avenge her own wrongs and how to protect herself, even resorting to physical violence if necessary. Whereas the typical blues speaker only wishes she could "fly like the eagle flies" and "scratch out the eyes" of her disrespecting man ("Hard Daddy" 16, 18), Cousin Minnie moves beyond fantasy revenge and actually takes action. In "Cousin Minnie Wins," Minnie shares her carefully crafted revenge on a man who "went around telling folks [she] wasn't nothing but his rag doll till his china doll comes" (291). Minnie took her time planning her revenge, and she took him by surprise. On the chosen day, he returned "home" to find no heat, no electricity, no phone, no furniture, no clothes, no food, and no Minnie! On another occasion, with a different man, Minnie hit the offender with a beer bottle so that "he were conked and crowned both all at once" ("Self-Protection" 193). Simple, of course, offers a chauvinistic view of her strategies.

> "[I]n protecting her ladyhood, Minnie does not always act like a lady. . . . It would have been more politer—and cheaper, too—had Minnie hit him with something that did not contain good alcohol," said Simple. "Or if she had screamed and throwed a glass. But Minnie did not scream. She just up and knocked the man out with a bottle. Should not a lady settle things in a more gentler manner? Maybe even faint first?" ("Ladyhood" 204)

However, when Boyd reminds Simple that Minnie is not one of the sheltered or wealthy "ladies" of antiquity, Simple agrees. "To remain a lady, Minnie often has to fight. It is not always easy for a colored lady to keep her ladyhood" (205).

During the Harlem Riot of 1964, Minnie forgets about her "ladyhood" and participates wholeheartedly in the urban outburst. However, whereas Simple himself was able to participate in the riot of 1943 and run off ("Feet Live Their Own Life"; *CW* 7: 22–23), Minnie gets struck by a bottle that was not aimed at her. Her injury also costs her a wig—another liability that Simple and other men would not have borne. Nevertheless, as Rita B. Dandridge emphasizes, Minnie exerts revolutionary energy in her efforts during the riot. Objecting to the admonitions of the so-called leaders for the masses to be "cool," Minnie imagines herself talking to those leaders. Empowered by her own actions and claiming that having been "stitched up" in Harlem Hospital had her "thinking better than before" ("Wigs for Freedom"; *CW* 8: 248), Minnie holds forth:

> I lost my forty-dollar wig in the riots, . . . [b]ut what is one wig more or less to give for freedom? One wig not to go slow. One wig not to be cool. One wig not to get off the streets. When it is a long hot summer, where else but in the streets, fool, can I be cool? Uncontrollable? Who says I was uncontrollable? Huh! I knowed what I was doing. I did not lose my head because when I throwed a bottle, I knewed what I was throwing at. I were throwing at Jim Crow, Mr. K. K. Krow—at which I aimed my throw. (251)

The rhyming words in her rhetoric signify the kind of street poetry that readers have heard from Simple in some of his pontifications, and they also signify the inherent poetry that Hughes evidently heard in his close observations of ordinary folks. Dandridge compares Minnie to Malcolm X in her outspoken and unrestrained efforts to quell Jim Crow (279–81).

Cousin Minnie even demonstrates her strength when she reveals that she has been diagnosed with a tumor. Reluctantly, she tells Simple about her situation:

> Jess, the doctors say I have a tumor, and when they say that, you are liable to have cancer. . . . I did not tell you I was sick before, I do not tell you I am sick now. But I am. Monday I go to be prepared for the operation. Maybe it might not take like vaccination. If it do not take, I am gone to Glory. If I go to Glory, maybe you will remember me who set beside you once on this bar stool. And if not, or if so, anyhow, good-by. ("Sympathy"; *CW* 8: 272)

Simple realizes that she leaves the bar without even telling him in which hospital she would be getting her surgery. Simple concludes,

"Minnie would borrow money from me at the drop of a hat. Yes, she would. But I guess she doesn't want to borrow sympathy" (272).

The variety of female characters in the Simple stories echoes the much smaller distinction drawn between Simple and his bar buddy and foil, Boyd. In his early discussion of Simple, Davis finds an appealing resonance in the divergent views represented by Boyd and Simple: "As we read these dialogues, we often find ourselves giving lip-service to the sophisticated Hughes [Boyd] side of the debate while our hearts share Simple's cruder but more realistic attitude" ("Jesse B." 22). Likewise, readers might admire the upward mobility and social aspirations Joyce Lane Semple represents while still appreciating the cavalier, fun life of Zarita or the pragmatic realism of Madam Butler, the landlady.

In her analysis of Joyce, Lynn Clarisse, and Cousin Minnie as freedom fighters, Dandridge notes that "Hughes severs his females from the traditional role of black matriarch" (283). This is perhaps the most significant common thread that all of these women from the Simple stories share with Madam Alberta K. Johnson. While the matriarch is one of the most pervasive archetypes in African American literature, Langston Hughes chose to focus upon the many other ways black women became vital members of their communities.

Works Cited

Barksdale, Richard K. "Comic Relief in Langston Hughes' Poetry." *Black American Literature Forum* 15.3 (1981): 108–11. *JSTOR*. Web. 17 June 2011.

――――. *Langston Hughes: The Poet and His Critics*. Chicago: ALA, 1977.

Borden, Anne. "Heroic 'Hussies' and 'Brilliant Queers': Genderracial Resistance in the Works of Langston Hughes." *African American Review* 28.3 (1994): 333–45. *JSTOR*. Web. 17 June 2011.

Dandridge, Rita B. "The Black Woman as a Freedom Fighter in Langston Hughes' Simple's Uncle Sam." *CLA Journal* 118.2 (1974): 273–83.

Davis, Arthur P. "The Harlem of Langston Hughes' Poetry." *Phylon* 13.4 (1952): 276–83. *JSTOR*. Web. 17 June 2011.

――――. "Jesse B. Semple: Negro American." *Phylon* 15.1 (1954): 21–28. *JSTOR*. Web. 17 June 2011.

_____. "Langston Hughes: Cool Poet." *CLA Journal* 11 (1968): 276–83. Rpt. in *Langston Hughes: Black Genius*. Ed. Therman B. O'Daniel. New York: Morrow, 1971. 18–38.

Govan, Sandra Y., and Helen R. Houston. "Recovering a Woman's Voice: Madam Alberta K. Johnson." *Langston Hughes Review* 17 (2002): 96–114.

Harper, Donna Akiba Sullivan. "Langston Hughes as Cultural Conservator: Women in the Life of a 'Negro Everyman.'" *Langston Hughes Review* 7.2 (1988): 15–21.

_____. *Not So Simple: The "Simple" Stories by Langston Hughes*. Columbia: U of Missouri P, 1995.

Hernton, Calvin C. "Black Women in the Life and Work of Langston Hughes: Feministic Writings of a Male Poet." *The Sexual Mountain and Black Women Writers: Adventures in Sex, Literature and Real Life*. New York: Anchor, 1987. 89–118.

Hughes, Langston. *The Collected Poems of Langston Hughes*. Ed. Arnold Rampersad and David Roessel. New York, Knopf, 1994.

_____. *The Collected Works of Langston Hughes*. Ed. Arnold Rampersad, et al. 16 vols. Columbia: U of Missouri P, 2001–03.

Hughes, Langston, and Arna Bontemps. *Arna Bontemps–Langston Hughes Letters, 1925–1967*. Ed. Charles H. Nichols. NY: Dodd, 1980.

Hughes, Langston, and Carl Van Vechten. *Remember Me to Harlem: The Letters of Langston Hughes and Carl Van Vechten*. Ed. Emily Bernard. New York: Vintage, 2001.

Jarraway, David R. "Montage of an Otherness Deferred: Dreaming Subjectivity in Langston Hughes." *American Literature* 68.4 (1996): 819–47. *JSTOR*. Web. 17 June 2011.

Klotman, Phillis R. "Langston Hughes's Jess B. Semple and the Blues." *Phylon* 36.1 (1975): 68–77. *JSTOR*. Web. 17 June 2011.

Martin, Dellita L. "The 'Madam Poems' as Dramatic Monologue." *Black American Literature Forum* 15.3 (1981): 97–99. *JSTOR*. Web. 17 June 2011.

Miller, R. Baxter. "Introduction: Langston Hughes and the 1980s—Rehumanization of Theory." *Black American Literature Forum* 15.3 (1981): 83–84. *JSTOR*. Web. 17 June 2011.

_____. "'No Crystal Stair': Unity, Archetype and Symbol in Langston Hughes's Poems on Women." *Negro American Literature Forum* 9.4 (1975): 109–14. *JSTOR*. Web. 17 June 2011.

Oja, Carol J. "Composer with a Conscience: Elie Siegmeister in Profile." *American Music* 6.2 (1988): 158–80. *JSTOR*. Web. 17 June 2011.

Rampersad, Arnold. *The Life of Langston Hughes*. Vol. 2. New York: Oxford UP, 1988.

Without Respect for Gender: Damnable Inference in "Blessed Assurance"

Steven C. Tracy

Dreams have always figured prominently in the works of Langston Hughes. In fact, one might proffer that much of Hughes's work is devoted to outlining, celebrating, and agitating on behalf of the dreams of oppressed and marginalized peoples worldwide, with particular focus on the dreams of African Americans. As a self-appointed "dream keeper" who knew the value of handling dreams with the greatest reverence and care, Hughes explored the way the dreams of various people were constructed in their minds and in the contexts of social and political realities and how they were dashed when either external or internal forces limited people's visions or capacities to understand how their plans and dreams encroached upon the plans and dreams of others. The idea of living the American dream of success measured in economic and hierarchical comfort, of course, is very much tied into notions of "normality" prevalent in society at any given time—one thinks of Edward Albee's 1961 production of *The American Dream*, in which absurd central characters "Mommy" and "Daddy" murder their adopted son for not exemplifying their notions of the American dream son. Those notions of the American dream, frequently privileging patriarchal, white, straight, and middle-class values, reflect a hegemony that privileges masculinity and heterosexuality as important components of the American dream as well. Hence, "deviation" from this heterosexual norm places the American dream of an "ideal" nuclear family out of reach.

Langston Hughes's short story "Blessed Assurance," first published in the collection *Something in Common* in 1963, has received some attention in recent years as a result of intensified debates regarding Hughes's sexual orientation. Arnold Rampersad, who finds "satire all around" in the story, focuses on the ridiculous males in the work and finds no "psychological questing into the sexual condition." He characterizes the story as the musings of Hughes, "the sophisticated voyeur" (2: 334). Conversely, Anne Borden asserts that Hughes employs irony in the story to "move homosexuality out of the realm of the dangerous and deviant in our minds," and suggests that it "creates dialogue on its possible uses in creating social change" (339)—an argument with which Charles I. Nero agrees (192). However, it is important to note that Hughes wrote the short story from the third-person limited point of view, offering only the interior thoughts of the father, John, and not of the other characters of the story. As a result, we must question some of the assumptions that John, and perhaps sometimes readers of the story, takes for granted regarding his son, Delly. John's state of mind, obvious homophobic prejudices, superficial judgments, and concept of what a "normal" American family is may well distort or obscure the reality of the situations in which he observes Delly.

What Hughes has highlighted here, of course, is the problem of the unreliability of the narrator, which adds an additional layer of nuance and complexity to his exploration of homophobic masculinity. In this case, the narration is in the third-person limited point of view, with John as a Jamesian "center of consciousness" to whose thoughts and opinions we have access. The particular advantage of this point of view is that it allows Hughes to plumb the depths of the father's feelings while maintaining a certain distance from those feelings, producing an ironic context for the information offered to the reader by John as well as a lens through which to view John's distorted feelings. As readers we must determine the author's distance from the father's attitudes by measuring the tone, particularly irony, with which Hughes portrays the father's attitudes towards his son, society, and ultimately himself. Considered in the context of Hughes's other work, which evidences the values of universal respect and tolerance, including a gendered advocacy of women's rights to safety, respect, and equality as revealed in his sympathetic portrayals of women and a particularly deep feeling for the needs and desires of children as demonstrated by his commitment to children's writing, Hughes's interrogations of the father's interior monologues are telling. The father, psychologically and socially crippled by feelings of his own inadequacy in relation to what he sees as his emasculated and subverted role in his marriage, filters the details of the story through this boiling and distorted alembic to produce "his" story, the attitudes of which are inversely proportional to Hughes's sensibilities.

The story is propelled frantically through the father's fear, expressed in straightforward and uncategorical terms, of his son's homosexuality. Delly, it seems, evinces characteristics that seem to the father more feminine than masculine. The father sees it as his duty to "fix" his son's defects by diverting him from the interests that embarrass the father but seem not to bother Delly at all. A number of these fears are superficial and shortsighted on the father's part: he thinks Delly's name is effeminate, and he worries about Delly's "excessive" sensitivity. Others are petty and cruel. Ultimately, fear leads John to challenge the authority of God, setting up the climax in which Delly, John, and Manley Jaxon form a perverse trinity in a church service where the blaspheming "god" John rains curses on his own son, Jaxon's spirit faints in ecstasy, and the three of them are rocked by John's unholy self-alienation. The climax mocks the moment of the evocation of God in the church service, setting John's hypocrisy and bigotry alongside the flash of the spirit produced by Delly's spiritual performance. However, the ambiguity of the relationship between Delly and Jaxon, and the possibility that John could be right about Delly's orientation, makes definitive interpretation of what "really" happens—homosexual or spiritual, or some combination of the two—impossible.

The story is not about Delly's homosexuality because we do not know whether he is, in fact, homosexual. We only know what his father thinks. Rather, the story demonstrates how prejudices that establish exclusive parameters for what the family is in the concept of the American dream—white, middle class, heterosexual—can distort our perceptions of reality, causing us to jump to unwarranted conclusions based upon partial and questionable "evidence." Significantly, at times Hughes seems to play with his readers by employing perversely humorous details in the story that, when recognized and deconstructed, deflate the false sexual implications suggested by the details. Ultimately, the story exposes the perversions of reality through which prejudicial perceptions based on societal gender constructions can put us and demonstrates how we act upon unfounded judgments rooted in hateful stereotypes. Furthermore, since John's desire to project the image of a family that fits the American ideal is so overwhelming to him that he prejudges and disrespects his son, Hughes's story constitutes an indictment of this manifestation of the American dream.

This is not to say that Hughes is not commenting on the horrors of homophobia—he most definitely is—but he comments on them through the veil of unverified accusation. Of course, Hughes was no stranger to attacks based on unfair or unverified allegations, which he had faced a few years earlier when he was called to testify before Senator Joseph McCarthy's subcommittee. The McCarthy chapter of American history arose from the ambitions of one man whose quest for power beyond the principles of democracy resulted in a narrative of the times that was filtered through his distorted vision. Many lives were destroyed out of fear that "weakness" would allow communists, whose supposed threat to the United States needed to be quashed in order to make the country safe, to overrun and destroy democracy from within. Of course, when Woodrow Wilson delivered a version of that phrase in 1917, the irony of an undemocratic "democracy" making the world safe for democracy was not lost on African Americans, who wondered when democracy would come home to roost.

In 1950, a little more than a decade before "Blessed Assurance" was published, Hughes had been named and attacked in *Red Channels: The Report of Communist Influence in Radio and Television* (Rampersad 2: 14). It was not his first run-in with the hobgoblins of political correctness—he was picketed in 1940 over "Goodbye Christ," and he had split with composer William Grant Still in 1949 when Still accused him of sabotaging their opera *Troubled Island* with his left-wing attitudes (Rampersad 2: 12). By 1953, when he appeared before McCarthy's subcommittee, Hughes, who had mounted a principled defense of fellow leftist W. E. B. Du Bois in 1951, was apologetic and badly shaken; though he did not "name names," he did renounce some past associations and "implicitly repudiated" the Left (Rampersad 2: 220). Later he also eliminated Paul Robeson from his book *Famous Negro Music Makers* (1955), under pressure from publishers. In his biography of Hughes, Rampersad suggests that Hughes, "as in the case of his sexuality . . . had allowed the expression of his radical political zeal to wither, to atrophy, to evaporate" (2: 220).

The connection between Hughes's bout with political correctness and his challenge to sexual correctness may well be informed by the political experience. After all, the story is *John's* vision of events—as the Red Menace was McCarthy's—and John dominates the narrative in such a way as to bully readers into accepting his assertions. Only through sly and nuanced irony does Hughes distance himself from John's attitudes and slowly deconstruct John's narrative. Just as McCarthy's speeches exploited Cold War tensions and fears of communism, John finds the sexual and social tensions in his own life so unbearable that he expresses and exploits sexual stereotypes and fears to distance himself from his son's "sexual heresy." Though John is not a demagogue as McCarthy was, largely because he fears implication in his son's sexual orientation, he becomes so overwhelmed by his feelings that they dominate his thought and narrative, crowding out dissent. Just as Edward R. Murrow and others objected to McCarthy's actions, Hughes's readers repudiate John's attitudes.

In a general sense, the story may be read as an attack on such unfair and unverified allegations, but we may also interpret the story as a metaphor for contemporary debate over Hughes's sexuality. That is, Hughes is confronting speculation about his own sexual orientation in the story, suggesting that for him, the matter of sexual orientation—and other issues—is personal, as previously noted in his poem "Personal." Furthermore, he perhaps suggests that such speculation regarding his sexuality is more a reflection of his critics' issues—as is John's speculation in the story—than his own.

Although the story is told from the third-person point of view, Hughes clearly offers us greater access to the thoughts of John than of anyone else. In fact, the story begins with a thought that John will not, out of his own sense of shame, speak out loud: "Unfortunately (and to John's distrust of God) it seemed his son was turning out to be a queer" (*Short Stories* 231). Furthermore, the statement immediately raises questions concerning point of view. What, the reader asks, is queerness? The use of the term by people situated differently in relation to the gay community connotes different meanings. On the one hand, it is a derogatory term used by enemies of the gay community that associates difference with immoral deviance. On the other, the term reverses the meaning by embracing the notion and nature of difference as natural. The clash between the two uses produces a dilemma. Is it felicitous difference, or is it an exponential strangeness that is a shock to conventional sensibilities? Then again, supporters might argue, what is wrong with unconventionality in a stagnating or repressive society—or anywhere? Where is the line between acceptable and unacceptable difference? And to whom should this all be submitted for approval? In the case of Hughes's story, John is the arbiter—or rather, the judge, jury, and executioner, empowered by centuries of homophobia and gender politics to impose his limited sense of normality and value upon the world.

It is an interesting opening statement because it puts John at odds with his God—a rather arrogant position for a presumably Christian person to take—based not on some kind of assurance (blessed or otherwise) regarding his son's homosexuality but on what *seems* to be the case. The sentence immediately exposes the father's homophobia, all the uglier for his derogatory epithet. Though such homophobic responses by parents would not have been uncommon at the time the story was written and indeed are not unknown today, such a baldly disdainful rejection of a son by a parent based upon suspicion is indeed shocking. When occurring within a sentence that criticizes a God who, in the Christian mythology, offered his own son in sacrifice for the good of the world, this father's rejection of his son is indeed anti-Christian, offering a clear criticism of the father. Indeed, he has put himself in the place of God, questioning and judging that deity, and he sacrifices his son not to save the world, but to save his own ego.

Of course, one source for the notion of the American dream is the Puritan notion of election, of being chosen by God. According to Puritan beliefs, people prosper in this world because God has chosen them and predestined them to heavenly rewards that are reflected in earthly success. In the story, John reflects a general sense of being beaten down by his lot in life, with his wandering wife and "effeminate" son, but he does not seem able to recognize his receding American dream family as a product of his own failures of sensitivity and perception. Although he clearly wishes to be among the elect and live vicariously through the "masculine" achievements of a heterosexual son, John interprets his son's supposed homosexuality as a punishment from God that separates his family from the norm. John resents what he perceives as God's judgment upon him.

John's basis for believing his son to be "queer" and a "sissy" centers on superficial perceptions he has regarding his son's looks and behavior that are based on gender stereotypes. In John's mind, several elements of his son's behavior add up to an effeminacy unnatural in heterosexuals. He agonizes rather ridiculously over his son's cleanliness, fashion sense, choice of frames for his glasses, cooperativeness with his sister, acceptance of chores John feels better left to sister Arletta, and lack of interest in football. Even though Delly is active in other sports, such as marbles, baseball, and tennis, his willingness to play dolls with his sister is enough to provoke criticism and suspicion from John. Hughes is, of course, mocking the attitude fostered in our society that males are not, or should not be, interested in or concerned about attitudes and behaviors that bespeak sensitivity, thoughtfulness, and fastidiousness about appearance, since the qualities that help males succeed in a patriarchal society are more individualistic and combative. Based on this circumstantial evidence, John reaches the conclusion that his son is homosexual, inferring that such behavior translates into a particular sexual orientation, whereas it may only reflect being brought up in a particular behavioral environment.

John may be particularly paranoid regarding Delly's sexual orientation because of what might be perceived as an external challenge to his own masculinity. In the story, John's wife has abandoned John and the children for another man. But even when he and his wife were together, she seems to have had the upper hand in the relationship, which during those social times may have been more typified by the man "wearing the pants" in the family. For example, the wife, whose name is never mentioned, forces the name Delmar on the child over John's objection—a decision John regrets and rather irrationally relates to Delly's "homosexuality." The name itself was actually the name of John's father-in-law. Thus, John's "male power" is being usurped by both his wife and her father, making John feel less dominant, less in control of a relationship that would have been conventionally dominated by males at that time. Furthermore, the name Delmar translates as "of the sea," which is itself a strong archetypal feminine symbol in classical mythology. This is either a source of John's worry or perhaps a sly bit of wordplay on Hughes's part that emphasizes once again the ambiguity of Delly's sexual status and Hughes's willingness to satirize through his ambiguous references.

The separation of John and his wife contains indicators of John's haunting self-doubt as well. When John's wife runs away, it is with a man described as making "more money than any Negro in their church," a man who owns a Cadillac and has racketeering connections. Indeed, the man is designated her "burly lover" (232). The outward trappings of success that symbolize the achievement of the American dream—money, possessions, and powerful connections—and a physical status that clearly seems imposing and challenging may indeed cause John to attempt to make up for his shortcomings and the fracturing of his family by longing for a more conventionally "masculine" demeanor in his son. In fact, it may also cause him to exaggerate the way he sees his son's demeanor because of his own wounded male pride. Delly likes his "not-yet-legal stepfather," an indication, perhaps, that John is not all he could be for Delly, causing Delly to seek a stronger male parent, or at least one who might not criticize and insult his behavior. John, in fact, seems peculiarly impotent throughout the story, usually thinking or muttering to himself but rarely acting in any effectual way. As a result, his own attitudes may be motivated by a deflated ego seeking relief in more masculine behavior from his son.

John does not seem to see such masculine behavior in Delly's relationship with the church's minister of music, Manley Jaxon. It is a sardonic choice of name by Hughes, particularly given John's supposition that Manley is homosexual as well. While John might opine that a homosexual's behavior is not "manly" at all, by naming the character "Manley," Hughes clearly implies that there is nothing inherently unmanly about being homosexual—a notion very likely wasted on John as well as on much of a mainstream America that clearly valued a macho and authoritative head of household. The surname may be a reference to the well-known entertainer and female impersonator Frankie "Half-Pint" Jaxon, adding another gender boundary–breaking element to the reference. The diminutive Frankie Jaxon was well known on the early vaudeville blues circuit, appearing regularly in New York in the early 1920s and then settling in Chicago in 1927—both locations well known to Hughes. Manley Jaxon is clearly a man, whether heterosexual or not, and a valued church member whose contributions do not seem to be affected by his possible sexual orientation, except in the prejudicial minds of those who might judge him based on gender prejudice. Clearly he is good at what he does, and he is a positive influence on Delly. He even seems to appreciate and validate Delly at a level that John cannot match, and there is nary a shred of evidence in the story that there has been any sexual contact between them. Just as with Delly, John seems to have no concrete support for his supposition regarding Jaxon's homosexuality, only what he perceives to be Jaxon's undue interest in his son.

The climactic point of the story, and the point of greatest humiliation for John, comes with Delly's performance of Jaxon's original anthem, which he has dedicated to Delmar. For John, such a dedication from one man to another itself is improper and indicative of an unnatural connection. Further, the core text for the anthem, taken from the book of Ruth in the Old Testament, expresses a deep attraction and devotion that implies, in conjunction with the dedication, a devotion of composer to the dedicatee. The composition's origin in the Book of Ruth is significant in that the Book of Ruth deals with an idyllic romance that is built around a quest for a home and emphasizes family, religious devotion, and love. These do not seem to be the prevailing values of John's household, where his own personal social and sexual status and viewpoint are exalted. The words of the anthem are spoken by Ruth to her mother-in-law, Naomi, when Ruth refuses to part with her after the males of the family die and the females are left widows. Delly, living with John, clearly likes his stepfather, probably because his own father is both critical and ashamed of him. His attachment to a male who is not a blood relative mirrors the same-sex attachment of Ruth and her mother-in-law. The fact that the words are spoken by one woman to another is a sign that love and devotion are not exclusively emotions exchanged in a heterosexual relationship. In fact, as is suggested by the hymn "Blessed Assurance," which gives the story its title, it is Delly's love for another man, Christ, that has "saved" him from a life of sin—another essential same-sex attachment. Additionally, Ruth's expressed love and devotion for Naomi indicate not homosexual love but family commitment. Therefore, John's supposition of an improper relationship as symbolized in the song is clearly undercut by the original source in the Book of Ruth. Hughes adds that one of the anthems that the church choir specializes in is "Jesu, Joy of Man's Desiring," which references the love of man for the male Jesus Christ and specifically indicates that such a "desiring" is not improper, underscoring Hughes's clear critique of gender-based stereotyping and homophobic paranoia.

Jaxon's choice of Delly to sing the lead part in the performance also incenses John, though again Hughes undercuts the implications of homosexuality in his treatment of Delly's performance. Jaxon's announced explanation of why Delly is given the lead is a rather bad sexual pun on Hughes's part. Rather than saying that the women's voices do not carry, or indeed creating some other "shortcoming," Hughes has Jaxon explain that the girls have no "projection." Obviously, the terminology can refer to the volume or carrying power of the voice, but it can also, in a double entendre, refer to the absence of a penis—no penile projection. However, readers might not even think of that second meaning at all if not for John's other suggestions of homosexual overtones. Once John sets our thoughts in motion along such lines, the idea that a homosexual Jaxon might prefer a singer with a "projection" enters the arena of innuendo.

Hughes's narrator introduces Delly's performance of the lead with a significant statement in the text: "So without respect for gender, on the Sunday afternoon of the program, Delmar sang the female lead" (234). Clearly, since Delmar is the subject of the sentence, it is he who has no respect for gender. Most immediately, this seems to be because gender is not important to the artistic performance of the song, which is best performed by Delmar. But the story also indicates that because gender is not physically or biologically based but rooted in societal constructions and attitudes that are harmful to Delly and, ultimately, John and Manley Jaxon as well, those gender constructions deserve no respect. When Delmar sings the female lead, he challenges the masculine gender constructions that cause his father to hate him. Ironically, even as he does this, he seems to confirm for his father the "queerness" that John believes he sees in him.

Although Delly is described as singing the female lead with a particular "sweetness" (234), his voice is compared to that of the sweet-voiced lead singer of the Soul Stirrers and later pop idol Sam Cooke.

Cooke was indeed possessed of a particularly sweet voice as evidenced in songs such as "Wonderful," recorded by the Soul Stirrers in 1956, especially in comparison to earlier gruff-voiced singers such as the howling and growling Blind Willie Johnson and Reverend Gary Davis and other church-wrecking "hard" leads in many of the gospel groups of the 1940s and 1950s, typified by Paul Foster of the Soul Stirrers and Julius "June" Cheeks of the Sensational Nightingales, acknowledged by many as "the hardest singing lead in gospel" (Darden 78). Indeed, Shane White and Graham White report that descriptions of African American singing ("screaming") during slavery included words such as savage, barbarous, harsh, primitive, wild, hideous, uncouth, and terrifying—all encapsulated under the title "impure" (52). Cooke helped bring gospel to a new "pop audience," and "[h]is youthful good looks and sensitivity to popular music trends helped gospel music extend its appeal to a new teenaged fan base" (Burford 357).

The sweetness of Cooke's voice was not indicative of sexual orientation but rather of a particular singing style very much a part of the range of vocal styles apparent in Afro-American culture, as evidenced by the high falsetto vocal styles of such 1920s and 1930s performers as King Solomon Hill, Joe Pullum, and Skip James. Cooke himself was heterosexual, as indicated in his biography—significantly titled *Dream Boogie* by author Peter Guralnik, as it portrays Cooke wavering between gospel and pop, God and the devil, in his pursuit of the American dream. His sweet pop recordings took a more guttural turn under the right circumstances, as in his Harlem Square Club 1963 recordings, which were described by commentator Cliff White in the recording's liner notes as being more "virile" than his pop recordings. One might, of course, see such a performer as the low-pitched, gruff-voiced Bessie Johnson as Cooke's female counterpart in this. The point is that a sweet or gruff singing style is not indicative of sexual orientation, as Hughes well understood, and such assumptions produce unwarranted conclusions.

Preachers and soloists in the African American church were notably objects of sexual attraction for parishioners because of their positions of authority and the vital connection between the evocation of spiritual and sexual energy, as Harlem Renaissance writer Nella Larsen describes quite clearly in her novel *Quicksand*. In "Blessed Assurance," the Reverend Dr. Greene notes that he "had seen other choir directors take the count" (234), not necessarily as a result of some homosexual attraction. Indeed, Delly affects elderly sisters and "swooning maidens" alike with his performance (234). Still, John interprets the events in the context of his own fears, assumptions, and preconceptions, and he arrives at a prejudiced perception of what happened at the church.

In the end, John tries to silence Delmar—"Shut up," he repeats incessantly—as Delmar sings the Frances J. "Fanny" Crosby–penned hymn "Blessed Assurance" (1873). Significantly, the chorus of the song emphasizes the personal nature of the hymn: "This is my story, this is my song." Reminding us at this point that the story comes to us through the consciousness of John, Hughes cleverly emphasizes the subjectivity with which John approaches this scene, as well as his son's life. John's attempt to silence Delly's voice and story is tantamount to the assassination of Delly's personality, character, and voice in favor of John's personality, character, and voice, represented by the narrative story he himself passes along. The two scenarios play out side by side in simultaneous irony. In attempting to silence Delmar, John is actually trying to quiet his own suspicions and fears and hide the shame that he feels Delmar, a perceived homosexual, brings upon him. Ultimately, though, the song may truly refer to John's lack of confidence in his own manhood and in his religion. Delmar continues to sing his song while John and Jaxon fall apart around him; he seems to have the blessing of Jesus and the ability to express it with beauty and grace. Hughes does not clarify Delmar's sexual orientation—we see speculation about it only through John's warped perspective. Thus, any critical certainty about it should certainly be identified with the reckless speculations of John, whose sense of shame and rejection of his son mark him as the true villain of the piece.

Ultimately, it is just these types of damning assumptions that Hughes attempted to fight all his life: assumptions about race, class, and gender that frequently found their genesis or affirmation in the construction of the American dream, with its promises of success in conventional, mainstream notions of normality. Having faced these elements in his own personal and political life, Hughes responded with the poem "Personal," which describes his religious views as being a private affair between him and God. However, continually driven by such challenges as the McCarthyist hysteria of the 1950s, Hughes provided "Blessed Assurance" four years before his death, a story that outlines his feelings in a public fashion. Perhaps his poem "Motto" most comprehensively expresses his philosophy of compassion and acceptance:

> *Dig and Be Dug*
> *In Return.* (lines 8–9)

Works Cited

Albee, Edward. *The American Dream.* New York: Penguin, 1960.
Borden, Anne. "'Heroic Hussies' and 'Brilliant Queers': Genderracial Resistance in the Work of Langston Hughes." *African American Review* 28 (1994): 333–45.
Burford, Mark. "Soul Stirrers." *Encyclopedia of American Gospel Music.* Ed. W. K. McNeil. New York: Routledge, 2010. 356–58.
Cooke, Sam. *Live at the Harlem Square Club.* Abkco, 1985. CD.
_____. *The Rhythm and the Blues.* RCA, 1995. CD.
_____. *Sam Cooke with the Soul Stirrers.* Specialty, 1991. CD.
Darden, Robert. "Julius Cheeks." *Encyclopedia of American Gospel Music.* Ed. W. K. McNeil. New York: Routledge, 2010. 78.
Guralnik, Peter. *Dream Boogie.* New York: Little, 2005.
Hughes, Langston. *The Collected Poems of Langston Hughes.* Ed. Arnold Rampersad and David Roessel. New York: Vintage, 1994.
_____. *Short Stories.* Ed. Donna Akiba Sullivan Harper. New York: Hill, 1996.
Larsen, Nella. *Quicksand and Passing.* New Brunswick: Rutgers UP, 1986.
Nero, Charles I. "Re/Membering Langston: Homophobic Textuality and Arnold Rampersad's *Life of Langston Hughes.*" *Queer Representations: Reading Lives, Reading Cultures.* Ed. Martin Duberman. New York: New York UP, 1997. 188–96.

Rampersad, Arnold. *The Life of Langston Hughes*. 2 vols. New York: Oxford UP, 1986.
White, Cliff. Liner Notes. *The Rhythm and the Blues*. RCA, 1995. CD. 23 MI 23
White, Shane, and Graham White. *The Sounds of Slavery*. Boston: Beacon, 2005.

Inspired by Hughes: Hughes's Dramatic Legacy in the Twenty-First Century_____
Leslie Sanders

[I]t is apparent today that [Hughes] almost always worked the right ground and broke and tilled it. So that today those who follow will find a field clearly marked out and in readiness for deeper harvesting.
—George Kent, *Blackness and the Adventure of Western Culture*

A 2007 column in *American Theatre* details various versions of *Black Nativity,* performed around the United States, as "inspired by Hughes." The phrase is apt. Perhaps the best known of Hughes's plays, *Black Nativity* is both a detailed text and an invitation to riff and re-create. The gospel play, a form he took up with gusto in the last decade of his career, is but one of the many he explored. Indeed, Hughes wrote plays in virtually every form, introducing to the American stage a variety of figures, narratives, and possibilities for engaging and portraying African American experience. In so doing, Hughes tendered the stage as an arena of possibility. His plays challenged demeaning forms of representation, deconstructing, for example, the inevitability of tragic outcomes in the folk play, while also depicting them, as in *Mulatto*. He dared to write comedies at a time when stage convention characterized the black figure as innately comic; he imbued accounts of historical struggles with hope. Hughes certainly deserves a major place in the history of African American theater. Yet whether, or perhaps in what manner, his many plays might be of more than simply historical interest on the stage is a challenge to scholars and practitioners alike.

Virtually all of Langston Hughes's plays and other theatrical works are now available in volumes 5 and 6 of *The Collected Works of Langston Hughes*, published by the University of Missouri Press. Ranging from short satiric skits to chronicle and gospel plays, full-length tragedies and comedies to operas, they reveal Hughes as willing to experiment with a wide array of theatrical techniques, satisfy a variety of audiences, and claim a variety of stages for black performance. Perhaps his most versatile form is one he evolved from his agitprop play in support of the Scottsboro Boys, *Scottsboro Limited* (1931), and from theater that he encountered during his travels in the Soviet Union and Central Asia, the Moscow theater in particular. Needing only a bare stage, minimal props, and a piano, *Don't You Want to Be Free?* (1938) recounts what Hughes insisted on calling "the emotional history of the Negro" using short vignettes, his own poetry, and blues music.[1] Hughes regularly updated the play to address issues current with various productions; for example, the original version advocates the organizing of black and white workers in class struggle, while a version performed in the early 1940s promotes the war effort. The form of *Don't You Want to Be Free?*, vignettes linked by an overarching narrative and augmented by poetry and music, would make up a good deal of Hughes's dramatic output for the rest of his career. Topical plays promoting the war effort (*For This We Fight*, 1943), urging people to vote (*The Ballot and Me*, 1956), and paying tribute to the civil rights movement (*Jericho-Jim Crow*, 1963) employ this form, as do the many gospel plays. *The Sun Do Move* (1942), which chronicles African American history from enslavement in Africa to participation in the Union Army in the Civil War, is similarly structured and is the first of Hughes's plays musically dominated by spirituals.

Easily adopted for any audience and purpose, educational or inspirational, this form, born of the political theater of the 1930s, is ideal for popular theater. Hughes composed these plays for lofts, community theaters, rallies, and the legitimate stage: *Jericho-Jim Crow*, staged off-Broadway, received the best critical reception of any of his plays. Distinctive in Hughes's plays is his use of music both as a backdrop and as a vital aspect of the narrative, and although none of these plays except the gospel plays seem to have been revived, *Don't You Want to Be Free?* was immensely popular in its day. It ran for 135 performances in Harlem and subsequently was performed at least 200 times in colleges throughout the country, as Hughes crowed in a 1952 letter to Karamu House directors and longtime friends Rowena and Russell Jelliffe (LHP).

Langston Hughes's lifelong engagement with theater is perhaps the least known aspect of his art. In 1921, the same year in which "The Negro Speaks of Rivers" found publication in the *Crisis*, his morality play for children, *The Gold Piece*, was published in *The Brownies' Book*. When he arrived in New York to attend Columbia University that same year, he sat "in the gallery night after night at *Shuffle Along*," the acclaimed work that heralded a decade of popular black musicals on Broadway (*Big* 85). The commercial success of such vehicles for a kind of black performance led Hughes later in the decade to dream, with Zora Neale Hurston, of a "real" Negro theater.

The need for such a theater, and what it might comprise both as text and as performance space, was articulated by W. E. B. Du Bois in 1926 as *about us*, *by us*, *for us*, and *near us*. His four tenets addressed a variety of issues that plagued the representation of black bodies and black life on the American stage. With the possible, albeit highly problematic, exception of the antebellum productions of *Uncle Tom's Cabin* in which its antislavery message was still potent, virtually nothing on stage depicted the harsh realities of African American existence or black inner life. Various entertainment forms did, however, emerge from the degrading conventions of minstrelsy and from the broader scope of vaudeville. These culminated in the form of black musical comedy that finally made its way to Broadway at the turn of the century, comprising a simple comic plot that served as occasion for music, dance, and repartee. Several at least met Du Bois's requirement of "by us," and while they sought success with mainstream audiences, they also challenged the conventions of minstrelsy and other strictures placed on black performance, such as taboos against showing romance or using a racially mixed cast. Yet they remained entertainments, important in many respects, but not a vehicle for serious representation and exploration of African American life.

Serious dramas depicting African American life emerged rather from the American Little Theatre Movement and in the form of folk drama. The work of the Irish playwright John Millington Synge and the 1911 tour of the Abbey Players from Dublin served as catalysts and inspiration for the growth of the American form, which was devoted to serious treatment of what its chief American proponent, Frederick Koch, called "the folkways of our less sophisticated people . . . leading simple lives." The plays' dramatic action, he writes, "may be found in man's desperate struggle for existence and in his enjoyment of the world of nature" (xv–xvi). White dramatists often deployed this genre to write about black life, creating the earliest plays to achieve general notice. The acclaim with which the Broadway performance of Ridgely Torrence's *Three Plays of Negro Life* was received in 1917 ushered in a period in which the serious portrayal of African American life found its place on the stage. Ten years later, Paul Green, a Koch student, won the Pulitzer Prize for his folk play *In Abraham's Bosom*.

Writing in Alain Locke's 1925 collection *The New Negro*, Montgomery Gregory, a drama professor at Howard University, recommends the folk play as the appropriate vehicle for what he terms "sincere and artistic drama" of "race life." He argues that "the only avenue of genuine achievement in American drama for the Negro lies in the development of the rich veins of folk tradition of the past and in the portrayal of the authentic life of the Negro masses of today," and dreams of a national Negro theater for the development of performance art and artists (159). Alain Locke, in the introduction to *Plays of Negro Life*, the 1927 anthology he edited with Gregory, similarly notes his preference for the folk play. Locke situates "Negro drama" within the developing "native American drama" and proposes that "[n]o group experience in America has plumbed greater emotional depths, or passed so dramatically through more levels of life or caught up into itself more of those elements of social conflict and complication in which the modern dramatist must find the only tragedy that our realistic, scientific philosophy of life allows us" (n.pag.).

These prescriptions for Negro theater and its plays are part of the larger debates during the period about how black life ought to be portrayed. Given the degrading images of African Americans with which

American culture is rife, representation of blackness in any genre was, and perhaps continues to be, haunted by images it must work to keep at bay. "[T]his sense of always looking at one's self through the eyes of others," as W. E. B. Du Bois puts it in *The Souls of Black Folk*, constrained artists and audiences alike (364).

Hughes began writing, then, at a seminal time for African American theater, and he was deeply conscious of the dangers of the medium itself. Two plays constitute Hughes's early attempts at creating "real" Negro theater, and both comprise significant challenges to the existing dramatic portrayals of black life. The first, arguably his apprenticeship in the field, was his ill-fated partnership with Zora Neale Hurston on the comedy *Mule Bone*. The details of their quarrel are perhaps better known than the play itself, which was not staged until 1991 because the writers "fell out." As a result, *Mule Bone*'s bold intervention into the genre of comedy and use of African American speech, custom, and lore, the combination of Hurston's short story and anthropological collecting and Hughes's plot, failed to achieve the impact its authors intended. However, critically, in its complex handling of the performance of black folkways, it insists on its authenticity and on the integrity of the community that expresses itself in this fashion. From it, Hughes learned how black comedy might shake loose from minstrelsy's shackles and allow African American culture and expression to provide both dramatic content and milieu.

Fresh from his collaboration with Zora Neale Hurston, Hughes began working on the other play with which he is often identified, the tragedy *Mulatto*. In this genre, too, Hughes challenged contemporary portrayals of black life. Hughes began working on the play while staying at the Hedgerow Theatre, near Philadelphia, the summer program of which included Eugene O'Neill's *Emperor Jones* and was to include Paul Green's *In Abraham's Bosom*. Both plays were highly influential, although the former, as Hughes recounts in *The Big Sea*, was derided by a Harlem audience: "Them ain't no ghosts, fool!" the spectators cried from the orchestra. "Why don't you come on out o' that jungle—

back to Harlem where you belong" (258). Although widely regarded as serious and sympathetic portrayals of black life, both plays depend on racist stereotypes; in both, the central black figure is primitive, irrational, driven by lust, and doomed. In the latter, Abe is mulatto, and his white blood is credited with what reason and ambition he possesses. In both plays, the central character's demise is justified by his own failings. The lynching that concludes *In Abraham's Bosom* is a punishment for patricide; the execution of Emperor Jones in O'Neill's play is a result of his own superstitious nature and his earlier overreaching.

In stark contrast to these and other dramatic portrayals of African Americans, Robert, the central character of Langston Hughes's *Mulatto*, is educated, articulate, and insistent on his right to respect, symbolically encapsulated in his persistent use of the front door of his father's house. Set in 1930s Georgia, the play depicts the volatile relationship between Robert and his father, Colonel Tom Norwood, who has lived with Cora, his housekeeper, "damn near like a wife" and formed with her an unacknowledged family (act 2, scene 2; *CW* 5: 44). Analyses of the play typically focus on the father-son conflict, and certainly much is made of it in the play. However, Harry Elam Jr. and Michele Elam argue that the play is not interested in the personal, as it generally has been read, but rather that it, and other works that feature the mulatto figure, "engage[s] a larger agonistic struggle over black masculine enfranchisement within the national citizenry," and "interraciality [acts] as a trope for the relationship between race, masculinity, and nation" (87). Certainly, when read politically, the play is virtually allegorical. Yet, the way in which Cora becomes the play's central figure after Robert kills his father and flees has not been explored. In a long soliloquy, she recounts her relationship with the Colonel and his fondness for his children and then expresses the horror of what is occurring as the lynch mob pursues her son, who returns to her and ends his own life in her bed. He has "gone to sleep," she tells the frustrated mob before falling silent. Interestingly, in a 1933 letter to his friend Harold Jackman about a possible production of the play, Hughes writes: "Note: Same set throughout. Action all takes place same day. . . . Mother's role is lead. Immediately after the murder, mood of play becomes halfmystic, strange, otherworldly—a play of puppets and symbols, tools of terror, not real people" (LHP).

Hughes wrote *Mulatto* for the great African American actor Rose McClendon, who was working at Hedgerow Theatre the summer he was there and began writing the play, and this may in part account for his conception of Cora. Yet, the African American experience from the perspective of black mothers had already preoccupied him. For example, his poem "Mother to Son" was published in the *Crisis* in 1922, and in 1931, as he was working on the play, he composed his poetic performance piece "The Black Mother." Through the figure of Cora, Hughes dignifies a particular painful and complex history of an intimacy born of power but rendered somewhat humane over time. In portraying Cora as possessing both dignity and agency, Hughes responds to a range of representations of black women as promiscuous or simply victims and broaches issues uncomfortable for proponents of racial uplift, as well as for those approving of plays such as *In Abraham's Bosom*.

Although *Mule Bone* and *Mulatto* are Hughes's first complete full-length plays, as early as 1928 he had begun notes for a "singing play" to be called *Emperor of Haiti*, later made into an opera called *Troubled Island* with music by the African American composer William Grant Still. The story of the most successful slave revolt in the African diaspora, *Emperor of Haiti* compresses the years 1791 to 1806 and attributes the leadership to a single hero, the successor of Toussaint Louverture, Jean-Jacques Dessalines, who declared himself Emperor of Haiti in 1804 and was assassinated two years later. Opening with the successful revolt, the play then turns to the court of Dessalines, depicting his downfall as caused by the betrayal of his mulatto advisors and his own illiteracy and distance from the masses. It premiered at Karamu in 1936, and Still had already proposed adapting the play into an opera.

The 1930s were a period of intense dramatic activity for Hughes. Most of his plays were written for black theaters: either Karamu House in Cleveland or theaters he founded. *Little Ham* (1936), *When the Jack Hollers* (1936, written with Arna Bontemps), *Emperor of Haiti* (1936), *Joy to My Soul* (1937), *Front Porch* (1937), and *Mulatto* (1938, using Hughes's original script)[2] were all performed at Karamu by the Gilpin Players, and, with the exception of *Mulatto*, written for them.[3] During the same period, he wrote *Harvest* (with Ella Winter, never performed), the one-act *Soul Gone Home* (not performed at the time), *Don't You Want to Be Free?*, written for his Harlem Suitcase Theater, and the full-length *The Sun Do Move* (1942), written for the Skyloft Players, a group he founded in Chicago. The scripts respond to a variety of impulses; however, principally Hughes sought to provide what he calls in his 1931 Rosewald Fellowship application "spiritually true dramas for the Negro theater" (LHP).

In 1926, the same year in which Hughes and Hurston articulated their dream of a "real Negro theater" and W. E. B. Du Bois laid out the requirements of his own vision, Hughes published his manifesto "The Negro Artist and the Racial Mountain." Declaring his audience to be the "low-down folks, the so-called common element, and they are the majority—may the Lord be praised! The people who have their nip of gin on Saturday nights and are not too important to themselves or the community, or too well fed, or too learned to watch the lazy world go round" (92), Hughes proclaims a new, and unselfconscious, direction for African American art:

> We younger Negro artists who create now intend to express our individual dark-skinned selves without fear or shame. If white people are pleased we are glad. If they are not, it doesn't matter. We know we are beautiful. And ugly too. The tom-tom cries and the tom-tom laughs. If colored people are pleased we are glad. If they are not, their displeasure doesn't matter either. We build our temples for tomorrow, strong as we know how, and we stand on top of the mountain, free within ourselves. (95)

As Shane Vogel points out in *The Scene of Harlem Cabaret*, Hughes's choice of the "low-down folks" as his audience flies in the face of the racial uplift movement and mentality that dominated the pages of the *Crisis* and dictated Alain Locke's choices in *The New Negro*. The manifesto that *The New Negro* comprises concerns how the Negro would enter the modern era, how African American folkways contributed to the larger culture, and how the production of high, rather than popular, art signaled worthiness to be fully included in American civilization. Locke sought to display and theorize a version of African American life and art that countered degrading stereotype and rose above the primitive. The volume's audience was white America. Hughes's declaration both counters and subverts that project. It seeks to explore and delight in the full range of black performance, recognizing how it will be judged and eschewing that judgment.

Vogel argues further that Hughes's manifesto speaks for what Vogel calls "the Cabaret School." He writes,

> Writers and performers of the Harlem Renaissance used the cabaret to imagine and enact alternative possibilities for racial, sexual and socioeconomic subjectivities that resisted the normalizing imperatives of uplift ideology. The centrality of performance and its expansive possibilities to the Harlem Renaissance was something that Langston Hughes always recognized. (36)

In his chapter focused on Hughes, "Closing Time: Langston Hughes and the Queer Poetics of Harlem Nightlife," Vogel employs nuanced readings of several Hughes poems of the cabaret in light of the social practices and legal strictures of Harlem nightlife to suggest the ethos of Hughes's queer sensibility. Vogel addresses the controversy over Hughes's sexuality that erupted in response to Arnold Rampersad's biography by moving the focus from historical archives to an examination of what Ann Cvetkovich calls "archives of feeling" (109). This intervention opens up myriad ways of reading Hughes's work that are provocative also for his work in the theater. Dimensions of two of his comedies from the 1930s, for example, are suggestive. The first is *Little Ham*.

When Hughes worked with his editor Webster Smalley on *Five Plays by Langston Hughes* in 1963, he moved the setting of *Little Ham* from the 1930s, when it was written, to the 1920s, changing some details to suit the new time frame. Not all the changes were, however, dictated by period. A few specific references were altered, references that specifically connect the world of Little Ham to the after-hours, demimonde cabaret world that Vogel demarcates as the domain of queer sociality. Set in Paradise Shining Parlor, Tiny's Beauty Shop, Tiny's apartment, and a Harlem ballroom, the plot of *Little Ham* is quite simple. In the course of events, its hero, Little Ham, breaks up with one woman to take up with another, who also discards a lover to be with him. He wins money in a numbers game, is hired as a runner by the white mobsters who take over the game halfway through the play, is arrested and released, and, with his new love, wins a dance contest in the comic finale. As in *Mule Bone*, the plot provides occasion for performance of the expressive culture of its characters, though they are urban, rather than rural, folk. They appear as a parade of types: West Indian, Deaconess, Lodge Lady, Staid Lady, and also Masculine Woman and Effeminate Youth. Masculine Woman, not compared to openly gay blues singer Gladys Bentley in the 1963 version, makes a brief appearance in act 1.

> *(A big MASCULINE WOMAN, looking exactly like Gladys Bentley, walks in and straight across to the cigar stand)*
> MASCULINE LADY. *(In bass voice)* Gimme a five cent cigar. *(MADAM offers her the box and accepts payment as EVERYBODY in the shop stares)* Is the number out yet?
> MADAM. Not yet.
> MASCULINE LADY. Then I'll pick it up later. *(Turns and strides out)*
> HAM. Whew! What's the world coming to? (*CW* 5: 225)

Effeminate Youth, as he is named on entrance although not in the cast of characters, is retained in the 1963 version of act 1 and given far more play. For example:

YOUTH. Can I get a polish?
HAM. You mean your nails?
YOUTH. I mean my slippers.
(Mounting the stand)
HAM. Well - er, are you - er, what nationality is you?
YOUTH. I'm a Creole by birth, but I never draw the color line.
HAM. I know you don't. Is you married?
YOUTH. Oh, no, I'm in vaudeville.
HAM. I knowed you was in something. What do you do?
YOUTH. I began in a horse-act, a comic horse-act.
HAM. A who?
YOUTH. A horse-act. I played the hind legs.
HAM. In other words, you was de horse's hips.
YOUTH. I used to be. But I got out of that. I've advanced.
HAM. To what?
YOUTH. I give impersonations.
HAM. Is that what they call it now?
YOUTH. I impersonate Mae West.
HAM. Lemme see.
YOUTH. Of course.
(Begins to talk like Mae West, giving an amusing impersonation of that famous screen star)
HAM. You a regular moving picture!
YOUTH. Indeed I am. (215–16)

In act 3, scene 2, the Master of Ceremonies announces the dance contest:

> Ladies and gentlemen, Lad-dees and gentel-mun! And gigolos! I have in my hand the Grand Silver Truckin' Trophy engraved with the name of Harlem's most prominent, high-toned society institution, the Hello Club. *(Applause)* This club has been ruling supreme amongst the Harlem Four Thousand for many years, and is known from Central Park North to the Yankee Stadium, and from the Harlem River to Sugar Hill, from the Ubangi Club to the Silver Dollar. (259)

This second explicit reference to Gladys Bentley, this time to the Ubangi Club where she held sway during the 1930s, certainly broadens the reach of "high-toned society" in ways such society would hardly approve.

Hughes called *Little Ham* a farce, a form that depends on highly exaggerated and unlikely situations ultimately for comic effect. Virtually all the central characters in the play are two-timing either spouses or lovers, sometimes narrowly escaping detection and at other times colliding, to rowdy but eventually harmless effect. Most pointedly, Ham's new love, Tiny, readying herself for a date with Ham, is caught by her lover, gun-toting Gilbert. She and Ham escape by locking Gilbert in the closet, from which he shoots harmlessly. Yet another source of comedy in the play is Ham's small stature and Tiny's massive girth, a stock comic image but also a suggestive gesture of gender reversal. Gender roles are cartoonish and lightly worn, a quality frequent in Hughes's comedies.

Also a farce, Hughes's comedy *Joy to My Soul* (1937) is set in the lobby of the Grand Harlem Hotel, which is rife with shysters of every description who prey on each other relentlessly. The Lady's Drill Corp of the Society of the Royal Sphinx, which is holding a convention at the hotel, twice marches through the lobby. Two characters, Prince Ali Ali and Princess Bootoo, crudely disguised, plan to prey on the convention; a third, medium Madam Klinkscale, advertises her powers, which seem to have some efficacy. The action revolves around a young and innocent millionaire from Shadow Gut, Texas, Buster Whitehead, who has come to meet his pen pal and fiancé, Suzy Baily. He is unaware that she, a hotel resident, is both ugly and twice his age. Fortunately, he instead meets and marries another innocent, the cigarette girl Wilmetta, thus assuaging the financial demands of two parasitic stepfathers. To make up for dropping Suzy, he gives her "oil well #3." Other plots are happily resolved: Prince Ali Ali is revealed to be Madame Klinkscale's first husband, and Klinkscale helps recover Princess Bootoo's back wages before resuming her marriage.

In *Joy to My Soul*, few are what they seem and disguise is rampant. Occurring within a twenty-four-hour period, the frenzied action and extremes of emotion in *Joy to My Soul* are, even more so than *Little Ham*, suggestive of the inclusive liminal spaces of the cabaret world. Farce, too, is a world of recognition and misrecognition, of levels of seeing, and of spectacle. The critic Eric Bentley writes regarding farce, "Like dreams, farces show the disguised fulfillment of repressed wishes" (x). *Joy to My Soul* is a comedy of desire in which cartoon innocents barely escape corruption and even the corrupt find a kind of redemption.

When Hughes turned to dramatic comedy again, twenty years later, it was to animate his great comic creation Jesse B. Semple, or Simple. Hughes had developed his collection *Simple Takes a Wife* (1953) into a play of the same name, and then, on request, adapted it into the musical *Simply Heavenly* (1957). A gently plotted rendition of Simple's musings, his courtship of the sweet and proper Joyce, and his adventures with Zarita, his "good time" girl, *Simply Heavenly* ends with marriage plans. Paradoxically, given Hughes's overtly political plays of the 1930s, *Simply Heavenly* raised some hackles. A United Service Organizations (USO) production in the South upset both whites, who objected to Simple's critical monologues, and blacks, who found the characters stereotypical. After seeing the New York production, writer and actor Alice Childress wrote to Hughes expressing discomfort about how white members of the audience in particular interpreted the play (LHP). Although the play went awry when performed on a commercial stage before a mixed audience, *Simply Heavenly* satirizes black self-consciousness. Called a "disgraceful stereotype" by a man in a bar in act 1, scene 3, the character Mamie turns on him: "Mister, you better remove yourself from my presence before I stereo your type! I like watermelons, and I don't care who knows it. . . . I ain't no pretender, myself, neither no passer." Asked what she means by "passer," Mamie responds, "Chitterling passer—passing up chitterlings and pretending I don't like 'em when I do . . . ." (*CW* 6: 192). The misrecognitions of white audiences and the disapproval of black bourgeois audiences restricted comic possibilities, at least on mainstream stages.

Hughes's last full-length play, the gospel musical *Tambourines to Glory*, is, as he describes in his author's note, "a dramatization of a very old problem—that of good versus evil . . . on the surface a simple play about simple people" (6: 281). He warns that the performers, therefore, had to be sensitive to the "complexities of simplicity." Essentially, the play attacks corruption in black churches through the story of goodhearted Essie and wily Laura, who start a church. Buddy Lomax, who is really the devil, takes up with Laura, and all is saved only by Laura's repentance. The play closed after three weeks on Broadway due to criticism of its view of the church and cool reviews.

The difficulties encountered by Hughes's last full-length plays are instructive. While the popularity of his gospel plays, *Black Nativity* in particular, continues unabated, even during his lifetime his chosen dramatic modalities encountered misapprehension. However, although prolific, his dramatic work was not where he entrusted his deepest ideas and emotions. After all, one of his greatest achievements, although also not appreciated at the time, is *Ask Your Mama: 12 Moods for Jazz* (1961), which is scored for performance, a practice he began in the early 1930s, took up again with *Montage of a Dream Deferred*, and then revived with *Mama*. Hughes's sense of performance included more than the stage, and he developed a performative frame for several of his long poems. Moreover, others artists, even during his lifetime, created theatrical pieces out of his poetry. Notably, the playwright Robert Glenn assembled a performance piece "by Langston Hughes" called *Shakespeare in Harlem* in 1961, and countless others have followed suit (Rampersad 2: 303).

When Hughes and Hurston's *Mule Bone* was finally performed in New York in 1991, the limitations of the play's characterizations of the rural folk became apparent. Although charming, funny, and beautifully restored, the play only really worked as a period piece. The cultural milieu no longer projected the authenticity that, in the 1930s, would have given it vibrancy. The situations appeared quaint, the language somewhat deliberate. However, adapted into a musical, *Little Ham* had a successful run in New York in 2001, eventually moving to an off-Broadway stage. Reviewers praised the music, in particular, and found the production charming. *Tambourines to Glory* did well in Washington, DC, in 2004, and *Joy to My Soul* was revived in Cleveland in 2006. Moreover, Hughes's comedies, including *Mule Bone*, continue to be performed in black regional theaters, by black theater companies, and on college campuses. The plays continue to delight African American audiences, in particular.

Hughes is, of course, one of the most beloved of African American writers, and his work is an endless source of inspiration. His most enduring work in theater, the gospel play, brings the sacred space of Christian worship into the theater and moves easily into the church; the plays understand and celebrate the ways in which the language of faith, both in music and word, expresses the soul of a people. Yet, they have not yet been considered as part of what Paul Carter Harrison terms Kuntu Drama; considering them within that continuum is a project for scholar and performer alike. *Mulatto*, too, should be revisited, taking into account Hughes's suggestions concerning the second act. Written and understood as realism, it also suggests dimensions beyond the literal that could be explored. The form of *Don't You Want to Be Free?* and Hughes's other work in political theater invites adaptation to a variety of messages and also to a range of poetic form, rap and spoken word in particular. Finally, as scholars and practitioners are becoming more comfortable with the ways in which Langston Hughes's sexuality inflects his artistic vision and practice, a revisiting of the comedies is in order to explore their gestures toward a more complex view of human sociality and their depictions of gender performance. *Little Ham*, especially, might benefit from drag; *Joy to My Soul* begs for outlandish and outrageous enactment. Hughes's theater in the twenty-first century is full of new possibility as well as pleasure in the familiar and much loved.

Notes

1. Hughes wrote this phrase on typescripts of *Don't You Want to Be Free?* that he sent out to interested parties.
2. The Broadway version of *Mulatto* was sensationalized by the producer, Martin Jones, who increased the sex and violence and included a rape scene. The script for the Broadway production has never surfaced. For an account of the Broadway production, see Rampersad 1: 311–315.
3. These are the dates of first performance at Karamu.

Works Cited

"After Langston Hughes." *American Theatre* December 2007: 14.
Bentley, Eric. "The Psychology of Farce." *Let's Get a Divorce! and Other Plays*. Ed. Eric Bentley. New York: Hill, 1958. vii–xx.
Du Bois, W. E. B. "Krigwa Little Theatre Movement." *Crisis* July 1926: 134.
_____. *The Souls of Black Folk*. 1903. *Du Bois Writings*. New York: Library of America, 1986.
Elam, Harry, Jr., and Michele Elam. "Blood Debt: Reparations in Langston Hughes's Mulatto." *Theatre Journal* 61 (2007): 85–103.
Gregory, Montgomery. "The Drama of Negro Life." *The New Negro*. Ed. Alain Locke. New York: Atheneum, 1992. 153–60.
Hughes, Langston. *The Big Sea*. New York: Hill, 1963.
_____. *The Collected Works of Langston Hughes*. Ed. Arnold Rampersad et al. 16 vols. Columbia: U of Missouri P, 2001–03.
_____. Langston Hughes Papers. James Weldon Johnson Collection. Beinecke Rare Book and Manuscript Lib., Yale U, New Haven.
_____. "The Negro Artist and the Racial Mountain." *Harlem Renaissance Reader*. Ed. David Levering Lewis. New York: Viking, 1994. 91–95.
Kent, George. *Blackness and the Adventure of Western Culture*. Chicago: Third World, 1952.
Koch, Frederick. "American Folk Drama in the Making." Introduction. *American Folk Plays*. Ed. Koch. New York: Appleton, 1939. xv–xvi.

Locke, Alain. "Introduction: The Drama of Negro Life." *Plays of Negro Life*. Ed. Locke and Montgomery Gregory. New York: Harper, 1927. n.pag.

Rampersad, Arnold. *The Life of Langston Hughes*. 2 vols. New York: Oxford UP, 1986–88.

Vogel, Shane. *The Scene of Harlem Cabaret: Race, Sexuality, Performance*. Chicago: U of Chicago P, 2009.

"Yo también soy América": Latin American Receptions of Langston Hughes's American Dream

Laurence E. Prescott

"Langston Hughes es el poeta universal de todas las razas oprimidas."
—Ildefonso Pereda Valdés, *Antología de la poesía negra americana* (1936)

Among twentieth-century writers and intellectuals of Latin America, few Anglo-American authors have earned as much respect, admiration, and attention as the poet, novelist, short story writer, and playwright Langston Hughes. Hughes's questioning of his society's values, his ability to discern and represent the issue of race not just as a problem of the United States but of the world, and his understanding of the broader concerns of poverty, discrimination, and oppression that dehumanized not only African Americans but other peoples as well motivated Latin American writers, poets, journalists, and others to appreciate and comment on his literary production. Indeed, his example as a committed writer encouraged Latin American contemporaries to explore and interrogate problems of race, class, and exploitation in their own cultures and societies. In particular, the simple yet penetrating verses of Hughes's poem "I, Too" resonated with many readers of Cuba, Mexico, Colombia, Peru, and other nations of the Americas who could easily identify with its message of resistance and pride. Often represented as "the darker brother," writers of multiracial Latin America often found in "I, Too" a reflection of their own cultural and economic realities and an affirmation of liberation, dignity, and hope in the triumph of the true meaning of America.

Primary evidence of Hughes's resonance among Latin Americans can be found in the numerous translations of his poetry, drama, and fiction into Spanish and also into Portuguese. Donald C. Dickinson and Edward J. Mullen have identified several Spanish versions of his poems that were published in anthologies and periodicals between the 1920s and the 1970s. Examining Hughes's impact in South America, Richard L. Jackson has shown that the North American author was and remains a literary and racial model to writers of Uruguay and Colombia as well as of Portuguese-speaking Brazil. More recently, in a lengthy article titled "'Yo también soy América': Langston Hughes Translated," Vera M. Kutzinski expands the research and study of Spanish translations of Hughes's poems.[1]

New archival investigations, as well as interviews I conducted with poets and writers of Latin America, have led to the finding of texts, previously unknown to North American scholars, that exemplify the profound and far-reaching reverberation of Hughes's literary voice throughout the Americas. In this essay I propose to examine some of the findings to show how and why Hughes, particularly in his poem "I, Too," articulates the hopes, aspirations, and needs of those who toil, struggle, and create and in doing so broadens the applicability of his poetic message and endears himself to peoples throughout the hemisphere.

Jackson has stated that Hughes's most popular poem among Spanish Americans was "Proem" or "Negro" ("African Diaspora" 29). In fact, however, the quantitative and qualitative data confirm that "I, Too" holds that distinction.[2] According to Mullen, the Cuban writer José Antonio Fernández de Castro's version of "I, Too" is the earliest known Spanish translation of verse by Hughes. Rendered as "Yo también honro a América," the translation appeared in the Cuban journal *Social* in September of 1928 ("Mexico and Cuba" 25).

Within weeks the translation came to the attention of the Peruvian writer Esteban Pavletich Trujillo, a young revolutionary and poet whose student activities had resulted in his deportation in 1925 from Peru to Central America, where he campaigned against the United Fruit Company and also joined the Nicaraguan Army of Liberation, becoming secretary of war to the group's charismatic leader, Augusto César Sandino. While in exile, Pavletich maintained ties to Peru and contributed to the two important periodicals that his compatriot, the Marxist philosopher and essayist José Carlos Mariátegui, founded and edited—*Amauta* in 1926 and *Labor* in 1928. The purpose of the latter publication was "to organize and create class consciousness among Peruvian workers" (Wise 119). The third issue of *Labor*, corresponding to December 8, 1928, included an article by Pavletich titled "Un mensaje y un anuncio" (A message and an announcement) in which he reproduces Fernández de Castro's translation of Hughes's poem and, more importantly, comments on the relevance of the poem's message to Latin American people's conditions and struggles.[3]

Pavletich discerned in "I, Too" a defiance and resistance to the common oppression and discrimination that African Americans and Latin Americans faced and struggled against in their respective homelands. Pavletich's reading of Hughes's poem constitutes or coincides with a cultural materialist reading. According to Hans Bertens, cultural materialism views the dominant sociocultural and political order (in this context, that of the United States) as "threatened from the inside, by inner contradictions and by tensions that it seeks to hide" (186). As Pavletich himself observes, "The youthful power and vigor of the American Empire have been able *to conceal* . . . within the deafening noise of the conquest of universal destinies, the germs of decomposition that *within its own bowels* conspire against its dubious future stability" (7; emphasis added).[4] To Pavletich, Hughes's poem exemplifies such an internal threat. The young Peruvian intellectual identifies the "strong, bitter and lyrical message" of "I, Too" as "the clamor of twenty million implacably oppressed human beings who, in spite of the Ku Klux Klan and the dawning of the Empire, 'also are America'" (7).[5] Pavletich opines that in "I, Too," Hughes "announces the broad destiny of his race." At the same time, he discovers in Hughes's poetics of the African American condition "so much of our common destiny."[6] Thus Pavletich found or made common cause between Latin Americans' struggles against capitalist exploitation and imperialist domination by the United States, on the one hand, and African Americans' struggles against racism and economic exploitation in the United States on the other.[7]

To Pavletich, Hughes's poetic discourse offered assurance that African Americans, by virtue of their history of enslavement and their courageous and unyielding fortitude in the face of racial discrimination and white supremacist violence, constituted a formidable force for the prospect of positive change in the United States. As the native-born group directly affected by the US nationalist fervor that generated the idea of racial superiority,[8] African Americans, Pavletich believed, held a unique position within the country and offered a singular perspective on their homeland, one that provided a keen awareness of and opposition to their nation's internal contradictions and unjust practices and paralleled Latin Americans' anti-imperialist stance and subversive discourse. Their pain, their anguish, and their labor had developed the nation's agricultural economy and had strengthened significantly its growth as a power. According to Pavletich, precisely because of the African American's separation "from the bourgeois machinery, [he] . . . today constitutes a dangerous poison for the body of the Empire, despite the barbarous antidote of the Ku Klux Klan" (7).[9]

Expanding upon this idea in a later section of his essay, Pavletich states, "If the North American agrarian regime was able to develop effectively, thanks—in large part—to the brutal enslavement of a race, the dynamic of the Empire has come about lubricated by the enslavement of a continent."[10] Both economic cycles, he points out, have been fueled by oppression and injustice, blood and exploitation. The result is, on the one hand, colonial oppressed classes and peoples ("pueblos y clases oprimidas coloniales"), and on the other, metropolitan oppressed classes and races ("razas y clases oprimidas metropolitanas"). Therefore, the Peruvian writer concludes, "Hughes's message speaks profoundly to our subversive consciousness, breathing into it new life and strengthening it. From different—yet convergent—camps, our voice joins his voice, breathless and full of longing" (8).[11]

Pavletich uses precise language and specific references pertinent to the United States that encapsulate the unique history of black people in the country and pinpoint their contemporary situation: slavery, racial superiority, oppression, injustice, Ku Klux Klan. But he does not limit his assessment of the African American condition to matters of race. As a Marxist-oriented thinker, he views race and class as linked. Indeed, they are two interrelated dimensions of the problem of oppression, exploitation, and discrimination. African Americans, he asserts, are "oppressed today as a race and as a class" (oprimidos hoy como raza y como clase). In his references to Latin America, however, Pavletich uses the term "esclavitud" (slavery) primarily in a figurative sense, just as Simón Bolívar and other privileged Creole leaders of the independence movement used it to describe their situation as colonized peoples under Spanish rule. Similarly, Marx and Engels would employ the term later to describe the proletariat. In other words, Pavletich does not mention or acknowledge the actual historical fact of African slavery in Latin America and its far-reaching social and economic consequences. Although he sees US imperialist ventures in Latin America as fueled by a consciousness of white racial superiority, he does not give equal consideration to the issue of race in Latin American societies.

This observation notwithstanding, Pavletich's essay is especially significant not only because it is one of the earliest critical commentaries on Hughes's work by a Latin American author but also because it identifies and links the conditions and struggles of racially discriminated and marginalized African Americans in the United States with those of politically dominated and socioeconomically oppressed peoples in Latin America. Laying bare attitudes and actions that denied and undermined the principles and promise of America—equality, inclusion, freedom, fairness, brotherhood—Hughes's poem allowed Pavletich to envision African Americans as a moral and social force capable of tempering the United States' drift toward imperial conquest. As Pavletich declares at the end of his essay, Hughes

> is and feels himself "America too" because he—he is twenty million men— was a laborer of this strong and arrogant North America, that owes him much, that owes us much. When the solid and united ranks of dissenters

impose new and wide continental roads, when our revolutionary action is joined to their revolutionary action—many others will join along the way—he will really be the "darker brother" in a free America in which there is room neither for slaves nor for slavers. (8)[12]

About a year after the publication of Pavletich's commentary, the Colombian journalist and critic Jaime Barrera Parra published his translation of Hughes's poem along with the original English text in an article titled "Los negros dentro de la civilización actual" (Negroes within the present civilization).[13] Editor of the literary supplement of *El Tiempo*, Bogotá, Colombia's leading newspaper, Barrera Parra was well aware of the avant-garde currents of the day and attentive to publications from the Americas and Europe. His article, which appeared in his "Notas del Week-end" column, offers a brief but cogent summary of the US radical Victor F. Calverton's essay "The Negro's New Belligerent Attitude." Published in the September 1929 issue of the journal *Current History*, the essay would later become the introduction to Calverton's *Anthology of American Negro Literature* (1929). While Barrera Parra also took note of poets Claude McKay and Countee Cullen, he was particularly impressed by the "impertinencia fanfarrona"—or brazen insolence—of "I, Too."

By virtue of his position with *El Tiempo*, Barrera Parra helped introduce younger writers into the Colombian capital's literary establishment. One of these was the poet Jorge Artel, who no doubt was familiar with Barrera Parra's column and who had probably read about Langston Hughes. Artel, a mixed-race native of the Atlantic coast who embraced his African heritage, found Hughes's work particularly engaging. In a statement on black literature written in 1932, Artel argues that those who aspire to express the pains, hopes, and dreams of black peoples in the Americas would do well to read, among other exemplary writings, the poetry of Langston Hughes and Paul Laurence Dunbar, which according to the Colombian poet had begun to reveal "the true image of the race and its unmistakable voice" ("La literatura negra en la costa"). Several years later, Artel included Barrera Parra's translation of "I, Too" in a public address that he titled "Modalidades artísticas de la raza negra" (Artistic modalities of the Negro race) and gave at a book fair (Feria del Libro) in his hometown of Cartagena de Indias. Characterizing Hughes as "the first . . . among Negro poets of North America," Artel glosses the poem as follows:

> I, too, am a man, like the white man. I, too, contribute with the strength of my spirit and my mind to the enhancement of the democracy in which I live. I, too, am beautiful because I have a soul just like the white man. I am a creator of art like the white man. And one day he and the caste he represents will see that my people have the same rights as theirs, and that the world and the sun and the joys of life were made for all. (16–17)[14]

Such statements of racial affirmation and insistence on equality by a black poet in a Latin American nation that espoused the ideology of mestizaje (the blending or amalgamation of racial groups and cultures), generally denied the existence of systemic prejudice and discrimination, and discouraged expressions of black pride were uncommon, fairly radical, and often met with censure—if not accusations of racism. In this case, however, Artel—no stranger to conflict and polemics—could not be wholly criticized for commenting on and interpreting the African American poet's words. Indeed, Hughes's message had emboldened him to criticize white supremacist attitudes and actions in Colombia indirectly and to bolster racial consciousness among Cartagena's black masses.

More than a decade later, Artel, then in self-imposed exile from Colombia, reached New York City where he sought out and finally met Langston Hughes, the poet laureate of Harlem. Recalling in 1960 the times spent at Hughes's home, he describes the poet as "a cordial man, inclined to the noble demonstrations of friendship and comradery. I met him in 1951; he had the extraordinary kindness of introducing me to several of his friends. . . . At his home in Harlem we used to converse at length on issues of America, human conflicts, political ideals. His is a generous spirit, without reservation" ("El autor de *Mulato*").[15] Three years later, in 1963, Artel published his translations of several of Hughes's poems in the Panamanian newspaper *La Hora*.[16] Finally, in 1967, on the occasion of Hughes's death, Artel paid homage to the poet in a public program that he organized at the University of Panama.

In addition to the mentioned writers, the Afro-Colombian novelist, short story writer, dramatist, essayist, and anthropologist Manuel Zapata Olivella must be included in any discussion of Langston Hughes's wider literary engagement with the American dream. In the early 1940s Zapata Olivella, then a young, leftist-thinking student and aspiring writer, had abandoned his medical studies to travel the roads of life. During his sojourn in the United States just after the end of World War II and in need of sustenance, he journeyed to Harlem to meet Hughes and seek his support. In *He visto la noche* (1953), his book of travel narratives about his experiences and observations in the United States, Zapata Olivella recounts succinctly the meeting with Hughes: "En el poeta encontré mucho más de lo que abrigara mi alma abatida: un amigo" (88; In the poet I found much more than what my battered soul hoped for: a friend). Their friendship, characterized by the reciprocal exchanges of autographed books and occasional correspondence, grew steadily and ended only with Hughes's death in 1967 (Prescott, "Brother to Brother").

Shortly after his return to Colombia in 1947, Zapata Olivella published an article entitled "Langston Hughes, el hombre" (Langston Hughes, the man) in which he narrates at length the meetings and conversations with Hughes, the generous hospitality and assistance extended to him, the poet's work ethic and eagerness to learn about the literature and condition of South American blacks, his impact on Zapata Olivella's own literary development, and, finally, Hughes's role in the African American struggle for freedom.[17]

The article served to give Colombian readers a more revealing portrait of the African American poet and writer who was known then largely through his publications. Zapata Olivella recalls Hughes's willingness to take time from his busy schedule to critique a short story that Zapata Olivella had hoped to sell to a New York newspaper. "I like the style . . . and the theme is interesting," he recalls Hughes saying. But Hughes offered strong constructive criticism as well: "I think you are neglecting the human passions in the description. In the novel, and particularly in the short story, man must be the central concern around which the narration turns. If there is no human sensibility deciphering the landscape, there is no life. Write it again in accordance with the main protagonist and someone will buy it" (12).[18]

To Zapata Olivella, the experience was especially beneficial; it enabled him to comprehend his own existential situation and to appreciate better "Langston Hughes, the man." He discovered in him a mentor "much more interesting, much more sensitive, much more human than his very own poetry; [showing] understanding toward young people who have still not discovered the mystery of the equation of art, but who are trying to decipher it through categorical imperatives" (12).[19]

Familiar with Hughes's first autobiography, *The Big Sea* (1940), which had been published in Spanish as *El inmenso mar* in 1944, Zapata Olivella identified deeply with his African American confrère not only as a friend and writer but also as a fellow wanderer (Prescott, "Brother to Brother" 93). "We had become acquainted only six hours before and it seemed we knew each other since childhood. It's the law of the vagabonds," he explains at the outset of his article (12).[20] Elsewhere, no doubt recollecting Hughes poem "The Negro Speaks of Rivers," he writes that Hughes "raises his vagabond voice that has the taste of the waters of the Mississippi, the wisdom of the Euphrates and the fecundity of the Congo . . ." (12).[21] Situating Hughes in the "revolutionary trenches" (trincheras revolucionarias) and among those who "have drunk in the miserable springs of the poor of the world," he asserts that "Hughes does not waste time on light palliatives nor lets resentment drag him to hatred; rather, he approaches reality with the moderation of the vagabond who has learned to take on all dangers, desiring for his race and the oppressed races of the world, the economic solution that makes them equal at its base" (12).[22]

Imbued with Marxist and liberal ideas from his own upbringing and readings, Zapata Olivella represents Hughes as a racial freedom-fighter who, despite setbacks to racial progress and the mounting threat of violence by the Ku Klux Klan, did not despair but saw beyond race to grasp the greater significance of class struggle. "Hughes does not believe in races but in opposing classes," Zapata Olivella concludes. "Hughes has faith in the proletariat that will liberate the oppressed" (16).[23]

If we consider Zapata Olivella's political orientation, it should not be surprising that he uses a Marxist language of machinery and oil—similar to the language Pavletich employed nineteen years earlier—to characterize the contribution and exploitation of enslaved Africans and their descendants within the US socioeconomic structure. Hughes, he repeats, "raises his vagabond voice . . . so that that very same North American people in their mad dash toward mechanization, do not forget the oil, the Negro who raises on his shoulders the miracle of the atoms."[24]

With the exception of *Pero con risas*, the Spanish translation of the novel *Not without Laughter* (1930), and the allusion to "The Negro Speaks of Rivers," Zapata Olivella does not mention Hughes's publications. But in conversations with Yvonne Captain-Hidalgo in the 1980s, he confirms the strong fraternal sentiment that his friend's poem had inspired in him: "Perhaps the [poem] that most influenced me in the sense of delighting me, in making me feel his brother, was "I, Too, Am America" (26).[25]

During the decade of the 1950s, Langston Hughes's engagement with Latin America continued unabated. But like many other intellectuals of the period, Hughes fell victim to the unrelenting attacks of Senator Joseph R. McCarthy of Wisconsin on persons identified as or suspected of being Communist Party members or sympathizers, or who were merely outspoken critics of US foreign policy or social ills.

If earlier writings by Hughes and his support of leftist causes made him vulnerable to the anticommunist hysteria sweeping the United States at that time, they most likely also strengthened his support from Latin American writers and intellectuals who opposed US policy in the hemisphere, including the coup d'état in Guatemala in 1954 and the continual bolstering of dictatorial regimes, such as that of the Somozas in Nicaragua.

New translations of Hughes's work appeared in anthologies of black poetry published in Mexico, Uruguay, and Argentina[26]; collections of poetry by French and English authors[27]; anthologies of contemporary US poetry[28]; and a variety of periodicals. These translations not only allowed previous generations of readers to reconnect with the poet and broaden their knowledge of his work but also introduced Hughes's name and writings to a new generation of readers. Among these was a group of students enrolled at the University of El Salvador who established the Círculo Literario Universitario (University Literary Circle) in 1956. The members of the Círculo published a monthly section in the newspaper *Diario Latino* in which they commented on literature, culture, and political issues.

One of the members of the Círculo, and perhaps its leading voice, was the aspiring poet and Marxist-oriented journalist Roque Dalton García, who in later years would gain international recognition as an original and revolutionary author. Among his early contributions to the Circle's monthly literary page was an article titled "Langston Hughes el ejemplo" (Langston Hughes the example), published in February of 1956. Identifying himself as a person incapable of understanding the concept of racial superiority that was evident in the United States and its concomitant practices of deprivation and discrimination, Dalton exalts and embraces the aesthetic counterweight of black poetry, asserting that "only we must understand the enormous beauty contained in the painful, prophetic, and eminently human Negro poetry."[29]

Within this poetic genre Dalton invokes the name of Langston Hughes, "un ejemplar poeta negro" (an exemplary Negro poet), as one of many "who have raised the flag of total redemption for the ridiculed, repudiated, and harried race."[30] He insists that the African American poet "is indicating roads of beauty to the desired future in which disappear the accursed pains that concomitantly have accompanied the Negro up to now." Hughes, Dalton continues, belongs to "the hemisphere of poets who tell the truth, to the hemisphere of poets committed to achieving a synthesis of the present pain and the certain hope of tomorrow."[31] To Dalton, Langston Hughes is thus "the logical and arrogant result of a pathetic state of homicidal actions and circumstances against a human sector that has been denied its humanity" and "a shining example" for the youth of America.[32] Reiterating Hughes's stature as a model, Dalton concludes that the poet is "an example that invites concern so that the truth will shine, in each throat, in each pen, above adversity and the interests that fight nightmarishly against him. An example that may give us the thirst for justice that all youth need, to fulfill the spiritual stature that their historical moment demands of them."[33]

Like Pavletich and Zapata Olivella, both of whom were relatively young writers of leftist persuasion, Roque Dalton also discerned in Hughes's writings a message that spoke to the needs, condition, and concerns of Latin American peoples, especially the youth of his generation, for whom the discourse of anti-imperialist and antidictatorial struggle paralleled that of the struggle of African Americans for freedom and against racism and discrimination. As Kutzinski states,

> The discourse of anti-US imperialism so pervasive in Latin America during the aftermath of the Spanish-Cuban-American War (1895–98), and quite inseparable from nationalist ideologies, provided translators and commentators alike with fertile ground for analogizing external and internal colonization: that is, they likened Latin American reactions to US neocolonial expansionism to the predicament of anti-black racism which Hughes scorned in so many of his poems. (551)

In short, as the title of Dalton's brief article denotes, Hughes provided to Latin American writers and intellectuals an example, a model, of committed literary art that successfully articulated the social and spiritual reality of a people. His literary art merged an awareness of the past with a vision of the future while also exuding aesthetic value simply and directly. Latin American writers and thinkers, Dalton suggests, could learn from Hughes's example.

Dalton's mention of several well-known poets of Spanish America and the United States[34] and use of undocumented quotations referring to Hughes suggest that he most likely had access to anthologies of black poetry, such as Toruño's *Poesía negra: Antología y ensayo*, published in México in 1953, or the second edition of Pereda Valdés's *Antología de la poesía negra americana*, published the same year in Uruguay. In fact, Toruño was editor of the "Sección Sábados de *Diario Latino*" in which the Círculo Literario Universitario was published. Using their original English titles, Dalton mentions four books by Hughes that were familiar to Latin American audiences: *Not without Laughter*, *The Big Sea*, *The Weary Blues*, and *Fine Clothes to the Jew*. The English usage suggests that Dalton was not personally acquainted with these texts. While he makes no reference to "I, Too," Dalton does cite verses from the poems "Negro" and "The Negro Speaks of Rivers."

Roque Dalton, Manuel Zapata Olivella, Jorge Artel, Jaime Barrera Parra, and Esteban Pavletich Trujillo are just a few of the many Latin American translators, commentators, and friends of Langston Hughes whose names, all too frequently, have been absent from scholarship devoted to Hughes's international reputation. Nevertheless, they are crucial to understanding his profound impact on the Latin American literati. His poems—and in particular "I, Too"—which captured the new dynamic spirit of African Americans while expressing their despair and enduring faith, readily found a receptive audience among the racially alienated and culturally marginalized citizens of Latin America. They understood his message well, for they, "too," wanted social change in their homelands. It is also important to remember that although Hughes was "black" according to the US hypodescent rule, which classified as black anyone of even distant African descent, for many Latin Americans he was a mulatto who could easily be one of them. Similarly, while the line "I am the darker brother" from "I, Too" is, understandably, usually construed within the US context to refer to African Americans, a reading of the verse within a broader continental context affords it a more general relevance to peoples of color throughout the Americas. Indeed, citizens of multiracial Latin America, who were commonly represented by Euro-Americans as darker-skinned peoples, often discerned in "I, Too" both a reflection of their own social, economic, and cultural realities and an insistence on the eventual triumph of the true meaning of the Americas as lands of freedom and opportunity. Moreover, despite the tendency of many in the United States to equate the name "America" with their country, the poem itself is neither racially nor geographically specific. Even though Hughes most likely had North America in mind, his use of the generic, all-encompassing toponym—"America"—confers to the poem a possibly unintentional ambiguity and flexibility that allow it to transcend national boundaries and encompass multiple historical and national contexts.

All available evidence indicates that Langston Hughes never set foot in Colombia, Peru, El Salvador, Panama, or many other lands of Latin America. Nevertheless, through his writings on everyday yet important concerns of the masses and the enlightened, through the many international friendships that he honored and maintained, and through his example as an able and dedicated poet who skillfully and unapologetically combined art and social commitment, he left a deep imprint on many Latin American writers.[35] In short, Langston Hughes engaged the Americas, and the Americas embraced Langston Hughes.

Notes

This essay is a revised and expanded version of a paper originally presented at the 2004 MLA Meeting in Philadelphia. I wish to thank Professors Dolan Hubbard and R. Baxter Miller for their interest and encouragement.

1. Asserting that she has "mapped the trajectory of every single known Hughes poem translated into Spanish and printed either in a book or in a periodical" (551), Kutzinski notes that prior to 1952 many of these translations had been circulating in anthologies and periodicals in Argentina, Chile, Costa Rica, Cuba, El Salvador, Mexico, Uruguay, and Venezuela (572). Kutzinski's research is both impressive and valuable. It does not, however, identify translations of Hughes's poems published in periodicals and anthologies in countries such as Colombia, Peru, and Panama.

2. Further evidence of the poem's significance for Spanish American poets and writers is Marcos Fingerit's anthology of African American poetry in Spanish translation, the title of which pays homage to Hughes's poem: *Yo también soy América: Panorama de poetas negros norteamericanos* (Buenos Aires: Ediciones Grifo, 1944). Kutzinski's research confirms that "I, Too" is Hughes's most translated poem in Spanish but does not mention Fingerit's collection (551).

3. The words "México, Octubre 1928" appear at the end of the article, indicating the place and date of the writing. Ironically, in that same year Mariátegui published his *Siete ensayos de interpretación de la realidad peruana*, in which he vilified the African influence in Peru. I know of no other publication on Langston Hughes's work that mentions or lists Pavletich's essay, and Wise does not mention it either.

4. The Spanish text reads: "La pujanza y el vigor juveniles del vasto Imperio Americano han podido *ocultar* . . . en el ensordecedor ruido de la conquista de los destinos universales los gérmenes de descomposición que *en sus propias entrañas* conspiran contra su dudosa estabilidad del porvenir" (7; emphasis added). All translations, unless otherwise noted, are mine.

5. The Spanish text reads: "el mensaje lírico, amargo y fuerte, de este gran negro poeta" and "el grito de veinte millones de hombres oprimidos implacablemente que, malgrado el Ku Klux Klan y la albura del imperio, 'son también América.'"

6. The Spanish text reads: "anuncia el ancho destino de su raza, en el que tanto hay de nuestro común destino."

7. It is important to note that the version of "I, Too" that Pavletich includes in his article does not use Fernández de Castro's first line ("Yo también honro a América"), but rather the verse that would become the first line of the translation that Mexican poet Xavier Villaurrutia would publish in 1931 in the journal *Contemporáneos* ("Yo también canto a América").

8. Pavletich writes: "(el) actual desorbitado concepto de superioridad racial que en gran proporción lubrica sus actitudes frente al mundo" (the present [US] excessive concept of racial superiority that in great part lubricates its attitudes toward the world).

9. The Spanish text reads: "Desasimilado del engranaje burgués, el negro en la actualidad constituye un peligroso tóxico para el organismo del Imperio, pese al bárbaro antídoto del Ku Klux Klan."

10. The Spanish text reads: "Si el regimen agrario norteamericano pudo ensancharse eficazmente gracias—en gran proporción—a la esclavitud brutal de una raza, la dinámica del Imperio se ha producido lubricada por la esclavitud de un continente."

11. The Spanish text reads: ". . . el mensaje de Langston Hughes habla muy hondo a nuestra conciencia subversiva, oxigenándola y fortaleciéndola. Desde campamentos diferentes—pero convergentes—nuestra voz se enlaza a su voz anhelosa y jadeante."

12. The Spanish text reads: "Es y se siente 'también América' porque él—él son veinte millones de hombres—fue obrero de esta América del Norte, fuerte y arrogante, que en mucho se le debe, que en mucho se nos debe. Cuando sólidas y conjugadas las filas de inconformes, cuando unida nuestra acción revolucionaria a su acción revolucionaria—otras más se sumarán en el trayecto—impongan anchos y nuevos caminos continentales, sí que será el 'hermano negro' en una América libertada en que no quepan esclavos ni esclavizadores."

13. Part of this discussion is based on my previous article "'We, Too, Are America': Langston Hughes in Colombia," published in the *Langston Hughes Review*.

14. The Spanish text reads: "Yo también soy un hombre, como el hombre blanco. Yo también contribuyo con la fuerza de mi espíritu y de mi inteligencia al engrandecimiento de la democracia en que vivo. Yo también soy bello porque tengo un espíritu como el espíritu del hombre blanco. Soy un creador de arte como el hombre blanco. Y un día éste y la casta que él representa, sentirán que mis gentes tienen iguales derechos que los suyos, y que el mundo y el sol y las alegrías de la vida se ha hecho para todos."

15. The Spanish text reads: "Es un hombre cordial, presdispuestos [sic] para las nobles manifestaciones de la amistad y el compañerismo. Lo conocimos en 1951, habiendo tenido la gentileza extraordinaria de relacionarnos con varios amigos. . . . En su casa de Harlem solíamos departir largamente sobre temas de América, conflictos humanos, ideales políticos. Es un espíritu generoso, sin reservas."

16. Though they appeared under the title "3 [i.e., Tres] Poemas de Huches Langston [sic]," there are actually translations of five poems: "Proenio" ("Proem"), "A una pequeña amante muerta" ("To a Little Lover-Lass Dead"), "A una bailarina negra de 'The Little Savoy'" ("To a Negro Dancer of the Little Savoy"), "Joven ramera" ("Young Prostitute"), and "Joven danzarina desnuda" ("Young Nude Dancer").

17. The article is divided into six separately titled sections: "Negros vagabundos" (Black vagabonds), "La jornada de trabajo" (The work day), "Un boleto para el teatro" (A ticket for the theater), "La lección de la vida" (The lesson of life), "Canto de amor y rebeldía" (Song of love and rebellion), and "El poeta y su raza" (The poet and his race).

18. The Spanish text reads: "Me gusta el estilo . . . y el tema se me hace interesante. . . . Creo que descuidas las pasiones humanas en la descripción. En la novela, y particularmente en el cuento, el hombre debe ser el tema central en torno al cual gire la narración. Si no hay sensibilidad humana descifrando el paisaje, no hay vida. Vuélve a escribirlo en función del protagonista central y habrá quien lo compre."
19. The Spanish text reads: "Langston Hughes, el hombre, mucho más interesante, mucho más sensitivo, mucho más humano que su propia poesía. Comprensivo, para con los jóvenes que aún no han descubierto el misterio de la ecuación del arte, pero que tratan de descifrarlo por imperativos categóricos."
20. The Spanish text reads: "Habíamos trabado conocimiento seis horas atrás y parecía conocernos desde la infancia. Es la ley de los vagabundos."
21. The Spanish text reads: "alza su voz de vagabundo que tiene el sabor de las aguas del Mississippi, la sabiduría del Eufrates y la fecundidad del Congo. . . ." Here Zapata Olivella obviously refers to three of the great waterways mentioned in Hughes's poem "The Negro Speaks of Rivers."
22. The Spanish text reads: "quienes como él han bebido en las fuentes míseras de los pobres del mundo . . . Hughes no se detiene en paliativos leves, ni se deja arrastrar al odio por el resentimiento, sino que enfoca la realidad con la mesura del vagabundo que ha sabido contraer todos los peligros, deseando para su raza y las oprimidas del mundo, la solución económica que las iguale por su base." Elsewhere Zapata Olivella describes Hughes as "el vagabundo de los siete ríos" (the vagabond of the seven rivers), a possible allusion to the seven sacred rivers of India and thus a poetic representation of Hughes as a world traveler.
23. The Spanish text reads: "Hughes no cree en razas sino en clases antagónicas. Hughes tiene fe en el proletariado que librará a los oprimidos."
24. The Spanish text reads: "alza su voz de vagabundo . . . para que ese mismo pueblo norteamericano en su loca carrera hacia el maquinismo, no olvide al aceite, al negro que levanta sobre sus espaldas el milagro de los átomos."
25. Zapata Olivella's words as recorded by Captain-Hidalgo are "Tal vez el [poema] que más me influyó en el sentido de entusiasmarme, en hacerme sentir hermano de él fue 'Yo también soy América.'"
26. See, respectively, Juan Felipe Toruño, ed., *Poesía negra: Antología y ensayo*; Simón Latino [Carlos Henrique Pareja], ed., *Los mejores versos de la poesía negra*; and Ildefonso Pereda Valdés, ed., *Antología de la poesía negra Americana*.
27. See Carlos López Narváez, comp. and trans., *El cielo en el río: Versiones de poemas del francés y del inglés*.
28. See Eugenio Florit, comp. *Antología de la poesía norteamericana contemporánea*.
29. The Spanish text reads: "a nosotros solamente, nos es dado comprender la enorme belleza que se encierra en la dolorosa, profética y eminente humana, poesía negra."

30. The Spanish text reads: "que han levantado la bandera de la redención total para la raza hostilizada, repudiada, escarnecida."
31. The Spanish text reads: "está señalando caminos con belleza al futuro anhelado, en que desaparezcan los dolores malditos, que de una manera casi concomitante han ido con el negro hasta ahora" and "en el hemisferio de los poetas que dicen la verdad, en el hemisferio de los poetas comprometidos en sacar una síntesis del dolor actual y la esperanza cierta del mañana."
32. The Spanish text reads: "resultado lógico y altivo de un estado patético de acciones y circunstancias homicidas en contra de un sector humano al que se ha querido negar la calidad de tal, es, para la juventud de América, un ejemplo luminoso."
33. The Spanish text reads: "Un ejemplo que invita a la preocupación por que la verdad resplandezca, en cada garganta, en cada pluma, por encima de la adversidad y los intereses que luchan dantescamente en su contra. Un ejemplo, que nos dé la sed de justicia que toda juventud precisa, para cumplir con la estatura espiritual que le reclama su momento histórico."
34. The poets are "Nicolás Guillén, Lewis Alexander, Regino Pedroso, Hugo Devieri, [Manuel] Arozarena, [Vicente] Gómez Kemp, Luis Palés Matos, Manuel R. Cárdenas, [and] Emilio Ballagas." Guillén, Pedroso, Arozarena, Gómez Kemp, and Ballagas were from Cuba; Alexander from the United States; Palés Matos from Puerto Rico; and Cárdenas from Venezuela. Devieri, who was Argentine, had also published a collection of *poesía negra* titled *Versos de piel negra: Antología de la poesía negra* (Buenos Aires: Editorial Mayo, 1945), which included translations of Hughes's poems "Song for a Dark Girl" ("Lamento de una muchacha negra"), "Cross" ("Cruz"), and "Union" ("Unión"). Kutzinski's article does not mention Devieri's anthology.
35. According to Dickinson, "The chief reasons for . . . [Hughes's international] popularity lie in his exposition of Negro music and American race relations—two topics of interest throughout the world" (117).

Works Cited

Artel, Jorge. "El autor de *Mulato*." *El País* 19 April 1960: 4.

_____. *Homenaje en honor de Langston Hughes[,] Luis Palés Matos [y] Rafael Hernández*. Panamá: Universidad de Panamá, 1967.

_____. "Modalidades artísticas de la raza negra." *Muros* 1 (1940): 16–20.

Barrera Parra, Jaime. "Notas del Week-end. Los negros de la civilización actual." *El tiempo* 6 Oct. 1929: 12.

Bertens, Hans. *Literary Theory: The Basics*. London: Routledge, 2001.

Calverton, V. F. "The Growth of Negro Literature." *Anthology of American Negro Literature*. New York: Modern Library, 1929. 1–17.

_____. "The Negro's New Belligerent Attitude." *Current History* 33 (1929): 1081–88.

Captain-Hidalgo, Yvonne. "Conversación con el doctor Manuel Zapata Olivella." *Afro-Hispanic Review* 4.1 (1985): 26–32.
Dalton, Roque. "Langston Hughes el ejemplo." *Diario Latino* 25 Feb. 1956: n.pag.
Devieri, Hugo, comp. *Versos de piel negra: Antología de la poesía negra*. Buenos Aires: Editorial Mayo, 1945.
Dickinson, Donald C. *A Bio-bibliography of Langston Hughes, 1902–1967*. 2nd ed. Hamden: Archon, 1972.
Fingerit, Marcos, comp. *Yo también soy América: Panorama de poetas negros norteamericanos*. Buenos Aires: Ediciones Grifo, 1944.
Florit, Eugenio, comp. *Antología de la poesía norteamericana contemporánea*. Washington: Unión Panamericana, 1955.
Góngora Mosquera, Juan. "Roque Dalton y la poética de la liberación." *Revista de crítica literaria latinoamericana* 17.34 (1991): 173–92. Web. 18 May 2011.
Hughes, Langston. *The Big Sea*. New York: Knopf, 1940.
———. *El inmenso mar*. Buenos Aires: Editorial Lautaro, 1944.
———. *Not without Laughter*. New York: Knopf, 1930.
———. *Pero con risas*. Trans. Néstor R. Ortiz Oderigo. Buenos Aires: Editorial Futuro, 1945.
———. "3 Poemas de Huches Langston [sic]." Trans. Jorge Artel. *La Hora* 15 June 1963: 8.
Jackson, Richard L. "Langston Hughes and the African Diaspora in South America." *Langston Hughes Review* 5.1 (1986): 23–33.
———. "The Shared Vision of Langston Hughes and Black Hispanic Writers." *Black American Literature Forum* 15.3 (1981): 89–92.
Kutzinski, Vera. "'Yo también soy América': Langston Hughes Translated." *American Literary History* 18.3 (2006): 550–78. *Project Muse*. Web. 19 Nov. 2006.
Latino, Simón [Carlos Henrique Pareja], ed. *Los mejores versos de la poesía negra*. Buenos Aires: Editorial Nuestra América, 1956.
Mariátegui, José Carlos. *Siete ensayos de interpretación de la realidad peruana*. Lima: Biblioteca "Amauta," 1928.
Mullen, Edward J. "Langston Hughes in Mexico and Cuba." *Review: Latin American Literature and Arts* 7 (1993): 23–27.
———. *Langston Hughes in the Spanish-Speaking World and Haiti*. Hamden: Archon, 1977.
———. "Langston Hughes y la crítica literaria hispanoamericana." *Memoria del XVII Congreso del Instituto Internacional de Literatura Iberoamericana*. Vol. 3. Madrid: Ediciones Cultura Hispánica del Centro Iberoamericano de Cooperación, 1978. 1395–1401.
———. "The Literary Reputation of Langston Hughes in the Hispanic World." *Comparative Literature Studies* 13.3 (1976): 254–69.
Pavletich, Esteban. "Un mensaje y un anuncio." *Labor* 3 (1928): 7–8.
Pereda Valdés, Ildefonso, comp. *Antología de la poesía negra americana*. Santiago de Chile: Ediciones Ercilla, 1936.
———. *Antología de la poesía negra americana*. Montevideo: B.U.D.A., 1953.

Prescott, Laurence E. "Brother to Brother: The Friendship and Literary Correspondence of Manuel Zapata Olivella and Langston Hughes." *Afro-Hispanic Review* 25.1 (2006): 87–103.

_____. "'We, Too, Are America': Langston Hughes in Colombia." *The Langston Hughes Review* 20 (2006): 34–46.

_____. *Without Hatreds or Fears: Jorge Artel and the Struggle for Black Literary Expression in Colombia*. Detroit: Wayne State UP, 2000.

Toruño, Juan Felipe, ed. *Poesía negra: Antología y ensayo*. México: Editorial Toledo, 1953.

Villaurrutia, Xavier. "Yo también canto a América." *Contemporáneos* (Mexico) 11 (1931): 157–59.

Wise, David O. "*Labor* (Lima, 1928–1929), José Carlos Mariátegui's Working-Class Counterpart to *Amauta*." *Revista de estudios hispánicos* 14:3 (1980): 117–28. *Periodical Archives Online*. Web. 12 May 2011.

Zapata Olivella, Manuel. *He visto la noche: Relatos*. Bogotá: Editorial "Los Andes," 1953.

_____. "Langston Hughes, el hombre." *Sábado* 23 Aug. 1947: 12, 16.

Langston Hughes, Modernism, and Modernity

John Lowney

Langston Hughes has long been celebrated for his innovative adaptations of African American vernacular and musical forms, from his blues and jazz poetry of the 1920s to his ambitious post–World War II jazz sequences, *Montage of a Dream Deferred* and *Ask Your Mama: 12 Moods for Jazz*. Hughes succeeded in writing poetry that is distinctively African American in its language and cultural references but also modern in its engagement with urban, mass cultural, and international social locations. It is interesting, then, that Hughes is not always recognized as a modernist poet, even though his experimentation with language and form has influenced subsequent generations of African diaspora poets. This essay will discuss how Hughes's critical engagement with modernity and his development of innovative poetic forms, especially those of his long poems, can be characterized as "Afro-modernist." Hughes's Afro-modernist poetics are based on the dramatic principle of montage, the dialogue of voices and discourses that occurs within poems as well as in sequences of poems. While this principle informs his earliest experimentation with vernacular forms of expression, I will discuss most intensively how *Montage of a Dream Deferred* and *Ask Your Mama* are exemplary Afro-modernist texts. Initially, I will explore the historical contexts of modernism. I will then consider a more theoretical understanding of modernism and modernity, including the poetics of dislocation with which modernism is usually associated. Finally, I will observe the expression of modernism and modernity in exemplary poems by Hughes.

Hughes began his literary career in the midst of the revolutionary political, social, and cultural changes that constituted modernity in the early twentieth century. Global change resulted from the devastation of World War I, the disintegration of European empires and the creation of new nation-states in these former colonies, and the Bolshevik Revolution in Russia. The early decades of the twentieth century also saw massive shifts in populations from rural areas to urban centers. Immigration, especially from southern and eastern Europe, and migration, especially of African Americans, to urban centers dramatically changed national identity in the United States. Corresponding with these processes of modernization were struggles for expanded access to democratic rights for women, workers, and racial minorities. New technologies also transformed society and the arts. World War I featured more advanced, and more brutal, weapons and modes of destruction. Not only did the war seem more chaotic and purposeless than any previous war, the numbers of dead and maimed were also unprecedented. At the same time, new modes of transportation created new ways of seeing and experiencing the world as well as increased mobility, but the introduction of automobile and air travel also resulted in unpredictable violence and chaos. Perhaps most importantly for writers, new communications technology such as the typewriter, the telephone, the tape recorder, the motion picture, and the radio created new modes of understanding the relationship between the speaker or writer and his or her audience. Coinciding with these technological changes were developments in the sciences that also challenged fundamental assumptions about perceptions of reality. Freud's theory of the unconscious, Einstein's theory of relativity, and Heisenberg's uncertainty principle made a case for the importance of irrationality, chance, and unpredictability.

Modernism, then, emerges from an intense consciousness of change, the feeling of living in totally novel times, of being disconnected from the past, of being a product of present technological and social change rather than part of a continuous tradition. What does this consciousness of change mean for modern artists? On the one hand, artists were compelled to find new modes for expressing this experience of newness: new forms, new styles, new languages. On the other hand, art became an especially powerful means for ordering what seemed like a chaotic world. Given the decline of religion and other traditional cultural institutions, art took on a greater importance for interpreting and making sense of the world.

There is another way to understand the relation of modernism to modernity, though, than through the assumption that the modern artist restores order and renews tradition in a chaotic world. For social groups whose access to cultural capital has traditionally been limited, such overwhelming change is not necessarily alienating. International modernism tends to be associated with a sense of cultural crisis, of the collapse of traditional myths and social structures, with a sense of anxiety about this collapse. But this collapse of traditional myths and social structures was potentially liberating for women, for example, who were gaining greater access to the public sphere. It was also potentially liberating for working people, whether they saw the Soviet Union as an exemplary communist state or not. And it was potentially liberating for people of color, whose demands for equality and justice were increasingly organized internationally as well as nationally within countries such as the United States. Afro-modernism, then, is a response to what was distinctive about Afro-modernity as well as to modernity in general. As Michael Hanchard writes, Afro-modernity "consists of the selective incorporation of technologies, discourses, and institutions of the modern West within the cultural and political practices of African-derived peoples to create a form of relatively autonomous modernity distinct from its counterparts of Western Europe and North America." Afro-modernity represents, then, "the negation of the idea of African and African-derived peoples as the antithesis of modernity" (247).

In the United States, the Afro-modernist response to modernity is usually identified with the New Negro (or Harlem) Renaissance. As a conscious recovery and reconsideration of African—as well as African American—cultural traditions, this reconsideration of what it means to be of African descent in the United States was at once a cultural and a political movement. It was, of course, a movement responding to the enormous social changes that had taken place among African Americans since Emancipation, from the promise of Reconstruction through the renewal of policies of racial discrimination, segregation, and injustice by the early twentieth century. The most notable change underlying the New Negro Renaissance was the massive migration of southern and, to a lesser extent, Caribbean blacks to northern urban areas such as Harlem. With the growth of black communities in urban centers, a new consciousness of black cultural identity emerged, especially among the younger generation that had grown up in the city. This identity affirmed pride in African heritage while aggressively challenging the social and political structures that limited African Americans from full participation as US citizens.

It is important to remember that the New Negro Renaissance was not limited to either Harlem or the United States, despite Harlem's importance as an African American cultural center in the 1920s. The New Negro Renaissance was part of a global movement that emphasized the right to self-determination for people of color worldwide. By the 1920s there were many institutions and organizations that contributed to the international dimensions of the New Negro Renaissance. These included the first Pan-African Congresses, which took place in Europe and featured the leadership of W. E. B. Du Bois; the Universal Negro Improvement Association, headed by Marcus Garvey, who had immigrated to New York from Jamaica; and the Communist Party and socialist organizations such as the African Blood Brotherhood, which included notable New Negro Renaissance writers such as Claude McKay. All of these organizations—and their media—stressed the shared interests of people of African descent and other people of color worldwide.

No writer better exemplifies the local and global implications of Afro-modernity than Langston Hughes. From his earliest years in the New Negro Renaissance through his involvement with the black power movement in the 1960s, he wrote with intimate knowledge of Harlem and a keen awareness of the international significance of African American culture. Recognition of Hughes's Afro-modernist poetics, however, has been limited by formulations of modernism that have excluded African American writing. New Critical formulations that privileged an exclusive canon of "high modernism" have had an especially misleading impact on literary history. Until the 1990s, modernism, with its formal preoccupations with alienation, fragmentation, epistemological uncertainty, and linguistic indeterminacy, was understood mostly as a European and Anglo-American phenomenon. Twentieth-century African American literature was, conversely, considered either antimodern or a culturally autonomous alternative to modernism. Such exclusive understandings of modernism overlook the plurality of modernisms as well as the interracial dimensions of modernism in the United States.[1] They overlook as well Hughes's association with international writers who aimed to "develop, even as they composed in the languages and styles of Europe and faced the challenge of European modernism, an aesthetic tied to a sense of myth, geography, history, and culture that was truly indigenous to their countries, rather than merely reflective of European trends" (Rampersad, "Approaches to Modernism" 67). These writers include poets whom Hughes translated, such as Federico García Lorca, Nicolás Guillén, and Jacques Roumain, as well as younger writers associated with the negritude movement, such as Aimé Césaire and Léopold Sédar Senghor.

The critical response to Hughes's early poetry suggests how controversial Afro-modernist writing was in the 1920s. The most common strategy for New Negro Renaissance poets was to write within traditional European and English poetic forms. The poetry of Claude McKay and Countee Cullen, for example, takes advantage of conventional forms to contrast dramatically the themes and language of the poems with the restrictions of form. That is, they chose to write in "respectable" poetic forms in order to reach their audience with provocative, socially critical ideas. Hughes represents an alternative response to modernity, as he seeks through formal experimentation inventive means to connect the African American past to the present. Hughes's poetry draws from a wide range of vernacular forms: folk tales, sermons, African American speech, and, most notably, the musical forms of the blues and jazz. In adapting vernacular forms for poetry, Hughes challenged more conservative readers of poetry, particularly African American intellectuals who associated poetry with high culture, rather than with night clubs or the streets. As his 1926 essay "The Negro Artist and the Racial Mountain" suggests, he did not only argue against middle-class moral and aesthetic norms; he explicitly identified his poetry with the expressive forms of the urban black working class, the "low-down folks, the so-called common element" (*Essays* 32). Hughes writes, "These common people are not afraid of spirituals, as for a long time their intellectual brethren were, and jazz is their child. They furnish a wealth of colorful, distinctive material for any artist because they still hold their own individuality in the face of American standardizations" (33). While the "common people" resist "American standardizations" individually and collectively, this resistance is not antimodern. Its defiance is identifiably urban and open to new social formations and technological means of expression. It is, as Hughes makes clear, a resistance that is based on the improvisational qualities associated with African cultural traditions *and* the modern sound of the blues and jazz. For Hughes, the popularity of the blues and jazz itself signified a generational revolt against established norms, including norms of what could be defined as African American folk expression, given that the blues and jazz were also commercially successful forms. Hughes recognized that while the blues had traditional roots in the songs of slave laborers, in the 1920s the blues sounded new and modern, as jazz sounded new and modern, because of the new contexts in which people heard African American music, whether in performance, through recordings, or on the radio.

Hughes's first two collections of poetry, *The Weary Blues* (1926) and *Fine Clothes to the Jew* (1927), were controversial because they celebrated the vernacular language as they dramatized the social tensions of urban African American working-class life. They furthermore transformed the musical forms of the blues and jazz into modes of social inquiry and social criticism, whether overtly or covertly. Poems such as "The Cat and the Saxophone (2 a.m.)," "Harlem Night Club," and "Jazz Band in a Parisian Cabaret" feature montages of voices and perspectives that evoke not only the double consciousness of African

American subjectivity but also the more insidious effects of the "color line." "The Cat and the Saxophone," for example, is structured as a dialogue of song lyrics (from "Everybody Loves My Baby, but My Baby Don't Love Nobody but Me") with the voices of musicians, drinkers, and dancers. While the lyrics are capitalized and the voices lowercase, the fragmentary lines create dramatic tension between performer and audience and between speakers responding to the music:

> BUT MY BABY
> Sure. Kiss me,
> DON'T LOVE NOBODY
> daddy.
> BUT ME.
> Say! (lines 9–14)[2]

The call-and-response structure of the poem underscores the unifying power of African American music, but at the same time the brokenness of the lines suggests a more anxious, more divided Afro-modernity. A similar effect is created with the more provocative interaction of blacks and whites in "Harlem Night Club." This poem evokes the nightclub as a site of interracial desire, a site that offers momentary release from the more restrictive world outside. Jazz is at once the source of this desire and its dramatic response, as the appeal to the jazz band to "Play, plAY, PLAY!" (3) begins and ends the poem, with the concluding reminder that "Tomorrow. . . . is darkness. / Joy today!" (20–21). Finally, "Jazz Band in a Parisian Cabaret" extends the interplay of nightclub voices to an international, multilingual location. Jazz is celebrated as a medium that can temporarily diminish class differences between "dukes and counts" (4) and "whores and gigolos" (5), or between "American millionaires" (6) and "school teachers / Out for a spree" (7–8). Its appeal is international as well, as the multilingual voices in the cabaret suggest, ranging from "May I?" (14), to "Mais oui" (15), to "Mein Gott!" (16), to "Parece una rumba" (17). As utopian as this cosmopolitan site of performance might seem, however, the poem's conclusion evokes a more ambiguous tension between the black performers and their white audience:

> Play it, jazz band!
> You've got seven languages to speak in
> And then some,
> Even if you do come from Georgia.
> Can I go home wid yuh, sweetie?
> Sure. (18–23)

While jazz is figured as a multilingual form of expression, the ironic if not demeaning statement "even if you do come from Georgia," followed by the vernacular proposition, compels us to consider whether the cosmopolitan idea suggested by the poem is as much an illusion as a temporary effect of jazz performance.

Hughes developed the montage form for more explicitly political purposes in the 1930s and 1940s, as his writing became increasingly identified with the urban, international, mass-cultural poetics of the popular front. There is considerable continuity, then, between the Afro-modernist engagement with the black working-class urban experience that he argues for in "The Negro Artist and the Racial Mountain" and the more polemical poetry he wrote during the Depression and World War II. The literary problem of mediating between the black "folk" and middle-class audiences informs his narrative fiction, drama, and, most popularly, his Simple stories as well as his poetry.[3] Hughes's Afro-modernist poetics found their fullest expression in the longer sequences he wrote after World War II, though, beginning with *Montage of a Dream Deferred*. Hughes's introduction to *Montage* explains the African American musical sources of its form:

> In terms of current Afro-American popular music and the sources from which it has progressed—jazz, ragtime, swing, blues, boogie-woogie, and be-bop—this poem on contemporary Harlem, like be-bop, is marked by conflicting changes, sudden nuances, sharp and impudent interjections, broken rhythms, and passages sometimes in the manner of the jam session, sometimes the popular song, punctuated by the riffs, runs, breaks, and disc-tortions of the music of a community in transition. (*Collected Poems* 387)

Montage, then, draws from the popular musical forms of Hughes's early poetry. In asserting how it relates to the social world it represents, however, Hughes identifies his poetry with the more experimental and more aggressive Afro-modernist sound of bebop. In the 1940s, the bebop sound of Charlie Parker, Dizzy Gillespie, Thelonious Monk, and others seemed harsher, noisier, and angrier than the more popular swing music, especially the swing music that had been popularized by white big bands. With its faster harmonic and rhythmic changes and its harmonic and rhythmic complexity, bebop seemed utterly discordant to its critics. At the same time, though, Hughes reminds us that bebop was traditional in its invocation of the blues even as it was defiantly modern in its reinvention of jazz forms.[4]

Montage expresses the social tensions of postwar Harlem through its formal and thematic evocations of bebop. The rapid movement between speakers and scenes suggests at once the anxious uncertainty of postwar Harlem and the corresponding sound of bebop. The poems that begin *Montage* illustrate how its montage form approximates the unexpected rhythmic and harmonic changes associated with bebop. The opening poem, "Dream Boogie," not only introduces the thematic motif of the "dream deferred" but also enacts the often abrupt movement of voice and mood that recurs throughout *Montage*. "Dream Boogie" begins with a direct address, "Good morning, daddy!" (1), and asks "Ain't you heard / The boogie-woogie rumble / Of a dream deferred?"

(2–4). The speaker then asks the listener what he hears when he listens more closely:

> You'll hear their feet
> Beating out and beating out a—
>
> *You think*
> *It's a happy beat?* (6–9)

Through this dramatic interruption of the poem's "boogie" rhythm, Hughes questions our expectations of African American popular music. Like bebop, "Dream Boogie" disrupts our expectations of rhythmic and harmonic continuity. In doing so, it accentuates the postwar urgency of the African American "dream deferred."

The poem that follows "Dream Boogie," "Parade," locates the problem of the "dream deferred" in a more recognizably political arena. The movement from the popular music of "Dream Boogie" to the formal ceremony of "Parade" seems unlikely, but "Parade" similarly accentuates the discrepancy of "black and white" perceptions of African American culture. Beginning with a participant's description of the procession, "Parade" is soon interrupted by "Motorcycle cops, / white" (13–14), who judge that "Solid black, / can't be right" (18–19). The police cannot "speed it / out of sight" (15–16), however; instead, the parade becomes a more determined act of resistance. An unidentified first-person speaker asks

> *I never knew*
> *that many Negroes*
> *were on earth,*
> *did you?*
>
> *I never knew!* (23–27)

In response to this question, another speaker affirms his right to march, as an individual and as a part of the collective black parade, and celebrates his "chance to let . . . the whole world see . . . old black me" (29–33). With the insistent repetition of "marching," which resonates with the wartime experience of black veterans, and with the repeated capitalization of "PARADE!", Hughes underscores the resolve of the marchers and translates this ceremonial event into an expression of black pride. The dramatic movement of "Parade," then, is not entirely different from the disruptive pattern of "Dream Boogie." Both poems are interrupted by shifts of voice and mood that are as thematically significant as they are formally suggestive of bebop. Through this opening montage of voices, whether interior or vocalized, Hughes introduces the psychological and social implications of the African American "dream deferred."

The dramatic juxtaposition of voices and scenes throughout *Montage* recalls the history of black struggle as much as the "community in transition" that was postwar Harlem. The concluding section of *Montage* suggests the international as well as national implications of its Afro-modernist portrayal of Harlem. As "Good Morning" suggests, the "dream deferred" is amplified, and complicated, by the growing immigrant and migrant populations that were transforming Harlem and all of New York City. "Good Morning" represents the testimony of a lifetime Harlemite who had seen generations of migrants from "Georgia Florida Louisiana" (13) and immigrants from "Puerto Rico . . . Cuba Haiti Jamaica" (9–11). He concludes, though, that their cultural differences are less significant than the racial barriers they encountered. They arrive

> wondering
> wide-eyed
> dreaming
> out of Penn Station—
> but the trains are late. (18–22)

While "the gates open," there are "bars at each gate" (23–25). In accentuating the shared predicament as well as the divisive conflicts of postwar African America, Hughes extends the "dream deferred" beyond the geographical boundaries of Harlem. By reiterating the mode of address that begins *Montage*, "Good Morning" reaffirms the critical power of African American music, especially bebop. Like the demanding Afro-modernist art of the bebop musicians whom Hughes celebrates, *Montage* itself defies the critical presumptions of black *and* white middle-class audiences. In adapting the confrontational stance of bebop, Hughes furthermore succeeds in renewing the mythic significance of Harlem as a site of African American collective memory.

Hughes's Afro-modernist writing became more decidedly international in the last two decades of his life, as his longest and most ambitious poem, *Ask Your Mama*, so dramatically exemplifies. Hughes's writing of the 1950s and early 1960s is informed by several overlapping concerns: the development of anticolonial liberation movements in Africa and the Caribbean, the movement for African American civil rights in the United States, and the growth of jazz as an increasingly international medium of expression. Hughes played an important role in shaping an international canon of African diaspora poetry after World War II, beginning with the landmark anthology he coedited with Arna Bontemps, *The Poetry of the Negro, 1746–1949* (1949). Hughes's role in promoting African writers became increasingly prominent by the 1960s, during which he edited two Pan-Africanist anthologies, *An African Treasury: Articles, Essays, Stories, Poems by Black Africans* (1960) and *Poems from Black Africa* (1963). This work coincided with Hughes's growing involvement with African diaspora cultural productions that combined music with the literary arts, including his collaboration with the jazz pianist Randy Weston on his groundbreaking recording *Uhuru Africa* (1961). It is not surprising, then, that *Ask Your Mama* features the interaction of African cultures in the Americas and Africa, with its evocation of Afro-Caribbean as well as African American music and its movement between different sites of black revolutionary struggle. In this context, jazz plays an explicitly political role in expressing the revolutionary desire for black liberation in the United States, Africa, and the Caribbean.

When *Ask Your Mama* was first published, readers struggled to comprehend its unfamiliar form and widely allusive content. The book is structured as a score for performance, as each section includes instructions for the kind of music meant to accompany it, and its wide-ranging reference to African diaspora history, geography, and music is demanding. Even its appearance is resolutely modern, as its shape resembles a record album, its pages are multicolored, and the words of the poem are printed entirely in capital letters. The structure of *Ask Your Mama* is clear enough: twelve movements, or moods, that are based on the theme introduced by "The Hesitation Blues": "How long must I wait? Can I get it now or must I hesitate?" Each of the twelve moods follows the African-American oral form of ritual insult known as "the dozens," and the twelve moods correspond with the twelve bars of "The Hesitation Blues." As definitive as this structure is, there is considerable room, as Hughes writes in his introductory notes, "for spontaneous jazz improvisation, particularly between verses, where the voice pauses" (*CP* 475). *Ask Your Mama* follows a pattern of juxtaposition not unlike that of *Montage*: the gaps between voices, scenes, and sections play as important a role for the reader's interpretation of the poem as the more noticeable thematic continuities. This structure also heightens the thematic significance of the poem's unpredictable movement between cultures.[5]

Hughes consistently stressed the cross-cultural importance of jazz in the 1950s and early 1960s. He defined jazz, however, within a continuum of African diaspora music rather than in a nationalist framework as a distinctively American form of music.[6] Ideological debates about the international significance of jazz and black music in general are integral to *Ask Your Mama*. The interaction of African American civil rights and African liberation movements is dramatized, often surprisingly, by the blend of African diaspora musical forms that Hughes invokes in the first mood of his long poem, "Cultural Exchange." Hughes also develops thematic patterns that recur throughout *Ask Your Mama* through the figures of black celebrities introduced in "Cultural Exchange." The various international locations of these figures transform jazz into an African diaspora form of "cultural exchange." Through its unpredictable patterns of movement, *Ask Your Mama* disrupts ideas of "culture" that assume hierarchical oppositions of white and black, European and African, American and African American, modernist and popular, and written and vernacular. This process likewise challenges readers' expectations of African American poetry, jazz, and modernism.

"Cultural Exchange" begins by stressing what is specific to racial formation in the United States. It does so, however, by satirizing racial stereotypes and reversing racial hierarchies. The initial "cultural exchange" takes place in the United States, "IN THE QUARTER OF THE NEGROES" (3), and the "ambassador" is "AN AFRICAN IN MID-DECEMBER / SENT BY THE STATE DEPARTMENT / AMONG THE SHACKS TO MEET THE BLACKS" (24–26). This reversal of the more familiar pattern of African American cultural ambassadors sent by the State Department to Africa not only contests the Cold War worldview of the United States as the center of "freedom" but also recalls the experience of racism by African diplomats who visited the United States in the 1950s. In reversing the more familiar route of "cultural exchange" between the United States and Africa, Hughes mocks naïve perceptions of cultural difference. At the same time, he emphasizes the challenges, as well as the potential, for Pan-Africanist alliances that are suggested later in the first mood and throughout *Ask Your Mama*.

"Cultural Exchange," then, underscores the uncertainty of the term *culture*, whether it evokes differences based on social class, nationality, or race. "Cultural Exchange" also describes the poem's act of reversing cultural expectations, beginning with the repetition of "quarter" in its opening lines:

> IN THE
> IN THE QUARTER
> IN THE QUARTER OF THE NEGROES
> WHERE THE DOORS ARE DOORS OF PAPER
> DUST OF DINGY ATOMS
> BLOWS A SCRATCHY SOUND. (1–6)

The "quarter" is introduced hesitatingly, but insistently, accentuating the economic sources and implications of racial segregation. "THE QUARTER OF THE NEGROES" is also a refuge, though, "AMORPHOUS" (7) to outsiders, but culturally distinctive to insiders in its creative capacity to improvise. If "THE DOORS ARE DOORS OF PAPER," with the economic, legal, and textual associations of "PAPER," and they are too insubstantial to withstand the wind, they are also more open to possible change.

The intercultural dynamic of uncertainty suggested by the opening lines of "Cultural Exchange" is intensified by the accompanying musical directions: "The rhythmically rough scraping of a guira continues monotonously until a lonely flute call, high and far away, merges into piano variations on German lieder gradually changing into old-time traditional 12-bar blues up strong between verses until African drums throb against blues fading as the music ends" (*CP* 477–78). This initial mix of African diaspora scenes and sounds undergoes numerous variations throughout *Ask Your Mama*. For example, the second mood, "Ride, Red, Ride," reiterates the book's title through Spanish variations in a sequence of Latin American, Caribbean, and African locations, featuring revolutionary leaders such as Fidel Castro and Patrice Lumumba, and asks again, "TELL ME HOW LONG — / MUST I WAIT? / CAN I GET IT NOW?" (4–6). The musical directions for this mood likewise feature a blend of maracas, calypso, and New Orleans jazz, reminding us of the creole roots of jazz in the United States. Such geographical and sonic blending, here and elsewhere in *Ask Your Mama*, complicates the term "NEGRO," suggesting cultural differences as well as cross-cultural commonalities. The multilingual array of proper names, place names, and names of contemporaneous, historical, and mythic figures has a similar effect: Hughes expands his readers' awareness of African diaspora history while contesting the reductive terms that structure Jim Crow racism. At the same time, however, "Ride, Red, Ride," like subsequent sections of *Ask Your Mama*, shows how the shared roots of slavery link Latin American and Caribbean "blacks" with African Americans, despite different histories of racial formation.

If *Ask Your Mama* can be considered "African American poetry's first Afro-Cuban jazz poem" (Kun 172), it looks back to earlier formations of Marxist and Pan-Africanist internationalism as much as contemporaneous African and Caribbean independence movements. *Ask Your Mama* likewise invokes earlier modes of jazz, blending traditional with new modes of jazz, not unlike the compositions of Charles Mingus, who accompanied Hughes on his 1958 poetry recording, *The Weary Blues*. "Shades of Pigmeat," the third mood of *Ask Your Mama*, exemplifies this sonic movement between cultures. It also exemplifies the tonal range of the poem's sense of humor, as humor serves as a political weapon as well as an emotional release from pain and disappointment. "Shades of Pigmeat" proceeds through a series of unlikely propositions that accentuate the absurdity of cultural prejudice. For example, "THE TALMUD IS CORRECTED / BY A STUDENT IN A FEZ" (24–25). This student is furthermore

> . . . TO JESUIT
> AS NORTH POLE IS TO SOUTH
> OR ZIK TO ALABAMA
> OR BIG MAYBELL TO
> THE MET. (26–30)

The juxtaposition of these "poles" with a sonic mix of "'Eli Eli' merging into a wailing Afro-Arabic theme with flutes and steady drum beat changing into blues" (*CP* 486–87) renders the logic of this proposition as absurd as the possibilities it imagines. If North and South are more alike than not, whether this geography is hemispheric or specific to the United States, then there is every reason to imagine Nigerian President "Zik" Azikiwe, Hughes's classmate at Lincoln University and an important theorist of Pan-Africanism, in Alabama. There is likewise reason to imagine Big Maybell, the rhythm and blues singer Mabel Louise Smith, performing at the Metropolitan Opera. There is reason to mix philosophical, religious, cultural, or musical modes in the spirit of "Pigmeat" Markam, the African American comedian, singer, dancer, and actor—in the spirit, that is, of African American traveling music, burlesque, and vaudeville shows. There is every reason, that is, to improvise as imaginatively as possible, to answer the urgent claims of Hughes's liner note for "Shades of Pigmeat": "Oppression by any other name is just about the same, casts a long shadow, adds a dash of bitters to each song, makes of almost every answer a question, and of men of every race or religion questioners" (*CP* 528).

By making "every answer a question" and by making its readers "questioners," *Ask Your Mama* asks us to consider new cultural combinations—Africa/America, North/South, or high/low—and new political alliances in order to address the question posed by the "Hesitation Blues": "How long must I wait? Can I get it now or must I hesitate?" As open-ended as this question is, as widely resonant as it becomes through the Afro-modernist form of *Ask Your Mama*, it expresses the social democratic ethos that motivates Hughes's writing throughout his career. In the final mood of *Ask Your Mama*, the "QUARTER" becomes twenty-five cents, "CHANGE" becomes pocket money, and "ASK YOUR MAMA" becomes a child's appeal to his mama for "SHOW FARE." Meanwhile, "bop blues" and "modern jazz" give way to "'The Hesitation Blues' very loud, lively and raucously" (*CP* 525). This raucous music is as much the sound of anger as the sound of sadness, but it is also the sound of defiant laughter, a rebellious renewal of the Afro-modernist jazz sound that Hughes first articulated in "The Negro Artist and the Racial Mountain": "the eternal tom-tom beating in the Negro soul—the tom-tom of revolt against weariness in a white world, a world of subway trains, and work, work, work; the tom-tom of joy and laughter, and pain swallowed in a smile" (*Essays* 35).

Notes
1. For contrasting accounts of the New Negro Renaissance as a modernist movement, see Baker, Douglass, Hutchinson, and Sanders.
2. All quotations from Hughes's poetry are from his *Collected Poems*. Quotations from his poetry hereafter will be cited parenthetically by line numbers.
3. The importance of leftist literary and cultural politics to Hughes's poetry is addressed at length in Dawahare, Graham, Smethurst, and Thurston.
4. See Tracy for the most comprehensive account of Hughes's literary engagement with African American music.
5. For cogent explanations of the structure of *Ask Your Mama* and its implications, see Jones, Kun 143-83, Miller, and Scanlon.
6. See, for example, "Jazz as Communication" and "The Roots of Jazz."

Works Cited

Baker, Houston A., Jr. *Modernism and the Harlem Renaissance*. Chicago: U of Chicago P, 1987.

Dawahare, Anthony. *Nationalism, Marxism, and African American Literature between the Wars*. Jackson: UP of Mississippi, 2003.

Douglas, Ann. *Terrible Honesty: Mongrel Manhattan in the 1920s*. New York: Farrar, 1995.

Graham, Maryemma. "The Practice of a Social Art." *Langston Hughes: Critical Perspectives Past and Present*. Ed. Henry Louis Gates Jr. and K. A. Appiah. New York: Amistad, 1993. 213-35.

Hanchard, Michael. "Afro-Modernity: Temporality, Politics, and the African Diaspora." *Public Culture* 11.1 (1999): 245-68.

Hughes, Langston. *The Collected Poems of Langston Hughes*. Ed. Arnold Rampersad and David Roessel. New York: Knopf, 1994.

_____. *Essays on Art, Race, Politics, and World Affairs*. Ed. Christopher C. De Santis. Columbia: U of Missouri P, 2002. Vol. 9 of *The Collected Works of Langston Hughes*. Ed. Arnold Rampersad et al. 16 vols. 2001-03.

Hutchinson, George. *The Harlem Renaissance in Black and White*. Cambridge: Harvard UP, 1995.

Jones, Meta DuEwa. "Listening to What the Ear Demands: Langston Hughes and His Critics." *Callaloo* 25.4 (2002): 1145-75.

Kun, Josh. *Audiotopia: Music, Race, and America*. Berkeley: U of California P, 2005.

Miller, R. Baxter. "Framing and Framed Languages in Hughes's *Ask Your Mama: 12 Moods for Jazz*." *MELUS* 17.4 (1991–92): 3–13.

Rampersad, Arnold. "Langston Hughes and Approaches to Modernism in the Harlem Renaissance." *The Harlem Renaissance: Revaluations*. Ed. Amritjit Singh, William S. Shiver, and Stanley Brodwin. New York: Garland, 1989. 49–71.

_____. *The Life of Langston Hughes*. Vol. 2. New York: Oxford UP, 1988.

Sanders, Mark A. "American Modernism and the New Negro Renaissance." *The Cambridge Companion to American Modernism*. Ed. Walter Kalaidjian. New York: Cambridge UP, 2005. 129–56.

Scanlon, Larry. "News From Heaven: Vernacular Time in Langston Hughes's *Ask Your Mama*." *Callaloo* 25.1 (2002): 45–65.

Smethurst, James. *The New Red Negro: The Literary Left and African American Poetry, 1930–1946*. New York: Oxford UP, 1999.

Thurston, Michael. *Making Something Happen: American Political Poetry between the World Wars*. Chapel Hill: U of North Carolina P, 2001.

Tracy, Steven C. *Langston Hughes and the Blues*. Urbana: U of Illinois P, 1988.

RESOURCES

Chronology of Langston Hughes's Life

1902	James Langston Hughes is born to James Nathaniel Hughes and Carrie Mercer Langston Hughes on February 1 in Joplin, Missouri.
1916	Hughes is elected poet of his grammar class.
1919	The young poet spends the summer in Mexico with his father.
1920	Hughes graduates from Central High in Cleveland, Ohio.
1921	Hughes publishes the lyric "The Negro Speaks of Rivers" in the *Crisis*, the publication of the National Association for the Advancement of Colored People (NAACP). He enrolls in Columbia University.
1922	Hughes drops out of Columbia and throws most of his books into the sea, except for Walt Whitman's *Leaves of Grass*. He begins to travel the world.
1923	Hughes writes the poem "The Weary Blues" and sails to West Africa aboard the West Hesseltine, a freighter.
1925	Hughes receives literary awards from both the *Crisis* and *Opportunity*, two of the most influential publications by African Americans.
1926	In January, Hughes publishes *The Weary Blues*, his first volume of poems and a milestone in American musical poetics. He enrolls at Lincoln University, a historically black institution in Pennsylvania.
1927	He meets fellow writer Zora Neale Hurston and tours the South with her. *Fine Clothes to the Jew* is published. Hughes meets the highly influential Charlotte Osgood Mason, who becomes his patron.
1929	Hughes graduates from Lincoln.
1930	Hughes breaks with Mason. *Not without Laughter*, his first novel, is published.

1931	Having been awarded the Harmon Gold Medal for literature, Hughes tours the South again. He meets Mary McLeod Bethune in Florida, travels to Haiti with former Lincoln classmate Zell Ingram, and visits the Scottsboro Boys in prison. The guest of Noël Sullivan, a prominent member of a well-respected family, he travels to San Francisco. *Dear Lovely Death*, a small pamphlet of poems, is published privately.
1932	Hughes ventures to the Soviet Union to work on an ill-fated film about race relations in the United States. Given a copy of D. H. Lawrence's short stories, he is inspired to write in the genre.
1934	*The Ways of White Folks* is published, and Hughes raises money for the defense of the Scottsboro Boys. He travels to Mexico upon news of his father's death.
1935	Hughes's play *Mulatto*, which would go on to set records for a production by an African American, is produced on Broadway.
1936	At least two and perhaps as many as six of his plays are produced by Karamu Theater, which he helped found in Cleveland.
1937	Hughes reports on the Spanish Civil War for the newspaper the *Baltimore African American*.
1938	He founds the somewhat leftist Harlem Suitcase Theater in New York. The International Workers Order prints perhaps his most polemical volume, *A New Song*, featuring the revolutionary poem "Let America Be America Again."
1940	Hughes's first autobiography, *The Big Sea*, is published.
1941	Awarded a Rosenwald fellowship, he leaves Carmel, California, for Chicago, Illinois, where he establishes the Skyloft Players. Later, he returns to New York.
1942	*Shakespeare in Harlem* is published. Hughes's play *The Sun Do Move* is produced by the Skyloft Players.

1943	Writing for the African American newspaper the *Chicago Defender*, he invents the comical character Jesse B. Semple.
1945	He collaborates with Mercer Cook to translate *Masters of the Dew*, a novel of Haitian peasant life by Hughes's friend Jacques Roumain.
1947	*Fields of Wonder* is published.
1949	*One-Way Ticket* introduces his famous comic character Madame Alberta K. Johnson, the poetic complement to prose character Jesse B. Semple. Hughes's opera *Troubled Island*, recounting the history of Haiti, is produced in New York.
1950	The opera *The Barrier* earns some acclaim in New York but fails on Broadway. *Simple Speaks His Mind* becomes the first book culled from Hughes's newspaper narratives.
1951	*Montage of a Dream Deferred* is published. Hughes's first experimental poetry book, it is designed as an extensive collage.
1952	*Laughing to Keep from Crying*, his second volume of short stories, is published.
1953	*Simple Takes a Wife* is published. Senator Joseph McCarthy investigates Hughes for his leftist leanings, calling him to testify in Washington, DC.
1956	Hughes's second autobiography, *I Wonder as I Wander*, is published.
1957	*Simple Stakes a Claim* is published.
1958	Based on one of his gospel plays, Hughes's second novel, *Tambourines to Glory*, is published.
1959	*Selected Poems*, which omits many of his more radical pieces, is published.
1960	*The First Book of Africa* and the edited anthology *An African Treasury* are published.

1961	*The Best of Simple* is published.
1963	*Something in Common, and Other Stories*, comprising ten new pieces and twenty-seven reprints, is published.
1966	Hughes concludes his narrative sequence about the comic character Simple and publishes *The Book of Negro Humor*. Funded by the United States government, he is recognized at the First World Festival of Negro Arts, held in Dakar, Senegal.
1967	*The Best Short Stories by Negro Writers* is published. Hughes dies on May 22 at the Polyclinic Hospital of New York. *The Panther and the Lash* is published posthumously.

Works by Langston Hughes

Poetry
The Weary Blues, 1926
Fine Clothes to the Jew, 1927
Dear Lovely Death, 1931
The Negro Mother and Other Dramatic Recitations, 1931
The Dream Keeper and Other Poems, 1932
Scottsboro Limited: Four Poems and a Play in Verse, 1932
A New Song, 1938
Shakespeare in Harlem, 1942
Jim Crow's Last Stand, 1943
Lament for Dark Peoples, 1944
Fields of Wonder, 1947
One-Way Ticket, 1949
Montage of a Dream Deferred, 1951
Selected Poems of Langston Hughes, 1959
Ask Your Mama: 12 Moods for Jazz, 1961
The Panther and the Lash: Poems of Our Times, 1967

Short Fiction
The Ways of White Folks, 1934
Simple Speaks His Mind, 1950
Laughing to Keep from Crying, 1952
Simple Takes a Wife, 1953
Simple Stakes a Claim, 1957
The Best of Simple, 1961
Something in Common and Other Stories, 1963
Simple's Uncle Sam, 1965
The Return of Simple, 1994
Short Stories, 1996

Long Fiction
Not without Laughter, 1930
Tambourines to Glory, 1958

Drama
Mulatto, 1935
Little Ham, perf. 1936
Don't You Want to Be Free?, 1938
Freedom's Plow, 1943
Street Scene, 1947 (lyrics)
Troubled Island, perf. 1949 (opera libretto)
The Barrier, 1950 (opera libretto)
Esther, 1957 (opera libretto)
Simply Heavenly, perf. 1957 (opera libretto)
Black Nativity, perf. 1961
The Gospel Glow, 1962
Five Plays, 1963 (ed. Walter Smalley)
Tambourines to Glory, 1963
Jericho-Jim Crow, perf. 1964
The Prodigal Son, perf. 1965

Nonfiction
The Big Sea: An Autobiography, 1940
Famous American Negroes, 1954
Famous Negro Music Makers, 1955
The Sweet Flypaper of Life, 1955 (photographs by Roy De Carava)
A Pictorial History of the Negro in America, 1956 (with Milton Meltzer)
I Wonder as I Wander: An Autobiographical Journey, 1956
Famous Negro Heroes of America, 1958
Fight for Freedom: The Story of the NAACP, 1962
Black Magic: A Pictorial History of the Negro in American Entertainment, 1967 (with Meltzer)
Black Misery, 1969 (illustrations by Arouni)
Arna Bontemps–Langston Hughes Letters, 1925–1967, 1980 (ed. Charles H. Nichols)
Remember Me to Harlem: The Letters of Langston Hughes and Carl Van Vechten, 1925–1964, 2001 (ed. Emily Bernard)

Edited Texts
The Poetry of the Negro, 1746–1949, 1949 (with Arna Bontemps)
The Book of Negro Folklore, 1958 (with Bontemps)
An African Treasury, 1960
Poems from Black Africa, 1963
New Negro Poets: U.S.A., 1964
The Book of Negro Humor, 1966
The Best Short Stories by Negro Writers: An Anthology from 1899 to the Present, 1967

Miscellaneous
The Langston Hughes Reader, 1958
The Collected Works of Langston Hughes, 2001–2003 (16 vols.; ed. Arnold Rampersad et al.)

Screenplay
Way Down South, 1939 (with Clarence Muse)

Translations
Masters of the Dew, 1945 (by Jacques Roumain; with Mercer Cook)
Cuba Libre, 1949 (by Nicolás Guillén; with Ben Carruthers)
Gypsy Ballads, 1951 (by Federico García Lorca)
Selected Poems of Gabriela Mistral, 1957

Children's Literature
Popo and Ffjina: Children of Haiti, 1932 (story; with Arna Bontemps)
The First Book of Negroes, 1952
The First Book of Rhythms, 1954
The First Book of Jazz, 1955
The First Book of the West Indies, 1956
The First Book of Africa, 1960

Bibliography

Barksdale, Richard K. "Langston Hughes: His Times and His Humanistic Techniques." *Black American Literature and Humanism*. Ed. R. Baxter Miller. Lexington: UP of Kentucky, 1981. 11–26.

_____. *Langston Hughes: The Poet and His Critics*. Chicago: ALA, 1977.

Berry, Faith. *Langston Hughes, Before and Beyond Harlem*. Westport: Hill, 1983.

Brown, Soi-Daniel. "'Black Orpheus': Langston Hughes' Reception in German Translation." *Langston Hughes Review* 4 (1985): 30–38.

Cobb, Martha. *Harlem, Haiti, and Havana: A Comparative Critical Study of Langston Hughes, Jacques Roumain, Nicolás Guillén*. DC: Three Continents, 1979.

Dickinson, Donald C. *A Bio-Bibliography of Langston Hughes, 1902–1967*. Hamden: Archon, 1967.

Emanuel, James A. *Langston Hughes*. New York: Twayne, 1967. Twayne US Author Ser. 123.

Filatova, Lydia. "Langston Hughes: American Writer." *International Literature* 11 (1933): 103–05.

Gates, Skip. "Of Negroes Old and New." *Transition* 46 (n.d.): 45–57.

Guillaume, Alfred Jr. "And Bid Him Translate: Langston Hughes's Translation of Poetry from French." *Langston Hughes Review* 4 (1985): 1–8.

Harper, Donna Akiba Sullivan. *Not So Simple: The "Simple" Stories by Langston Hughes*. Columbia: U of Missouri P, 1995.

Hubbard, Dolan. "Bibliographical Essay." *A Historical Guide to Langston Hughes*. Ed. Steven C. Tracy. New York: Oxford UP, 2004. 197–234.

Hudson, Theodore. "Langston Hughes's Last Volume of Verse." *CLA Journal* 11 (1968): 345–48.

Huggins, Nathan. *Harlem Renaissance*. New York: Oxford UP, 1971.

Hughes, Langston. *The Collected Poems of Langston Hughes*. Ed. Arnold Rampersad and David E. Roessel. New York: Knopf, 1994.

_____. *The Collected Works of Langston Hughes*. 16 vols. Ed. Arnold Rampersad et al. Columbia: U of Missouri P, 2001–03.

Hughes, Langston, and Carl Van Vechten. *Remember Me to Harlem: The Letters of Langston Hughes and Carl Van Vechten, 1925–1964*. Ed. Emily Bernard. New York: Knopf, 2001.

Jackson, Blyden. "A Word About Simple." *CLA Journal* (1968): 310–18.

Jemie, Onwuchekwa. *Langston Hughes: An Introduction to the Poetry*. New York: Columbia UP, 1976. Columbia Introd. to 20th-Cent. Amer. Poetry.

Kearney, Reginald. "Langston Hughes in Japanese Translation." *Langston Hughes Review* 4 (1985): 27–29.

Kent, George E. "Langston Hughes and the Afro-American Folk and Cultural Tradition." *Langston Hughes: Black Genius*. Ed. Thurman B. O'Daniel. New York: Morrow, 1971. 183–210.

Killens, John. "Broadway in Black and White." *African Forum* (n.d.): 66–76.

King, Woodie. "Remembering Langston Hughes." *Negro Digest* 18 (1969): 27–32, 95–96.

Kinnamon, Keneth. "The Man Who Created Simple." *Nation* 205 (1967): 599–601.

Kramer, Aaron. "Robert Burns and Langston Hughes." *Freedomways* 8 (1968): 159–66.

Lewis, David Levering. *When Harlem Was in Vogue*. New York: Knopf, 1981.

Locke, Alain. "The Negro in American Literature." *Anthology of American Negro Literature*. Ed V. F. Calverton. New York: Modern Library, 1929.

———. "The Negro Poets of the United States." *Anthology of Magazine Verse for 1926, and Yearbook of American Poetry*. Ed. William Stanley Braithwaite. Boston: Brimmer, 1927.

McLaren, Joseph. "Langston Hughes and Africa: From the Harlem Renaissance to the 1960s." *Juxtapositions: The Harlem Renaissance and the Lost Generation*. Ed. Loes Nas and Chandré Carstens. Cape Town: U of Cape Town, 2000. 77–94.

———. *Langston Hughes: Folk Dramatist in the Protest Tradition, 1921–1943*. Westport: Greenwood, 1997. Contributions in Afro-Amer. and African Studies 181.

Meltzer, Milton. *Langston Hughes: A Biography*. New York: Crowell, 1968.

Mikolyzk, Thomas A. *Langston Hughes: A Bio-Bibliography*. New York: Greenwood Press, 1990. Bio-Bibliog. in Afro-Amer. and African Studies 2.

Miller, R. Baxter. *The Art and Imagination of Langston Hughes*. Lexington: UP of Kentucky, 1989.

———. "Café De La Paix: Mapping the Harlem Renaissance." *South Atlantic Review* 65.2 (2000): 73–94.

———. "Framing and Framed Languages in Hughes's *Ask Your Mama: 12 Moods for Jazz*." *MELUS* 17.4 (1991–92): 3–13.

———. "Langston Hughes, 1902–1967." *A Historical Guide to Langston Hughes*. Ed. Steven C. Tracy. New York: Oxford UP, 2004. 23–62.

———. *Langston Hughes and Gwendolyn Brooks: A Reference Guide*. Boston: Hall, 1978. Ref. Pubs. in Lit.

———. "Reinvention and Globalization in Short Stories by Langston Hughes." *MELUS* 30 (2005): 69–83.

Mitchell, Loften. *The Story of the American Negro in the Theater*. New York: Hawthorne, 1967.

Mullen, Edward J. *Critical Essays on Langston Hughes*. Boston: Hall, 1986. Critical Essays on Amer. Lit.

O'Daniel, Therman B., ed. *Langston Hughes: Black Genius*. New York: Morrow, 1971.

Ostrom, Hans A. *Langston Hughes: A Study of the Short Fiction*. New York: Twayne, 1993. Twayne's Studies in Short Fiction 47.

Parker, John. "Tomorrow in the Writing of Langston Hughes." *College English* 10 (1949): 438–41.

Patterson, Louise. "With Langston Hughes in the USSR." *Freedomways* 8 (1968): 511–17.

Pool, Rosey. "The Discovery of American Negro Poetry." *Freedomways* 8 (1968): 152–58.

Presley, James. "The American Dream of Langston Hughes." *Southwest Review* 48 (1948): 380–96.

Rampersad, Arnold. *The Life of Langston Hughes.* 2 vols. New York: Oxford UP, 1986.

Roessel, David. "The Letters of Langston Hughes and Ezra Pound." *Paideuma: A Journal Devoted to Ezra Pound Scholarship* 29.1–2 (2000): 207–42.

Tracy, Steven C. "Introduction." *A Historical Guide to Langston Hughes*. Ed. Tracy. New York: Oxford UP, 2004. 3–22.

_____. *Langston Hughes & the Blues*. Urbana: U of Illinois P, 1988.

Trotman, C. James, ed. *Langston Hughes: The Man, His Art, and His Continuing Influence*. New York: Garland, 1995. Garland Ref. Lib.

Woods, Gregory. "Gay Re-Readings of the Harlem Renaissance Poets." *Critical Essays: Gay and Lesbian Writers of Color*. Ed. Emanuel S. Nelson. New York: Haworth, 1993. 127–42.

CRITICAL INSIGHTS

About the Editor

R. Baxter Miller (PhD Brown, 1974) is professor of English and African American studies at the University of Georgia. The editor of the *Langston Hughes Review*, he has written or edited ten books, including the internationally acclaimed *Black American Literature and Humanism* (1981) and *The Art and Imagination of Langston Hughes* (1989), which won the American Book Award for 1991. Much of his revised oeuvre appears as *A Literary Criticism of Five Generations of African American Writing: The Artistry of Memory* (2008). His *Black American Poets between Worlds, 1940–1960* (1986) was more focused on a period. His critical study *On the Ruins of Modernity: New Chicago Renaissance from Wright to Kent* was published by Common Ground in 2011. Miller has published widely in such journals as *American Literary Scholarship, Southern Literary Journal, Journal of the Midwestern Modern Language Association, Mississippi Quarterly, MELUS, African American Review, South Atlantic Review, American Studies of Eastern Europe*, and *International Journal for the Humanities*. As complement to his American focus, he has presented many of his research findings in Paris, France; Kumasi, Ghana; and Cambridge, England. In 2007 he received a Department of State grant, on behalf of the American Embassy, to deliver a course of lectures at the Belarusian State University and Minsk Linguistic University. In 2001 he received the Langston Hughes award for his work as "scholar, editor, and steward" of the legacy, and in 2010, the Ford-Turpin honor for distinguished scholarship.

Contributors

R. Baxter Miller is professor of English and African American studies at the University of Georgia. The editor of the *Langston Hughes Review*, he has written or edited many books, including *Black American Literature and Humanism* (1981), *Black American Poets between Worlds, 1940–1960* (1986), *The Art and Imagination of Langston Hughes* (1989), and *A Literary Criticism of Five Generations of African American Writing: The Artistry of Memory* (2008). His critical study *On the Ruins of Modernity: New Chicago Renaissance from Wright to Kent* was published by Common Ground in 2011. A former president of the Langston Hughes Society, he is the founder of the Division of Black American Literature and Culture in the Modern Language Association.

Donna Akiba Sullivan Harper, the Fuller E. Callaway Professor of English at Spelman College in Atlanta, was educated at Hampton University, Oberlin College (BA), and Emory University (MA and PhD). A founding member and past president of the Langston Hughes Society, she authored *Not So Simple: The "Simple" Stories by Langston Hughes* (1995) and edited four collections of short fiction by Hughes. She has published numerous articles and book reviews. In addition, she has presented several conference papers on her research findings throughout the United States and in special presentations in Wuhan, China (2007), as well as Ankara and Istanbul, Turkey (2010). A life member of the College Language Association and a past member of the Executive Committee of the Association of Departments of English of the Modern Language Association, she is passionately committed to increasing the ranks, including the diversity, of the professoriate. She coordinates the UNCF-Mellon Undergraduate Fellowship Program at Spelman and directs the UNCF-Mellon Summer Institute at Emory University.

Dolan Hubbard is professor and chair of the Department of English and Language Arts at Morgan State University in Baltimore, Maryland. He previously served as an associate professor at the University of Georgia (1994–98), where he held a joint appointment in English and African American Studies. A graduate of Catawba College (1971) in Salisbury, North Carolina, he earned his MA at the University of Denver (1974) and his PhD in English at the University of Illinois at Urbana-Champaign (1986). He is a past president of both the Langston Hughes Society (2000–06) and the College Language Association (1994–96), the nation's preeminent organization of literary and linguistic scholars who are primarily African American. A former editor of the *Langston Hughes Review*, he is author of *The Sermon and the African American Literary Imagination* (1994), which was named an Outstanding Academic Book by *Choice* for 1995. He is editor of *Recovered Writers/Recovered Texts: Race, Class, and Gender in Black Women's Literature* (1997) and *The Souls of Black Folk: One*

Hundred Years Later (2003) and a member of the editorial board of *The Collected Works of Langston Hughes*, for which he edited volume 4, *The Novels: Not without Laughter and Tambourines to Glory.*

Hans Ostrom is professor of African American studies and English at the University of Puget Sound. His works of scholarship include *Langston Hughes: A Study of the Short Fiction, A Langston Hughes Encyclopedia*, and the five-volume *Greenwood Encyclopedia of African American Studies,* edited with J. David Macey. Ostrom has also published *The Coast Starlight: Collected Poems 1976–2006* and two novels, *Three to Get Ready* (1991) and *Honoring Juanita* (2010). A Fulbright Senior Lecturer at the University of Uppsala in 1994, Ostrom has also taught at the University of California, Davis, where he earned his PhD, and at Johannes Gutenberg University in Mainz, Germany.

John Edgar Tidwell has won awards from the National Endowment for the Humanities and the American Council of Learned Societies, among several others, which have enabled him to publish widely in African American literature and to focus especially on writers Sterling A. Brown, Frank Marshall Davis, Langston Hughes, and Gordon Parks. He has published *Writings of Frank Marshall Davis, A Voice of the Black Press* (2007), *Black Moods: Collected Poems* (2002), *Livin' the Blues: Memoirs of a Black Journalist and Poet* (1992), *Sterling A. Brown's A Negro Looks at the South* (with Mark Sanders, 2007), *Montage of a Dream: The Art and Life of Langston Hughes* (with Cheryl R. Rager, 2007), and *After Winter: The Art and Life of Sterling A. Brown* (with Steven Tracy, 2009). His essays, interviews, book reviews, and editorial work have appeared in such prestigious periodicals as *Callaloo*, *African American Review*, *CLA Journal,* the *Journal of American History*, *Kansas History*, and the *Langston Hughes Review*. He and Carmaletta M. Williams have collaborated on *My Dear Boy: Carrie Hughes's Letters to Langston Hughes, 1926–1938*, a book-length manuscript under press consideration.

Christopher C. De Santis is professor of African American and US literatures and director of graduate studies in the Department of English at Illinois State University. De Santis is the editor of *Langston Hughes and the Chicago Defender: Essays on Race, Politics, and Culture, 1942–62* and two volumes in *The Collected Works of Langston Hughes*: *Essays on Art, Race, Politics, and World Affairs* and *Fight for Freedom and Other Writings on Civil Rights*. His most recent book is *Langston Hughes: A Documentary Volume*. De Santis has also published numerous articles and reviews in *African American Review, American Studies, American Book Review, CLA Journal, Contemporary Literary Criticism, Langston Hughes Review, The Oxford Companion to African American Literature, The Southern Quarterly,* and other books and journals.

Joseph McLaren teaches African American and African literature at Hofstra University, where he is professor of English. He has taught at Mercy College, College of the Virgin Islands, Long Island University, the State University of New York at Purchase, and Rutgers University. He has traveled extensively in Africa and has presented papers at international conferences in Senegal, Ghana, Nigeria, South Africa, Morocco, Egypt, Kenya, Eritrea, Belize, Guadeloupe, Barbados, Trinidad, Jamaica, Sardinia, and Israel. His publications include a variety of articles on literature and culture. He is the author of *Langston Hughes: Folk Dramatist in the Protest Tradition, 1921–1943* (1997). In addition, he coedited *Pan-Africanism Updated* (1999) and *African Visions* (2000) and edited two volumes of the *Collected Works of Langston Hughes—Autobiography: The Big Sea* (2002) and *Autobiography: I Wonder as I Wander* (2002). With the legendary jazz artist Jimmy Heath, he coauthored *I Walked with Giants* (2010), Heath's autobiography.

Carmaletta M. Williams is executive director for diversity, equity, and inclusion and professor of African American studies at Johnson County Community College (JCCC) in Overland Park, Kansas. She earned her BA and MA in English from the University of Missouri–Kansas City and her PhD from the University of Kansas. She has won a number of distinguished teaching awards including the Burlington Northern Santa Fe Faculty Achievement Award, five Distinguished Service Awards from Johnson County Community College, the Carnegie Foundation for the Advancement of Teaching and Council for Advancement and Support of Education's Kansas Professor of the Year, and the League for Innovation's Innovation of the Year award for her videotape, "Sankofa: My Journey Home," about her Fulbright-Hays Award study in Ghana, West Africa. Williams traveled to Guinea, West Africa, where she established a faculty exchange between L'Ecole Nationale de Poste et Telecommunications and JCCC. She was invited to South Africa to interview citizens about their experiences during and after apartheid. She was awarded JCCC's first Diversity Award in September 2005. She has published many scholarly works, including *Do Nothing Till You Hear from Me: Langston Hughes in the Classroom* for the National Council of Teachers of English.

W. Jason Miller, an associate professor of English at North Carolina State University, has written *Langston Hughes and American Lynching Culture* (2011) along with scholarly articles on novelists such as Willa Cather and William Faulkner. He has published his own poems in various journals including the *South Carolina Review*. In addition, he has contributed entries on the blues and gospel music, including one on Langston Hughes, to the *New Anthology of American Poetry*. He has also served as an executive committee member of the National Council of Teachers of English's Assembly on American Literature. He completed his undergraduate degree and MA at the University of Nebraska at Kearney and his PhD at Washington State.

David Roessel is the Peter and Stella Yiannos Professor of Greek Language and Literature at the Richard Stockton College of New Jersey. He is the associate editor, with Arnold Rampersad, of *The Collected Poems of Langston Hughes* (1994) and the coeditor, with Nicholas Moschovakis, of *Mister Paradise and Other One-Act Plays by Tennessee Williams* (2005). His book *In Byron's Shadow: Modern Greece in the English and American Imagination* won the 2001 Modern Language Association Prize for Independent Scholars.

Sharon L. Jones is associate professor in the Department of English Language and Literatures and director of African and African American studies at Wright State University in Dayton, Ohio. She earned a BA and MA in English from Clemson and a PhD in English from the University of Georgia. She is coeditor of *The Prentice Hall Anthology of African American Literature* and author of *Rereading the Harlem Renaissance: Race, Class, and Gender in the Fiction of Jessie Fauset, Zora Neale Hurston, and Dorothy West* and *Critical Companion to Zora Neale Hurston: A Literary Reference to Her Life and Work*. Her areas of expertise include American literature to 1900, twentieth-century American literature, and African American literature. She became president-elect of the Langston Hughes Society in 2010. She is a former guest editor for a special issue of the *Langston Hughes Review*.

Steven C. Tracy is professor of Afro-American studies at the University of Massachusetts, Amherst. He has authored, edited, coedited, or provided introductions for over thirty books; provided over seventy contributions to book publications edited by others; written over fifty CD liner notes; and taught, lectured, and presented papers in the United States, Canada, England, France, Belgium, the Netherlands, Israel, and China. A singer and harmonica player, he has opened for B. B. King, Muddy Waters, Sonny Terry and Brownie McGhee, Canned Heat, and others, and recorded with Steve Tracy and the Crawling Kingsnakes, Albert Washington, Big Joe Duskin, Pigmeat Jarrett, and the Cincinnati Symphony Orchestra. His book project *Touched by the Blues: Futuristic Jungleism, Ragmentation, and the Bluing of American Literature* will be published in 2012. He is on the Fulbright Senior Specialist roster until 2015.

Leslie Sanders is university professor in the Department of Humanities at York University, Toronto, Canada. Her areas of expertise are African American and African Canadian literature and theater. She is the author of *The Development of Black Theatre in America* (1988) and the editor of two volumes on the dramatic works of Langston Hughes, part of *The Collected Works of Langston Hughes*, for which she was also a general editor. In addition to her work in African American literature, she has written about several African Canadian writers, especially Austin Clarke, Dionne Brand, and Djanet Sears, and about African Canadian documentary film. She is on the editorial board of *New Dawn: Journal of Black Canadian Studies*, has served on *Modern Drama*, and has edited two issues of *Canadian Woman Studies/Cahiers de la femme*. She is webmaster for African Canadian Online, which developed out of one of her courses.

Laurence E. Prescott, professor of Spanish and African American studies at Penn State University, teaches courses in Latin American literature and civilization and Afro-Hispanic literature and civilization. His research interests include Afro-Colombian literature, postcolonial studies, and inter-American literary relations. A former Fulbright Scholar, he has published *Without Hatreds or Fears: Jorge Artel and the Struggle for Black Literary Expression in Colombia* (2000), a *Choice* magazine 2001 Outstanding Academic Title, and *Candelario Obeso y la iniciación de la poesía negra en Colombia* (1985). With Colombia Truque Vélez he coedited the groundbreaking, six-volume *Colección presencia Afrocolombiana* (2008). His articles and reviews have appeared in the *Latin American Research Review*, *Afro-Hispanic Review*, *Revista de estudios Colombianos*, *Revista Iberoamericana*, *Callaloo*, and other journals, as well as in scholarly books. His projects include a study of African American life and culture in Latin American travel writing and a bibliography of Afro-Colombian writers.

John Lowney is a professor of English at St. John's University, where he teaches courses in twentieth-century American and African American literary and cultural studies. He is the author of two books on twentieth-century American poetry, *History, Memory, and the Literary Left: Modern American Poetry, 1935–1968* (2006) and *The American Avant-Garde Tradition: William Carlos Williams, Postmodern Poetry, and the Politics of Cultural Memory* (1997). He has published many essays on African American literature, modern and postmodern poetry, and American literature and culture of the 1930s. He is pursuing research on jazz, internationalism, and literary Afro-modernism.

Index

Africa, 124
African American theater, development of, 240–41
African diaspora, engagement with, 69, 286–91
Afro-modernism, viii, xiv, 17, 275–91
American dream, the, 223, 229
American Dream, The (Albee), xiii
Annjee (*Not without Laughter*), 140
Arletta ("Blessed Assurance"), 229
art, role in racial uplift, 105
Artel, Jorge, 261
Ask Your Mama, 14–16, 287–91
"Aunt Sue's Stories," 62, 141
autobiography, 121–36

"Backlash Blues, The," 69
Baily, Suzy (*Joy to My Soul*), 249
"Ballad of Roosevelt, The," 176
Barrera Parra, Jaime, 260
bebop, 283
Bentley, Gladys, 247
"Big Meeting," 200–201
Big Sea, The, 121–28
"Bird in Orbit," 15
"Birth," 12
black aesthetic, development of, xi, 105–18
Black Christ, 196
black woman, the, xii, 55–67
"Blessed Assurance," 201–5, 223–36
blues, the, 87–99, 176–91, 279–80
"Blues I'm Playing, The," 8
Bontemps, Arna, 149–55
Book of Ruth (biblical), 205, 232
Boyd (Simple stories), 215
Brown, Sterling A., 92–97

cabaret reading, 246–50
Carmon, Walt, 190
"Carolina Cabin," 11
"Cat and the Saxophone, The," 281
censorship, 165–66
Chesnutt, Charles W., 108
China, 133
Christianity, 57–61, 75, 81, 161, 194–205, 228–32
"Christ in Alabama," 160–64
civil rights movement, 77, 171, 215
Clark, Gwyn (Kit), 145–46
Clark, Homer, 148
communism. *See* socialism
Communist Party, 186–89
community, 98
Cooke, Sam, 233–34
Cooper, Anna Julia, 109
"Cora," 65
Cora ("Father and Son"), 203
Cora (*Mulatto*), 243–44
"Crazy Blues, The" (Smith), 92–93
critical reception. *See under* Hughes, Langston
Cuba, 129
Cullen, Countee, 31, 95, 279
"Cultural Exchange," 288

Dalton García, Roque, 265–67
Delmar (Delly) ("Blessed Assurance"), 202–5, 223–36
Depression. *See* Great Depression
Dessalines, Jean-Jacques (*Emperor of Haiti*), 244
dialect, use of. *See* vernacular, use of
"Dream Boogie," 283
"Dream Deferred," 165–69
Du Bois, W. E. B., 71, 110

Effeminate Youth (*Little Ham*), 248
Emperor Jones, The (O'Neill), 242
Emperor of Haiti, 244
Essie (*Tambourines to Glory*), 251
Esther, 167

faith, test of, 199–202, 228–29
family, xi, 138–56
family systems theory, 140
"Father and Son," 9, 203
Fine Clothes to the Jew, 90, 179
Fire!!, 22
food imagery, 167–69
functional relationships, 138, 149

García Lorca, Federico, 46, 278
Gilbert (*Little Ham*), 249
"Good Morning," 285
Great Depression, 9
Great Migration, 74, 277
Gregory, Montgomery, 241
Guillén, Nicolás, 278

Haiti, 129
Haman (*Esther*), 167
"Harlem." *See* "Dream Deferred"
"Harlem Night Club," 281
Harlem Renaissance, 71–74, 126, 277–78
Harper, Emerson and Ethel (Toy), 149
Harper, Frances Ellen Watkins, 107
Harriette (*Not without Laughter*), 140
history, 69–84
"Homesick Blues," 179
homosexuality, 201–4, 223–25, 247
Hughes, Carrie, 144–45, 152
Hughes, James, 123, 147
Hughes, Langston
    and Arna Bontemps, 149–55
    and the blues, 87–99
    career, ix, 4, 10–13, 22–24

and the Communist Party, 186–89
critical reception, 19, 31–37, 50
early life, 20, 122, 141
and the Harlem Renaissance, 71–74, 126
historical context, 6, 16, 275
international reception, 41, 255–68
and McCarthyism, 13, 226–27
and socialism, 75
Hurston, Zora Neale, 23, 127, 242

imperialism, 257–58, 266
In Abraham's Bosom (Green), 242
"I Remember the Blues," 90
"I, Too," 256–57, 261–64, 267
I Wonder as I Wander, 128–36

Japan, 133
Jaxon, Manley ("Blessed Assurance"), 202, 225, 231–35
jazz, 279–87
"Jazz Band in a Parisian Cabaret," 281
John ("Blessed Assurance"), 228–30, 235
Johnson, James Weldon, 6, 32
Johnson, Madam Alberta K., 66, 208–13
Joy to My Soul, 249–50

Langston, Mary, 63, 141
Langston Hughes Review, 43
Langston Hughes Society, 43
Larsen, Nella, 234
Latin America, reception in, 255–68
Laura (*Tambourines to Glory*), 251
leftist criticism, 35, 187–90
Lewis, Bert ("Father and Son"), 9, 203
Little Ham, 246–49
Little Ham (*Little Ham*), 247–49
Locke, Alain, 4, 182
Lomax, Buddy (*Tambourines to Glory*), 251

lynching, x, 158–74
Lynn Clarisse (Simple stories), 215–16

Madam Alberta K. Johnson. *See* Johnson, Madam Alberta K.
"Madam and Her Madam," 211
"Madam and the Fortune Teller," 66
Madam Klinkscale (*Joy to My Soul*), 249
Madam (Simple stories), 216
Madam poems, 66, 207–13
Madam to You (Siegmeister), 213
Mamie (*Simply Heavenly*), 250
Marxism. *See* socialism
Masculine Woman (*Little Ham*), 247
Mason, Charlotte Osgood, 127, 145–46, 185
Matthews, Victoria Earle, 109
McCarthy, Joseph, 13, 83, 226
McCarthyism, 13, 226–27
McKay, Claude, 279
"Mexican Market Woman," 64
Minnie (Simple stories), 218–20
"Mississippi," 172–73
modernism, viii, xiv, 17, 275–91
Montage of a Dream Deferred, 282–85
Mordecai (*Esther*), 167
"Mother to Son," 57
Mr. Parkes ("Big Meeting"), 200
Mulatto, 134, 243
Mule Bone, 242

"Negro, The," 171–72
"Negro-Art Hokum, The" (Schuyler), 112–13
"Negro Artist and the Racial Mountain, The," 114–16, 181, 245
"Negro Mother, The," 59–60
"Negro Speaks of Rivers, The," 69
New Negro, The (Locke), 241

New Negro Renaissance. *See* Harlem Renaissance
Nigger Heaven (Van Vechten), 73, 118, 127
"Northern Liberal," 73
Norwood, Thomas ("Father and Son"), 203
Norwood, Thomas (*Mulatto*), 243
"Nothing but Roomers," 217
"Not What Was," 16

"On Imagination" (Wheatley), 107
"On the Road," 197–99

"Parade," 284
parent-child relationship, 203–4, 223–36
Paris, 124
patronage, 118, 127
Pavletich Trujillo, Esteban, 256–59
"Poet to Patron," 191
political poetry, 75–81, 158–74, 180–91
Prince Ali Ali (*Joy to My Soul*), 249
Princess Bootoo (*Joy to My Soul*), 249
propaganda, 72, 79

queer reading, 47, 201, 223, 247

race relations, 129–33, 158–74, 261, 267
Rainey, Ma, 87–89, 94–97
Randolph, A. Phillip, 71
reception, critical. *See under* Hughes, Langston
Reed, James and Mary, 143
Reverend Dorset ("On the Road"), 198–99
"Revolution," 180
"Ride, Red, Ride," 289
Robert (*Mulatto*), 243
Roumain, Jacques, 278
Russia. *See* Soviet Union

Index 319

Sargeant ("On the Road"), 199
Schuyler, George, 112–13
Scottsboro Boys, 160–64
Scottsboro Limited, 178
Semple, Jesse B. (Simple), 24, 207
Semple, Joyce Lane (Simple stories), 214–15
"Shades of Pigmeat," 290
Shakespeare in Harlem, 36
Simple. *See* Semple, Jesse B.
Simple stories, 209, 214–21
Simply Heavenly, 217, 250
slavery, 258
socialism, 75, 77
"Song for Billie Holiday," 7
Souls of Black Folk, The (Du Bois), 110
South, the, 129
Soviet Union, 23, 130–32
Spanish Civil War, 135–36
"Strange Fruit" (Holiday), 167
"Strange Hurt," 65

Tambourines to Glory, 251
Tempy (*Not without Laughter*), 140
theatrical works, 45, 238–52
Till, Emmett, 170–74
Tin Pan Alley, 93
Tiny (*Little Ham*), 249
"To Maecenas" (Wheatley), 106

"To Negro Writers," 119
"Town of Scottsboro, The," 183
travel, 21, 80, 124, 129–34
"Troubled Woman," 64

USSR. *See* Soviet Union

Van Vechten, Carl, 6, 73, 117, 210
vernacular, use of
  in *Ask Your Mama*, 15
  critical reception, 32–33, 179
  in "Mother to Son," 57
  in "Negro Mother, The," 59–60
  as representative of authentic experience, 73
Voice from the South, A (Cooper), 109

Washington, Booker T., 71
Ways of White Folks, The, 35, 78
Wheatley, Phillis, 106
Whitehead, Buster (*Joy to My Soul*), 249
Wilmetta (*Joy to My Soul*), 249
women, depictions of, xii, 55–67, 207–21
World War II, 75, 136

Zapata Olivella, Manuel, 262–64
Zarita (Simple stories), 217
Zarita (*Simply Heavenly*), 250